Remembering India's Villages

Remembering India's Villages

Edited by
Santosh K. Singh

AAKAR

Remembering India's Villages
Edited by Santosh K. Singh

First Published 2021
Reprinted 2023

ISBN 978-93-5002-720-2

Published by
AAKAR BOOKS
28 E Pocket IV, Mayur Vihar Phase I
Delhi 110 091 India
www.aakarbooks.com

Laser Typeset at
Sakshi Computers, Delhi

Printed at
D.K. Fine Art Press, Delhi

Contents

Introduction
India's Villages: A Lost Theme and Its Return

Santosh K. Singh

Ordinarily there has been a deafening silence around the word "village" or "rural" in contemporary India; only to be broken by exceptional moments such as the recent pandemic induced home-bound returns of the rural migrants or a spate of suicide cases reported from the countryside or some protests by the farmers for a better deal with the state. This silence is not new though; it has existed for at least the last three decades, if not more, beginning from the year 1991 when the new economic regime of what was referred to as LPG (Liberalization, Privatization and Globalization) was heralded. Ideally a space which, even by a conservative estimate, accounted for nearly two-thirds of India's more than a billion population should have been bustling with activities and leading the agenda of the present and future India, the rural scenario, in reality, however, looks bleak. The newspapers and other media platforms are awash with scary headlines with alarming regularity- " vanishing villages", " death of villages", "ghost villages", to name a few-giving rise to additional rings of despondency and despair to the already sunken morale of those who continue to exist and occupy this space. A village in that sense today is reduced to a space which is a forced (out of no option) choice of habitation. The charm of urban, especially among youths, is addictive. But this is not without reason, it has a history; a past strewn with false promises, moral trappings, even divinization and eulogies celebrating its pristine setting thereby backgrounding its abject poverty, inequalities and miseries of all sorts.

It is not that the villages were always in the dumps, at least in spirit, like the way they are today. For a long time they were considered the pivot of Indian society, the cradle of the great Indian civilizational virtues (Ray 1973). Beteille had rightly observed (1980: 108): "The point to bear in mind is that the importance of the village within Indian civilization is to be understood not simply in demographic but also in normative terms. The village was not merely a place where people lived; it has a design in which were reflected the basic values of Indian civilization". The ancient religious texts always gave primacy to the idea of the village and bestowed sacredness to the space and its overall solidarity. Many rituals began by invoking the Gram devata, the village-god, even before the principal deities. Understandably, as a predominantly rural/ peasant society, villages always figured as the quintessential and an integral part of Indian society. During the colonial period, villages again became central to the larger framework of colonial govern-mentality, and this too not just as the unit of revenue collection but also as part of figuring out the natives and its life universe in order to nurture and perpetuate the colonial interests of the British regime. This unleashed a slew of measures, such as census, to unpack the enigma called Indian society and understand its constitutive logic better. Caste, religion and village stood out as three indispensable significant tropes for studies and research related to Indian society. That a number of the census commissioners and administrators had a close association with the discipline of anthropology clearly suggest how serious the colonial government was in this project of enumeration, especially its socio-cultural dimensions and complexities. The then prevalent anthropological tradition too favoured the entire process; of identifying microcosms to examine and study the evolution from a simple to complex forms. Villages in this framework emerged as the unit of study of Indian society.

The much hyped and glorified phrase of "Little Republics" used for the villages of India by the British administrator, Charles

Metcalfe, and others, was part of that design (see O' Malley 1934/75; Cohn 1968; Inden 1990). So powerful was the ring of romanticisation around the villages that many, including Karl Marx, fell prey to it. Not to speak of the nationalist leaders like Gandhi and others who insistently foregrounded the virtues of village life and idealized its core characteristics as an equal, harmonious and peaceful world. Gandhi in particular, though ordinarily had a pragmatic view, but was rather overwhelmed by this purported exotic imagination of village India as the ideal model on which the new nation would be configured and built around, leading to what he later called Gram swaraj. Gandhi was clearly attracted by the overt simplicity and pastoralist charm of the village India. While Nehru and others had slightly different imaginations but they all played second fiddle to the larger Gandhian meta-narrative of and about village which had overwhelming mass appeal and popular endorsement. In other words, village India had that haloed sacredness about it that not many dared to interrogate. It needed a leader like B.R. Ambedkar, however, to question that imagination; and to offer an alternative, a more real sense of the rural in India. Ambedkar attempted to debunk this myth-making about India's villages as harmonious, ideal space for human habitation. Behind the idyllic facade of village India, Ambedkar contested, existed the cesspool of retrograde and inhuman caste practices. In his response, Ambedkar in fact argued just the opposite of what Gandhi and his associates articulated—that the possible road map of an independent India—passed through not the dingy, congested by-lanes of the villages of India but through the highways of its modern urban pockets. Ambedkar highlighted the significance of urban spaces in future India as an escape route where the erstwhile lower castes and untouchables will have the possibility of an equal, dignified world. Yet, Ambedkar's was the marginal voice at that moment of India's history; the halo around village India only got further illuminated with Gandhi and others fully convinced that the progress and development strategies of the new, free nation had to keep the villages at its core. True, Nehru was the architect of modern India and that he invested heavily in modern projects like big dams, heavy industries and establishing new industrial townships to initiate India's urban-based growth stories; yet, in principle he too followed the Gandhian prescription, or at least did not disagree with it in the initial years (Jodhka 2002; Gupta 2005).

Post-Independence, expectedly, India's development planning agenda kept its promised focus on the villages. The First Five Year plan (1951-56) was both a testimony and commentary on this. Likewise, the Community Development Programme (CDP) which was inaugurated in 1952 had a clear Gandhian stamp on it. If the First Five Year plan focused on the primary sector, land distribution, irrigation infrastructure to strengthen the agrarian economy, etc., the CDP which was launched on a pilot basis had rural income, health, sanitation and agriculture productivity at its core. In other words, the charm of the countryside continued to enthral the planners and the policy makers. At least, in the early years of the post- independence era the trend continued till there was reorientation of focus towards industry and the secondary sector under the Nehruvian model of growth and development which was ushered in with a clear focus on heavy industries with renewed vigour. The new thinking was to generate employment in the manufacturing, non-agrarian sectors to essentially remove some pressure off the rural economy. Emphasis on towns and cities, youth skill enhancement, training programmes for creating a skilled labour force etc. were initiated at a large scale. This is not to say that villages completely disappeared from the imagination of the planners. Villages continued to be a place where the majority of Indians, almost three- fourths lived. It is for this reason—the value of numbers in democratic electoral politics—that appears to have forced the political class to keep its one foot in the villages, even if it was largely for the lip service and tokenism (See Rudolph and Rudolph 1987).

By the beginning of the 1980s, even the Bollywood mainstream cinema had almost abandoned the idea of the village as a site of imagination and creativity. A tradition that had a rich repertoire with some iconic films such as *Do Bigha Zameen, Mother India, Upkaar, Naya Daur*, and many such, which had a successful run and popularity, was on the wane. A new imagination took over. Amitabh Bachchan, as an angry young man, was the mascot of that departure; the new tide of Indian cinema. His characters were mostly urban and had deep anguish towards the system and the state. Rural was relegated further even in popular imagination. Across the 1990s even the locations for picturization moved westward, giving rise to what some refer to as the NRI phase of Bollywood where exotic locations from Europe and the US became indispensable. Indeed the characters, stories and landscape became overly diasporic, global and urban. The rural folks did not have enough charm or popular appeal left in them to qualify for a lead role in any mainstream cinema. It was a new India: aspirational and gung-ho about anything urban. The moral compass of the Indian society had undergone irreversible make up.

The rural or the village, however, re-emerged at the turn of the 21st century. But this was not because the people at the helm, the political class, realized their mistakes or lapses. Rather, this reappearance happened in the background of a crisis. Owing to decades of colossal neglect and apathy, the countryside was gradually collapsing; wide cracks were now visible (Gupta 2005). An unprecedented agrarian crisis in the form of farmers' suicides caught the attention of the nation (Mohanty 2011). In popular perception the farmers were always perceived as poor but sturdy and fighters, not ones to give up. Hence the spate of suicides reported from the hinterland, by that too from the erstwhile Green Revolution pockets, shook the nation. When the stories of suicides started getting reported from the land of Punjab and Maharashtra, the silence around the countryside showed signs of being disrupted. The advent of mass media, especially mobile technology, released a new energy and awareness across the countryside. The city though always had a pull, but the return was as much celebrated. Like the protagonist of *Do Bigha Zameen* (1957) the city was a land of opportunities but also compromise. The return to his village, to save his mother earth, was the ultimate accomplishment for Sambhu Mahto, the struggling marginal farmer who undertakes the journey to Calcutta to earn money, and to save his land from the avaricious landlord who wanted to grab his land to set up an industry. The film ends with Mahto returning to his village but unable to save his land. Yet, the last scene of the film shows him unsuccessfully attempting to grab a fistful of *matti*, the soil, from the sacred earth, and smearing it on his forehead. By the turn of the 21st century, that "return" lost its moral wherewithal. The return from a city to village, which earlier carried a ring of reunion, or at least a sense of fulfilling a private promise, now was loaded with despondency and defeat. This is not to romanticise the milieu. What is however obvious that the collapse of the agrarian economy for various reasons, mainly historical and structural, triggered off a slew of new processes that gradually began to reconstitute (and also interrogate) its ethos. Its impact, however, could be seen and felt in the deep interiors of the village and its socio-cultural universe. The aggressive entry of the market, facilitated by the new economic regime, into the rural landscape towards the last decade of the 20th century further accelerated the process of reconstitution.

The change and reconstitution of the rural has happened at such a large scale and with such a swift pace, and is so deep, that the decades of "shutting off the village", left the people associated with the renewed quest for enquiry with a sense of surprise (See Jodhka 2014, 2016; Thakur 2014). The usual conceptual kit and frameworks proved inadequate. For instance, the land that commanded such a profound socio-cultural centrality in any village study earlier, now had a completely different connotation, it was less of socio-cultural and more of an economic entity. The large-landholding castes moved their household to nearby towns but continued to keep one foot in the village and another in the city because the land could not be transported in the city-ward truck that they first boarded with their families, in search of better education, health facilities, and, more importantly, quality of life that an urban location offered unlike their rural homes. The land was effectively "de-moralized". Land that largely sustained the idea of the village showed signs of cracks in its cultural and organic linkages with the people. Other significant accessories such as animal population and traditional equipment such as wooden ploughs and wheels etc. too gradually began to disappear. With this, came down crashing the traditional jajmani system. The specialists—who used to provide the essential equipment for the agrarian economy and society such as potters, barbers, blacksmiths, basket makers and rope makers—all steadily looked urban-ward, for a better future for its next generation. The inbuilt asymmetries of power and inequality, cocooned in the caste envelope, in the system of Jajmani progressively pushed its subaltern-actors towards a more secular and civil occupational zones. Aspiration is perhaps the most understudied theme in studies on India in general and its villages in particular. The fact is aspiration is substantially mental and cognitive; it does not necessarily require any validation from the material. By the turn of the new century, both the young zamindar and the landless agriculture farm labour from the lower strata, turned into an aspirational next generation. All pervasive mobile technology of communication and access to the outer world added wings to their imagination. Dwindling farm fortunes encouraged the flight of that imagination. The nearest railway station, no wonder, therefore, became a site of significant merit, so much so that a commentator found it to be the most crucial space to study villages today anthropologically (Thakur 2014).

It is clear that the crisis in the agrarian scenario is factual. But does that also mean that the villages are disappearing or vanishing? True, agriculture, as the mainstay of the rural economy is in deep distress, but does that spell doom for the space called the village? A more objective and real assessment could be possible only if we cease to look at the villages as mere economic units, bereft of any social and cultural agencies and networks. A more real response or line of understanding would be to look at villages as space that is drastically getting reconstituted and reconfigured. And not disappearing. Villages have changed in terms of their signposts, but they still exist as spaces. The present volume attempts to remind us exactly that: the very presence of the rural and its continued significance with all its old and new complexities. The first three chapters, while retaining the substantive core, dwell upon the theoretical and conceptual contours of the idea of village India, observed from three different perspectives. while Dev Nath Pathak looks at the realm of rural as a site of tri-logue between Gandhi, Ambedkar and Tagore; Bhavya Chitranshi and Anup Dhar pose the question: What if, the 'rural is the future; and *not* the past? Priyasha Kaul explores how Bollywood contributed to the romanticized idea of the rural. Dev's essay seeks to revisit a potential tri-logue among three thinkers of modern India, and to argue that contrary to popular perception, the rural is actually set to mutate rather than decline. Engaging with this tri-logue, the paper promises to justify the need of revisiting the critical romantic utopianism that is common in the three thinkers. The essay takes recourse to cinematic popular representation of the village to illuminate his arguments. Priyasha Kaul in her chapter entitled. "Rural Frames: Bollywood Imagination of Village India" underlines how the village has long been a central feature of popular Indian imagination about the nation and society. The essay, in the main, underlines the journey of Indian society fresh out of colonial rule to post-liberalization in the last quarter of the 20th century, and how cinema captured this trajectory and in turn shifted its frames. Chitranshi and Dhar in their essay ask some piercingly pointed questions. They interrogate stubborn existing formulations—rural as an inferior, ugly other of the urban, rural sites as backward past of the developed today and such—and instead propose to look at the question of the rural, through a mutually and dynamically constitutive dialectic, that of the circuits of global capital and the third world. Set in the backdrop of a rich review of literature, the essay draws from a micro study to embellish their expansive theoretical spectrum.

Ishita Dey's paper argues for a shift from macro to micro level engagement of the discipline to the village life world. She advocates a new methodological turn towards multispecies ethnography while arguing that only when studies factor in the relationship and sociality that human establish with the non-human world that a deeper understanding of entrenched identities and dynamics of the village interior could be explored.

The essay by Bidhan Chandra Dash while retaining the theoretical rigour of the preceding chapter also marks the entry of substantive field-based micro-level views in the volume. The chapter by Dash entitled, "Violence on Dalits in Village India: Metaphors, Marginalities and the 'Problem of Exit'" seems to respond to the debates around romanticization of the rural and the overbearing influence of Gandhian thinking. Dash brings in the Ambedkarite perspective to village study in India by taking up a theme that remained almost non-existent in traditional village studies dominated by the functionalist perspective. Anchoring his arguments to the key ideas of Ambedkar, who clearly disagreed with the much prevalent notion of village India as an ideal and utopian space, Dash's essay brings into focus the less talked about themes of village India.

Ishita Mehrotra in her essay questions the nature of change in the rural areas via her study of caste, class and gender in occupational patterns of three villages of Uttar Pradesh. She interrogates the claim of modernity and proposes that India's pursuits of capitalist modernity are based on exploitation of traditional hierarchies, where women and especially Dalit women from labouring households fare the worst. Mehrotra therefore challenges the falsity of modern announcements around the process of neoliberal development model as pursued in India. Critiquing the top down model of development paradigm and its inbuilt exclusionary mechanism the paper by Anjana John highlights the flawed understanding of infrastructural power in today's rural India. The paper is based on action research of electrifying the Baiga hamlet in a village of Madhya Pradesh that aims to study how social inequalities influence and impact on the distribution of energy in India.

As the crisis in the agriculture sector loomed large and deepened in the 1990s onwards, many experts suggested agribusiness as a model for India's agriculture. This was also the juncture when the world was experiencing intense globalization and the role of alternative, more technology-market intensive template of agriculture was being advocated and stressed as the way out and for the rejuvenation of village economy and society. This new model or alternative imagination about agriculture brought pressure on the conventional system of knowledge and its integral components such as land, seed, water, people and fertilisers. However given the capital, technology and resource intensive nature of the business model its tenability becomes an issue given that a significant portion of the farming community in India happens to be marginal. Besides, these propositions have serious cultural implications and a complex set of factors do dictate the process of movement from traditional to modern agriculture. Chandri Raghava Reddy and Prasanth Kumar Munnangi's chapter based on study of a village in Telangana underscore the complexities around the transition of agricultural knowledge from what they call from Polyvalent to Monovalent knowledge system. Whereas the paper by Santosh K. Singh highlights the significance of the social and cultural dimension of agribusiness in a village and how contrasting world views underline two sets of communities, thereby indicating the ambivalences in the business model. These studies in general underline the sensitivity with which such models need to be pursued, for there are non-economic factors too which require due consideration. Understandably, the entry of multinational agribusiness giants in the agriculture sector has severely affected the self-sufficiency aspect of the rural community and one of the key segments of that self-sufficiency has been the world of seeds. Shalini Bhutani's ethnography of seed-business under the title "Sammamma's Seeds: The Price She Pays" brings in the nuances around the politics of GM seeds and how it affects the lives of smaller stakeholders and marginal farmers.

Like seeds, land is another sector of agrarian life that has been massively under negotiations and corporate pressure. Increased urbanization led to the boom in real estate industry which then triggered a trend for land acquisition. The paper by Sukhwant Singh Sidhu attempts to assess the social impact of land acquisition on the stakeholders of rural Punjab. Sidhu highlights the phenomenon of land acquisition based on his work in Mohali, Punjab, which has been under avaricious gaze of the state development apparatus since long given its proximity to the city of Chandigarh. The study is significant as the state of Punjab which is historically known for its agriculture and sturdy entrepreneurial farmers but has lately been experiencing decline of agrarian fortunes and the farmers who are quitting the field. The cases of suicide and disenchantment of the younger generation with farming have been reported from the state. In this background the paper argues how the land which was once associated with one's honour is being seen as panacea when it comes to selling the land.

Over all, the volume is a compilation of a range of issues concerning the village India, from across its humongous length and breadth. It is in its thematic diversity that its central focus lies. It is only recently that books and works on rural India have started appearing on the catalogues of new arrivals in the libraries of universities and colleges. May this volume add to the contemporary buzz around the village/rural in India and invite young students and researchers to engage with the theme and its enormous diversity. It is only then that the silence around it as a research theme will be broken and a new beginning of village studies would then be possible. The academic research interest towards rural among the young generation of scholars has been missing lately, and it is only through more studies and researches in the universities and colleges that the lost world of village India may be revived and retrieved. The near drought of contemporary works on the theme of villages of India too contributed to the policy negligence and it is hoped that with more academic publications and writings this critical theme will regain its deserved position all over again, as it was in the early 60s and 70s, all over again. Remembering India's villages, therefore, is a tiny step in that direction. Remembering here is futuristic; and not a wistful looking back, primarily an invitation to remind ourselves that the time has come to get real with the rural. And the villages are not going anywhere; they are just being reconstituted.

REFERENCES

Beteille, Andre. 1980. The Indian Village Past and Present in E.J. Hobsbawm et. al., *Peasants in History*, Published by Sameeksha Trust, Delhi: Oxford University Press.

Bhalla, A. and P. Bumke. (eds.) 1992. *Images of Rural India in the Twentieth Century*, New Delhi: Sterling Publishers.

Ray, Nihar Ranjan. 1973. *Nationalism in India*, Aligarh: Aligarh Muslim University Press.

Cohn, B.S. 1968. Notes on the History of the Study of Indian Society and Culture. In M. Singer and B.S. Cohn (eds.) *Structure and Change in Indian Society*, Chicago: Aldine Publishing.

Gupta, Dipankar. 2005. Whither the Indian Village?: Culture and Agriculture in "Rural India", *Economic and Political Weekly*, February 9, 2005.

Inden, R.B. 1990. *Imagining India*, Oxford, UK. Basil Blackwell.

Jodhka, Surinder S. 2002. Nation and Village: Images of Rural India in Gandhi, Nehru and Ambedkar, *Economic and Political Weekly*, Vol. 37, No. 32 (August 10-16, 2002), pp. 3343-3353.

Jodhka, Surinder. S. 2014 (January). What's Happening to the Village? Revisiting Rural Life and Agrarian Change in Haryana, Delhi: CAS Working Paper Series, CSSS/JNU.

Jodhka, Surinder. S. 2016. Revisiting the Rural in 21st Century India, *Economic and Political Weekly*, June 25, 2016, Vol. 51, Nos. 26 and 27.

O'Malley, L.S.S. 1934/75. *India's Social Heritage*, New Delhi: Vikas Publishing House Pvt. Ltd.

Rudolph, Lloyd I. and S.H. Rudolph. 1987. *In Pursuit of Lakshmi: The Political Economy of the Indian State*, Delhi: Orient Longman Ltd.

Singh, Santosh K. 2020. "Village as Home", The Viral Condition, Identities Virtual Symposium, Published and Hosted by the Journal *Identities: Global Studies in Culture and Power*, Routledge, Taylor and Francis Group. Article Link: https://www.identitiesjournal.com/the-viral-condition-virtual-symposium/village-as-home

Singh, Santosh K. 2016. De-ploughing the "Rural": Urban Myths About Rural Consumption, *Economic and Political Weekly*, Vol. 51, Issue No. 25, June 18, 2016 (Web exclusive).

Thakur, Manish. 2014 (January). Understanding Ruralities: Contemporary Debates, Delhi: CAS Working Paper Series, CSSS/JNU.

1

Imagination of Village: A Tri-logue with Gandhi, Tagore and Ambedkar

Dev Nath Pathak

Is the village no longer a premise of thinking, reasoning and imagining? It seems there is a strong inclination towards an answer in the affirmative. Following a conjecture, social scientists proposed a decline in the idea of the village. We have heard phrases such as shrinking or vanishing or diminishing village. This chapter tends to suggest otherwise. It proposes to perceive a mutation in the idea of the village rather than decline. This is revealed through intermittent references to popular cinematic instances. Although studying cinema is not a prime objective, the cinematic nuggets may aid in elucidating a point about critical utopias. In the main, the essay seeks to revisit a potential tri-logue among three key thinkers of modern India who made vivid interjections on the question of the village. The three thinkers are namely, M.K. Gandhi, Rabindranath Tagore and B.R. Ambedkar. A dramatic criteria of selection of the three is: they tend to offer a complicated turf with high decibles of disagreements. In other words, the three thinkers put together aid in unravelling currents and counter-currents of a debate conducive for a holistic imagination of the village in India. Engaging with the tri-logue, this chapter justifies the need to revisit the critical romantic utopianism that is common in the three thinkers.

Setting the Stage

The village has for long been viewed as a convenient entry point for understanding 'traditional' Indian society. Even though tradition itself is a perpetual process[1] it makes sense as to how people's subjectivity may be shaped. In a popular imagination and related subjectivity the village is a signifier of the authentic native life, a social and cultural unit uncorrupted by outside influence. Many popular cinematic tales in India, from Raj Kapoor's *Jis Desh Me Ganga Behti Hai* (The Country Where Flows the River Ganga, dir. Radhu Karmakar, 1960) to Govinda starrer *Jis Desh Me Ganga Rahta Hai* (The Country Where Lives Ganga, dir. Mahesh Manjrekar, 2000), vindicate this romantic imagination of the village. In this imagination, as Nandi noted elsewhere, the village "has become the repository of traditional wisdom and spirituality, and of the harmony of nature, intact community life and environmental sagacity—perhaps even a statement of Gandhian austerity, limits to wants and anti-consumerism" (2001: 13). The village indeed becomes an ideological ploy, inviting glib deliveries of platitutudes. However, if there is the 'infantilised village' inspired by romantic utopianism, as Nandi noted, there is also the village as a 'geriatric responsibility'. The latter refers to the village as a theatre of performance by various stakeholders, inclusive of thinkers, leaders, as well as sociologists. For, the sublatern cannot speak, the city-bred scholars will lend voices. And these voices can be mistaken for that of the villagers. The complication of the villages are often ironed out by the iron fist of city-dwelling intelligentsia.

This is what seems to be the case with a large part of academic interest in the idea of the village. For the professional sociologists and social anthropologists, the village represented India in microcosm, and hence sociological studies of the village was significant since independence. Nothing is original about such a sociological premise. The picture of the villages resonant with the national imagination are quite varied though. Cinematic as well as social scientific accounts underline division and hierarchy in the midst of romantic utopias about villages. They duly cast aspersions on the imagination of the village as a serene, pastoral, agrarian paradise. The filmmaker Mehboob Khan showed it in *Mother India* (1957) much more poignantly than the tribe of sociologists and social anthropologists could do with empirical data. A schematic ambivalence in imagining the village allowed Mehboob Khan to enlist the anomalies of rurality, based on caste and gender disparties. It also emphasised the exploitative socio-religious and economic institutions and unequal ownership of land. And while doing so, stress social scientists, the cinematic imagination did not compromise on the affective components, viz. emotions and everydayness. The village as a microcosm of India was fraught with social divisions and inequalities, in Mehboob Khan's *Mother India* as much as in Louis Dumont's *Homo Hierchicus*[2] (1970). This befitted the age when modernisation became synonymous with nation-building in post-independent India. Almost in tune with the Nehruvian idea of modern India, where scientific advances and technological progress were cherished values, *Hum Hindustani* (We, The Indians, dir. Ram Mukherjee, 1960) shifted the romantic glance from villages to the towns. For much of sociological research, the village remained a convenient setting for field work generating substantive discussions around caste, occupations, kinship, religion, landholding patterns and the like in post-independent India. From contributing to the state initiatives of community development programmes to reaching the point where the sociologists pronounced "vanishing" of villages[3], it is curious that a rich and complex trope of romantic-utopianism has been pervasive.

In this wake, it is imperative to unravel a discursive trope comprising streams of thoughts in the writings, speeches, and actions in the intellectual history of modern India. The essay in the remaining curates a tri-logue of M.K. Gandhi, Rabindranath Tagore and B.R. Ambedkar. Juxtaposing the thoughts of these three thinkers underlines the components of a possible futuristic vision, a romantic utopia, at the conceptual cusp of tradition and modernity. Arguably, a specific notion of 'Indian modernity'[4] brings the three thinkers in intellectual and ideological proximity despite an array of disagreements. The peculiarity of Indian modernity lies in the intellectual scheme wherein tradition and modernity are not irresolvable binary opposites. Instead, they are Janus-faced, in unfinished critical dialogue. In this scheme, there is little scope for revivalism or disintegration of traditions, as they seem to thrive on the advances of modernity. This intellectual scheme supports a sense of creative ambivalence that is evident in the logic of thinking of the trinity of modern Indian social thoughts.

Before embarking on the thoughts of the trinity, it is important to steer clear of another set of crucial issues. The creative ambivalence is also reflected in historical and sociological engagement with the notion of the village in modern India. The alleged sociological reduction of the village into tried and tested categories ought to be placed in the scheme of colonial investigative modalities[5]. The colonial modalities unfolded two ways of seeing the village, one as a unit for colonial administration and the other as an epistemic category. Henry Sumner Maine, Karl Marx and B.H. Baden-Powell, among others in this ilk, looked at the Indian village more as a unit of knowledge about Indian society than a mere unit of colonial administration. However, the two are not exclusive of each other and overlaps could be underlined in the history. Suffice to say the two strands of seeing the village belonged to the same historical pale of perspectives. Moreover, unlike the colonial administrators, the national(ist) leadership did not see the village simply as a constituting 'basic unit' (for administration or as a unit of knowledge) of Indian civilisation. For most of them, the village represented 'the real' India, the nation that needed to be recovered, liberated and transformed. Even when they celebrated village life, they did not lose sight of the actual state of affairs marked by scarcity and ignorance, constraints and anomalies[6]. Even after the British relegated the Indian village to the backseat in favour of caste as a category for understanding Indian society, the notion of the self-sufficient village republic continued to stir the nationalist imagination. Needless to say, the native's visualisation of the village was not free from ideology and utopias. This was very well rooted in the historical context. However, what makes this visualisation worth revisiting is the realism in romance, tranformative zeal in reconstruction of the past, and a locally significant idea of modernity embedded in the history of India.

In the wake of sociological reductions (allegedly a narrow reconstruction) of the category of the village, it is rather daunting to propose for a romantic utopian notion of the village. The discursive realisations in this chapter may seem regressive, ahistorical, and anti-intellectual at times. Such a dismissive approach to the romantic utopian village is premised on another kind of romantic-utopian imagination. It is that of smart cities pertaining to aspirational dreams that has replaced the village, a realm of scarcities and deadends. Various models of smart cities is at the price of an imagination of village in contemporary India. Being romantic about rurality in contemporary India may be dubbed even as an anti-developmental stance. In this framework the villagers and small town dwellers are migrant workers in the cities. It got empirically vindicated when migrant workers began to return to the villages and small towns during the lockdown and pandemic in 2020. With migrant workers socio-cultural components of the villages have been making space in the city-spaces. This means villages did not disappear even in a relatively regulated 'urban villages' in megacities. The 'village in mind' in such cities become visible on the occasions of festivities when teeming numbers of villagers queue up to board a train in the big cities to travel back to villages.

This is the complex context in which it is imperative to revisit the tri-logue with the three key thinkers of modern India. The tri-logue, at least in this chapter, is a hinge for deliberating the possibility and significance of romantic utopianism in order to rethink the village in India. And, that is why it is also important to steer clear of the dominant (sociological and historical) approaches to these thinkers and thereof notion of the village. This chapter will push the readings of the predecessors aside, if not trash them, for broadly two reasons. The predecessors have been too much conditioned by historicity. It has not been possible to fathom the merit of civisational-mythological ruminations in a historically conditioned approach. Though an eye at historicity is relevant for many examinations, it could delimit the perspective too. Such an approach operationalises various kinds of linear binaries. The linearity of binary opposition in the historically conditioned readings seldom allows to engage with the trinity beyond their 'discordant disagreements'[7]. It reduces the trinity as intellectuals-at-war on the issue of village in the institution of modern education.

The dominant scheme of analysis in social science does not seem to leave the space to see the trinity complementing each other on the notion of the village. Each is squarely separated from the other. This is a kind of historicity of location that enabled in grasping the peculiarities in modern India. If one broadens the scope of historicity it would perhaps reveal that the dominant historical framework allegedly disabled to take note of the continuum of past and present, tradition and modernity, socio-religious and secular, collective and individual. Secondly, the predecessors' predominant interest in the idea of the village and thereof socio-cultural lives is characterised by a new milieu and values in modern India. The new milieu enjoins upon the intelligentsia to configure the possible emancipation from anything which binds to the past. And the village, a concrete storehouse of the alleged anachronistic allegiance, must be overcome in this scheme. Such reformist zeal concealed in social science approaches to the village overlooks the potential sources of enchantment that a village spatially and socially embodies. Just like religion did not disappear with modernisation and nation building, villages are hard to die!

With these modest disclaimers, adequately hinting at what this essay is seeking to do, this is imperative to draw attention to the key premise upon which a tri-logue of the three thinkers is envisaged. This premise entails, on one hand, an orientalist imagination of the villages, typically articulated in Metcalfe's words, "dynasty after dynasty tumbles down, revolution succeeds revolution. Hindu, Pathan, Mughal, Maratha, Sikh, English all are masters in turn, but the village communities remain the same. In times of trouble they arm and fortify themselves. A hostile army passes through the country. The village communities collect their cattle within their walls and let the enemy pass unprovoked"[8]. On the other hand, there was a recognition that the village was not as unchangeable as the essentialist anthropological prophesy, for example Dumont's (1970), may have echoed. It changed enabling sociologists' to go overboard and announce a possible disappearance of the ideal village. In this ambivalent historical scheme, village was a central category for the three historical icons, Gandhi, Tagore and Ambedkar. This ambivalent schema engendered the possibility of double-barrel romantic utopianism about the village, seeking to see value of communitarian lives and transformative politics at once. Despite the variations in the line of arguments and propositions, the three represent a dialogic kinship on the fact that the village represented the core of the traditional social order of India. They however disagreed, both, on the merits of traditional Indian village life, and also on the place it should have in the envisioned India of the future[9]. But, to be a devil's advocate, the stress on disagreement among the three thinkers, a case in the conventional and predominant readings and popular politics, could obscure the depth of vision, anxiety and expectations which the three seem to have about the village. Keeping their disagreements aside, though it comes into the picture at the onset of the following section, one can still imagine an engagement with the tri-logue of the trinity underpinning the re-imagining of the village.

Trinity Revisited: A Critical Romantic-Utopia for the Future

It is not easy to strike a tri-logue with the trinity given their disagreements. If it was still managebale between Rabindranath Tagore and M.K. Gandhi, it seemed almost impossible between B.R Ambedkar and Gandhi. But then, one should be reminded of an insightful proposition, Palshikar made elsewhere, "personality clashes need not be the decisive factor in the assessment of thought. Also, we need to accept that immediate political interests of Gandhi and Ambedkar clashed. Ambedkar began his political career as the leader of the untouchables and continued to claim to be the authentic representative of the untouchable community. Gandhi, on the other hand, appeared to be denying the existence of separate interests of untouchables in the context of the freedom struggle. Ambedkar was always suspicious of the social content of the freedom struggle and believed that Gandhi was not adequately sensitive to this. Since Gandhi was at the helm of the freedom struggle, Ambedkar thought it necessary to position itself against Gandhi. Given these historical circumstances, is it necessary that we sit in judgment to decide the case in favour of either Gandhi or Ambedkar?" (2014)[10]

Thus, this tri-logue shall seek to engage with the trinity without subscribing to the discordant disagreements in the prevalent readings of the three thinkers and actors of modern India. Instead, in the following, the essay shall present the thought system of the three in order to unravel the structures of romantic, futuristic, utopias in them. This is despite the recognition of the nearly high-decible of disagreements among them.

Born in the 1860s in two regions separated by the bulk of the country, both Tagore and Gandhi were townsmen. Tgaore was born and brought up in Calcutta and Gandhi's family too was town-based, rather than village-based. This is to underline the spatial location despite the fact that the distance between the town and village was duly blurry in the colonial India. So one can say, they lived with the sense of the village in their respective locations in the towns. Yet, they turned to the concrete body of the village in adult life after they had formed a view of the world in which the village stood for the core values of the Indian civilisation[11]. Difference between perspectives of prominent leaders with regard to the village is quite evident: for Gandhi the village was a site of authenticity while for someone like Nehru it was a site of backwardness and for Ambedkar, a site of oppression. Gandhi has been rightly known as the ideologue of the village, centring it as the fulcrum of ideal India, *swaraj*.

> My idea of Village Swaraj is that it is a complete republic, independent of its neighbours for its wants, and yet interdependent for many others in which dependence is a necessity. Thus every village's first concern will be to grow its own food crops and cotton for its cloth. It should have a reserve for its cattle, recreation and playground for adults and children. Then if there is more land available, it will grow useful money crops, thus excluding ganja, tobacco, opium and the like. The village will maintain a village theatre, school and public hall. It will have its own waterworks ensuring clean supply. This can be done through controlled wells and tanks. Education will be compulsory up to the final basic course. As far as possible every activity will be conducted on the co-operative basis. There will be no castes such as we have today with their graded untouchability. Non-violence with the technique of Satyagraha and non-cooperation will be the sanction of the village community[12].

Gandhi went on to discuss the governance of the village by the Panchayat annually elected by the adult villagers, male and female, possessing minimum prescribed qualifications. As evident, for Gandhi, the village was a 'republic' of self-suffciency, a place where "a tiger and a goat drank water at the same watering hole and lived together cordially and happily."[13] The Indian village had a design, a way of life, which had the potential of becoming an alternative to the city and technology driven capitalist west. The binary conception of village and city, rural and urban is hinged on an ideal notion of the village, derived from India's civilisational past. But, is it free from the acknowledgement of the degenerating village, historical encounters and structural impacts on the village? As he asserted, "the nearest approach to civilisation based upon non-violence is the erstwhile village republic of India. I admit that it was very crude. I know that there was in it no non-violence of my definition and conception. But the germ was there"[14]. Such optimism despite the admission of anomalies could be possible only because Gandhi's town and village coexisted in spite of the cognitive binaries that he mentions.

The Gandhian acknowledgement of crudeness in the past is also a marker of his inclination to change. But, what kind of change? Gandhian dismay about the nature of changes that the Indian village life had gone through during the British colonial rule was explicit on many occasions. In his view, these changes had impaired the villagers, made them less creative and more dependent on the outside world. In his words, "...the villager of today is not even half as intelligent or resourceful as the villager of fifty years ago. For, whereas the former is reduced to a state of miserable dependence and idleness, the latter used his mind and body for all he needed and produced them at home"[15]. It would be thus unjustifiable to suggest that Gandhi held a linear, unequivocal, simple, romantic notion of the village without recognition of the structural anomalies of the past and distorting encounter of colonialism. That Gandhian idealism about the village impaired a fuller understanding of the village cannot be the starting point for a discussion on Gandhi's imagination of the village. Any oversimplification of Gandhian imagination in social sciences only impaired the possibility of Gandhian growth in India.

The idea of an ideal in Gandhi was fraught with the awareness of the contemporary challenges and complexity of the past. It was this creative ambivalence, rather than plain nostalgia, in Gandhi's visualisation of the village that underpinned his actions and thoughts. While he asked for revival of the 'spirit of traditional village life', he also found many flaws with the actually existing villages. It was not that all these rural ills were a consequence of the western/urban influence. Two aspects that he commented quite frequently on were the practice of untouchability and a general lack of cleanliness. He repeatedly talks about reviving the village, particularly its 'defunct handicrafts' to save the peasant from the adverse ramification of industrialisation and inevitability of moving to the cities. A closer look at his writings tends to suggest that his vision of the village was essentially 'a futuristic one', representing an alternative society that was different from the modern-industrial West, and its colonial clones in South Asia. His villages would have had similarities with what Sir Henry Maine (1871) had spoken of in his lectures on village communities in the east and west at Oxford. Maine's objective was to cull out a comparative jurisprudence from the eastern village society following the methodological suit of comparative mythology. For Gandhi, a village was not a purely given entity. His writings reflect more of a sensitive reformist rather than someone interested in giving a revivalist urge. And hence, his stress was on the idea of village swaraj, as underlined in the quote above.

Gandhi eschewed a discourse of representation by which the village is already marked as the 'epistemological other' of the city. An epistemological other that stands in conceptual contrast, loaded with superiority and inferiority, would amount to a blind romance. Instead, he aspired to show it as a realm of possibilities, a 'dream of mind', for the idea of swaraj. In arguing for responsible technology, communal (community bound) accountability, and social and economic sharing, Gandhi was at once also challenging Nehru's semantic conflation of village and primitivism, as well as outlining his vision of the village as a site for social change and as the arena for a new civil order[16] . In a letter to Jawaharlal Nehru (dated October 5, 1945), Gandhi incisively emoted,

> While I admire modern science, I find that it is the old looked at in the true light of modern science which should be re-clothed and refashioned aright. You must not imagine that I am envisaging our village life as it is today. The village of my dreams is still in my mind. After all every man lives in the world of his dreams. My ideal village will contain intelligent human beings. They will not live in dirt and darkness as animals. Men and women will

> be free and able to hold their own against anyone in the world. There will be neither plague, nor cholera nor small pox; no one will be idle, no one will wallow in luxury. Everyone will have to contribute his quota of manual labour. I do not want to draw a large-scale picture in detail. It is possible to envisage railways, post and telegraph offices, etc. For me it is material to obtain the real article and the rest will fit into the picture afterwards. If I let go the real thing, all else goes[17].

Evidently, it is a dream with reality in sight. His objection is to the vantage point where one is compelled to either dream or be real. Gandhi indeed placed the village in the scheme of reasoning which he fashioned meticulously to propose an idea of India. Dislocating Gandhi's imagination of villages from that scheme of reasoning for the convenience of analysis could be vulnerable to the interpretative politics of analysts. For example, in sociological rumination, the Gandhian imagination of the village is reduced to a simpler matrix of civilisation. In a typical reading of this kind there is a proposition which reveals the sociological convenience qua intellectual myopia. It presents a linear, neat, and reprehensible tripartite classification of stages of Gandhian imagination. At first, the Gandhian imagination of the village is seen in the scheme of Indian civilisation, at the second, the village is a counterpart of the city. The civilisational glory of the village results in a bad romance. In it, village-life presents a critique of, and an alternative to, the modern Western culture and civilisation. And lastly, at the third phase, it is Gandhi's notion of actual existing villages and imperative to reform. This tripartite division, suitable for a sociologist's classificatory scheme, operates with a simpler notion of Indian civilisation, and a foggy one. It divides Gandhian imagination without admitting any possibility of interlinkages of the three parts, akin to the integrated whole called civilisation. And hence, such an approach remains oblivious of Gandhian ambivalence. Whereas, in the foregoing part of this essay, a holistic sense of Gandhian idealism about the village deems it as a civilisation category, in the process of making rather than a finished entity of the past.

To take a jump cut, Tagore and Gandhi represented the quintessence of Indian thought and life in the modern age. Tagore operated with a qualitatively different scheme of thought and reasoning, leading him to be critical of Gandhi's ideas. In 1919, Tagore warned against an instrumental view of satyagraha or an overly enthusiastic notion of passive resistance. "Passive resistance is a force which is not necessarily moral in itself; it can be used against truth as well as for it. The danger inherent in all force grows stronger when it is likely to gain success"[18]. This was an explicit critique of the nationalist reduction of the idea of swaraj. And needless to say it also underlined Tagore's scepticism about the Gandhian notion of the self-sufficient village. Although Gandhi recognised the crucial importance of Tagore's dissent, calling him the Great Sentinel, Gurudev[19], he held his ground. For instance, about the spinning wheel, Gandhi remarked, "A plea for the spinning wheel is a plea for recognising the dignity of labour"[20]. In a society ridden with caste-based division of labour and a complex set of discriminative practices and taboos, Gandhi›s insistence on spinning, along with cleaning latrines, community kitchens, etc., is more than symbolic. But then, Tagore had his poetic vision. It led him to propose yet another futuristic view in which local and universal were Janus-faced.

In a compelling set of essays written between 1915 and 1940, Rabindranath Tagore articulated a social vision for a just, humane, collectively owned socio-economic structure, i.e. villages. At the core of his thought was the cooperative principle. But his vision, like that of Gandhi, was not unaware of the crisis at hand. He wrote: "Today our villages are half-dead. If we imagine we can just continue to live, that would be a mistake. The dying can pull the living only towards death."[21] Tagore echoed scepticism about the solutions proposed by the elite, such as charity or moral enlightenment of the wealthy class. Instead, he sought an ethical model of production. What would that entail? Tagore's vision went far beyond notions like 'social responsibility' that are in vogue today. To him, ethical production required that resources (such as land and capital) are collectively owned by the producers themselves. Tagore's insightful observation is worth recalling when socio-economic fermentation among the agrarian workers and farmers in contemporary India is palpable. This would ensure that the produce is also collectively owned, and that all producers have a say in determining their share of value in the product of their work. The typical small farmer, indebted and impoverished, was much in need of such a structure. And in the same breath, Tagore has been an advocate of a transition to a re-localised, cooperative, society in close touch with the land.

Tagore employs metaphors from nature as well as culture, to elucidate his thoughts. He compares, for example, the village to a married wife and maid-servant, and suggests,

> Villages are nearer to nature than towns, and in closer touch with the fountain of life. They possess a natural power of healing. It is the function of the village to provide people with their elemental needs, with food and joy, with the simple poetry of life and with those ceremonies of beauty which the village spontaneously produces and in which she finds delight. But when constant strain is put upon her, when her resources are excessively exploited, she becomes dull and uncreative. From her time-honoured position of the wedded wife, she descends to that of a maid-servant. The city, in its intense egotism and pride, remains unconscious of the hurt it inflicts on the very source of its life, health and joy. Our modern cities, in the same way, feed upon the social organism that runs through the villages. They appropriate the life stuff of the community and slough off a huge amount of dead matter, while making a lurid counterfeit of prosperity. Thus, unlike a living heart, these cities imprison and kill the blood and create poison centres.[22]

In the same romantic breath of a poet, Tagore doubles as a deep ecologist to plead with us not to fall prey to the narrow, parochial, localisation of imagination. He bridges the gap between near and afar, earth and sky, local and universal, as he says,

> Have I not known the sunshine to grow brighter and the moonlight deeper in its tenderness when my heart was filled with a sudden access of love assuring me that this world is one with my soul? When I have sung the coming of the clouds, the pattering of rains has found its pathos in my songs. From the dawn of our history the poets and artists have been infusing the colours and music of their soul into the structure of existence. And from this I have known certainly that the earth and the sky are woven with the fibres of man's mind, which is the universal mind at the same time.[23]

Tagore's vision of self-realisation, in the framework where universal and particular met, involved reviving the multiplicity of local communities within India's geographical vastness, and for India to foster unity in diversity of Asia and lead the West towards the self-realisation of the world. Tagore was no revolutionary in the typical sense of the word, and accepted the necessity of private property, at the same time regarding his rural reconstruction projects as his 'life's work'. This may seem self-contradictory unless read with due sensitivity.

> If we could free even one village from the shackles of helplessness and ignorance, an ideal for the whole of India would be established. That is what occurred to me then and that is what I still think. Let a few villages be rebuilt in this way, and I shall say they are my India. That is the way to discover the true India.[24]

The italicised phrases (by this author) are suggested to be Tagore's moot propositions about village-India, true India, shackled in helplessness (historical, material, and structural conditions), in ignorance (of the inherent tendencies qua civilisational constitution) and the imperative to rebuild them (the reformist zeal). It is a neat blending of civilisational utopia of visionary, sociological realisation of an organically linked thinker, and reformist vision in the wake of the critical consciousness that stem from a thinker's reasoning. Tagore's manifesto about the community development or the upliftment of the village community too is a case in point. It was expressed in an essay *Swadeshi Samaj* (Indigenous/Indian Society) in 1904[25]. This essay was the first comprehensive statement of his social philosophy. He analysed the causes of the disintegration of village life and made concrete suggestions for its reconstruction. His scheme centred on the reorganisation of village life through concerted efforts. The salient features therein are: Concept of Community Development, Village Reconstruction and the Community College Movement, revival of cottage industries to mitigate the poverty of the masses; intimate cooperation between rural workers and villagers and curtailment of expenditure at socio-religious ceremonies.

Tagore laid great weight on the need for collective enterprise in villages. The use of labour-saving machinery was indispensable, but it would be possible only if collective cultivation were introduced through the initiative of union executives. In Tagore's scheme of rural reconstruction the material aspect was not left out. Tagore always thought, "true happiness depends more on the habit of the mind than on the size of the purse"[26]. For Tagore the task of rural reconstruction was aimed to 'rebuild man'. And hence, in another essay he states two objectives—first to educate the villager in self-reliance, secondly to implement the concept of 'life in its completeness' with 'music and readings'[27]. "Tagore wanted to develop these limited villages completely—its essential strength would be a cooperative society"[28]. As it may appear that Tagore sought to bridge the gap between city and village through the 'Sriniketan experiment', combining science and spirituality, modernity and tradition, universal and local. The traditional handicraft was made more durable by giving the touch of science and these artisans formed a single group to promote their product with the exporters. Tagore, beyond charity, wanted to make the rural economy independent and only paying heed to cottage-industry was not enough. To uplift the rural economy the role of agriculture cannot be denied and to sustain the rural economy, expertise in agriculture was vital. The goal of self-reliance was the basic premise in Tagore's scheme of rural-economic reconstruction. This is nor far-fetched that Tagore's advocacy was distinguished from the nationalist and economic thinking of the nationalist movement, viz. swadeshi and swaraj. Instead, his stress was on 'constructive swadeshi' which could enable the masses to produce before falling prey to jingoism and boycotting foreign goods.

With a fair amount of critical distinction of thought, in disagreement with Gandhi, Tagore operated with his own share of romanticism about the future of India. He aspired and endeavoured to show that it was a realisable utopia, like Gandhi did. And within this version of romantic utopianism, there is a creative ambivalence, as elucidated above. It sought to see value in the village while admitting the imperative of changes. It forged the relation of local and universal in the positive spirit of reform.

Radically opposed to Tagore and Gandhi, stands Ambedkar's dispassionate plea. As he told the constituent assembly, "I hold that these village republics have been the ruination of India... what is the village but a sink of localism, a den of ignorance, narrow-mindedness and communalism?"[29]

For Ambedkar, the village presented a microcosmic model of the Hindu social organisation. It was 'the working plant of the Hindu social order, where one could see the Hindu social order in operation in full swing'[30]. The Indian village was not a single unit. It was divided into two sets of populations: 'touchables' and 'untouchables'. For Ambedkar, the governing normative structure of the village was in no way close to the ethos of democracy. The village life was marked by experiences of exclusion, exploitation and untouchability. He expressed it duly, "This is the village republic of which the Hindus are so proud. What is the position of the untouchables in this Republic? They are not merely the last but are also the least...in this Republic there is no place for democracy. There is no room for equality. There is no room for liberty and there is no room for fraternity. The Indian village is the very negation of the Republic[31]. For Ambedkar this kind of village was a colony of upper castes where Dalits are humiliated and decimated.

Ambedkar indeed positions himself against Gandhi, and attacks caste, Hinduism, and the village in continuity. For, one is integral to the other, and hence if one wants to understand Ambedkar's critique of villages, one ought to be reading Ambedkar saying, "There are many occupations in India which, on account of the fact that they are regarded as degraded by the Hindus, provoke those who are engaged in them to aversion. There is a constant desire to evade and escape from such occupations, which arises solely because of the blighting effect which they produce upon those who follow them, owing to the slight and stigma cast upon them by the Hindu religion. What efficiency can there be in a system under which neither men's hearts nor their minds are in their work? As an economic organisation caste is therefore a harmful institution, inasmuch as it involves the subordination of man's natural powers and inclinations to the exigencies of social rules"[32].

Thus, for Ambedkar, the Indian villages are representative of Hindu colonialism designed to exploit the untouchables. The untouchables have no rights. They are there only to wait, serve and submit. Towards this, "every Hindu village has a ghetto. The Hindus live in the village and the untouchables live in the ghetto"[33].

And this is not useful for the Hindus either. Ambedkar suggests, "The caste system prevents common activity; and by preventing common activity, it has prevented the Hindus from becoming a society with a unified life and a consciousness of its own being"[34].

One has to see, as Ambedkar suggests, how the larger structure of the Hindu village is a working plant of the Hindu social order, an order based on exclusion and inclusion. In contrast to Metcalfe who saw Indian village communities as 'little republics', Ambedkar sees them, unlike Gandhi and Tagore, as 'republics of humiliation'. To him, 'the Indian village is the very negation of [the idea of] a republic'[35]. And hence, Ambedkar's appeal to fellow Hindus is, "the Hindus must consider whether the time has not come for them to recognise that there is nothing fixed, nothing eternal, nothing *sanatan*; that everything is changing, that change is the law of life for individuals as well as for society. In a changing society, there must be a constant revolution of old values; and the Hindus must realise that if there must be standards to measure the acts of men, there must also be a readiness to revise those standards"[36].

However, it remains noteworthy that Ambedkar too, despite condemning the village communities for their conservatism and ignorance, could not deny them the virtue of stability essential for social and economic progress. Without it, the vagaries of parliamentary democracy will be under a brake[37]. If the village community does not become an engine of social reengineering, it shall continue to get restricted to being a 'stink of localism'. In this regard, it is worth recalling the observation of Palshikar (2014), "The discourses of Gandhi and Ambedkar were not antithetical. Therefore, it is possible to think in terms of common concerns and potential grounds for dialogue between the two discourses. Further, both Gandhi and Ambedkar were concerned with the question of emancipation"[38].

The question of emancipation was crucial in Ambedkar's imagination of India. It was emancipation at both, inner and outer, spiritual and material domains of lives. And hence, it seems, Ambedkar upholds Buddha over Marx, Buddhism over communism, as he notes,

> The blessing of liberality consists in the householder living with the mind the freed from the taint of avarice...Greed, avarice, ill

> will, sloth and drowsiness, distraction and flurry and doubt are stains of the mind. A householder who gets rid of such stains of the mind acquires great wisdom, abundant wisdom, clear vision and perfect wisdom. ....The Buddha's method was different. His method was to change the mind of man: to alter his disposition: so that whatever man does, he does it voluntarily without the use of force or compulsion. His main means to alter the disposition of men was his Dhamma and the constant preaching of his Dhamma. Buddha's way was not to force people to do what they did not want to do, although it was good for them. His way was to alter the disposition of men so that they would do voluntarily what they would not otherwise to do[39].

With this spirit of Buddhism by his side, Ambedkar declared, "If you ask me, my ideal would be a society based on *Liberty, Equality, and Fraternity*."[40]

Steering clear of tempting linearity of agreement-disagreement in a debate, a tri-logue emanates from the intellectual, political and social positions that the three thinkers hold. Each is speaking to the other, and trying to marshal their specific fragments in the larger whole of imagining village India. The holistic implication of the tri-logue is an invitation to think of Indian villages with critical awareness of the stifling impacts of caste structure, hegemony of Hinduism, narrowness of nationalism, and unwanted intervention of the Western projects of modernisation. While doing so, the tri-logue also enjoins upon the minds with critical consciousness to rethink villages, as an ideal unit of India. There are various methods of actualising the envisioned ideal. Each method may vary from, or partially overlap with the other. Needless to say, the difference in methods does not amount to throwing the baby away with the bathwater, so to say. The three thinkers of modern India operate with differently constituted utopianism about the village. Each seeks to bring about transformation. For Gandhi, the transformation hinges on the imperative of *swaraj* while for Tagore it is needed to be aware of the stifling localism qua nationalism. Thus Tagore would envisage the village as a self-sufficient entity where local and universal could thrive at once in the register of aesthetic naturalism. Ambedkar's critical utopia entails the egalitarian tenets of Buddhism on one hand and the ideals of modernity characterised by the three appeals consequent of the French Revolution—*Liberty, Equality, and Fraternity*. Reading the three thinkers in one-breath amounts to a tri-logue which aids in critical comprehension of the entity called the village, as well as engendering romantic utopias on how to reimagine a village-India. It is however a creative ambivalence in the utopias of the three thinkers that is emphatic, and of relevance across epochs in the history of modern India.

In the Aftermath of the Tri-logue

Post-independent India carried forward the schematic ambivalence akin to that of the tri-logue of the trinity. By studying a village, the pioneering Indian sociologist M.N. Srinivas claimed, one could generalise about the 'social processes and problems to be found occurring in great parts of India'[41]. Building upon such anthropological interest, the village perceived not merely as a place where people lived. It was seen as a structure infused with the basic values of Indian civilisation[42]. A kind of villageism in the 1960s dominated the disciplinary glances, and thus enthusiasm for Panchayati Raj, community development, as part of nation building were aloft in the post-independence period. The village was to be the laboratory of directed (instructed and programmed) cultural change (Dube, 1964). Many policy decisions and the massive rural development programmes directed the post-colonial state's attention towards the village. This persisted even in the reconstituted panchayats post the 73rd amendment in the Constitution of India. It was believed that women, Harijans and other disadvantaged sections should take their rightful place in village India post-independence. The sociological and social anthropological rhetoric[43] and researches placed the village as a marker of India in continuum with the above tri-logue. Though the tri-logue pinned up the engagements with the village, it seems less impactful in academic, administrative, governance, and commonsense. The imagination of nation building seldom reflects on the tri-logure, inherent critical insights.

Centrality of the village for the first generation of sociologists/ social anthropologists in India however sits uneasily with some of the recent pronouncements in the prognostic sociological reasoning. For example, Gupta avers, 'the village is no longer a site where futures can be planned' (2004: 11). He adds further, 'the village is shrinking as a sociological reality, though it still exists as space' (Ibid: 9). In post-liberalised India this is tempting to toy with the idea of the vanishing village. In the 1990s, cinematic, urban-nostalgic, representation of the village was nearly abysmal. Cities, with various avatars, seemed to have won over villages in popular tales. Diaspora imagination prevailed upon the tabloid depiction of the village, such as in *Dilwale Dulhaniya Le Jayenge* (The Big-Hearted Will Win the Bride, 1995, dir. Aditya Chopra)[44]. This is in a particular context of the liberalised economy that accommodated goods from across the commercially connected world. Similar dispositions however had a mention much before the technical opening of the economy and globalisation becoming a buzzword, for example *Purab Aur Paschim* (East and West, 1970, dir. Manoj Kumar), *Des Pardes* (Nation and Foreign Land, 1978) among others. The latter struck a connection between London and a village in north India, even though diaspora imagination of the roots-in-village back in India (a typical notion of homeland) was on the nationalist register.

Lately the popular cinematic imagination showed more inclination to the complexity of villages, rather than depiction along nationalist jingoism. *Peepli* (*Live*) (2010, dir. Anusha Rizvi and Mahmood Farooqui), in the wake of globalisation is an instance. The village resurfaced, in the genre of crime-thriller, as grey countrysides. For example, in *Ishqiya* (2010, dir. Abhishek Chaubey), and *Paan Singh Tomar* (2012, dir. Tigmanshu Dhulia) inter alia. The register of the popular portrayal of the village has undergone a metamorphosis, no doubt. It is now a village with ambivalence, that was an essential feature of the tri-logue conducted above. There cannot possibly be a plain and simple narrative of village beating the nationalist drum. It is a village constituted by its good and bad, possibility and constraint. It is a better off situation for villages in popular cinema. Now they truly look like villages. The anomalies of villages are more about existential issues of everyday life connected with the mediated manipulations, politics without morality, comedy of errors, and political honour.

This leads to a relevant situation in which a tri-logue with the trinity makes sense. Rather than spending time in dealing with the empiricists' obsessive conclusions emerging from de-humanised statistics, it is worth dealing with the omnipresent rurality. The latter enables a glance through the ranks and files of cities in India today. This is everywhere, in pavement-dwellers' settlements, underneath a city flyover or overbridge, in the small pockets of rurality known as the urban village, as well as in the erstwhile village which may have attained demographic changes.

Much before the sociologists began to marshal details for an empiricist idea of the village, emphasising decline, Nandy (2001) had noted a triumph of the colonial city. The latter was India's new self on a triumphant march to diminish the idea of the village. The colonial city, 'the new self, identified with history, progress, becoming' (Ibid: 13). In Nandy's reading, the village is no longer a village-in-itself but a counterpoint to the city. It is a fantasy village, for the city. The village was more of a dystopia for those city-dwellers who wished to explore their selves on the register of nostalgia, a kind of villageism. Critically revisiting Nandy, it is possible to show concrete corporeality of the dystopia called the village. If there was a grand colonial self, there perhaps emerged other varieties of micro-selves within. These myriad micro-seleves were as affective as the bulldozer driver of the village that Srinivas (1976: 294) discussed as Rampura.

The city and village no longer seem to work as binaries of the past. They have intermingled, as have the dwellers of these spaces. In this context, many micro-selves in India today do not operate with the plain and simple register of the village as endangered species going to be lost to the urban tides of post-colonial India. If there is nostalgia, it is perhaps of a qualitatively different variety, worth exploring on some other occasion. Suffice to say, the new selves with the dreams of development do not see the village and city disentangled from each other. Likewise, many extensions may be spotted as growing out of the tri-logue of the trinity in post-independent India. In this exceeding plurality of forms and expressions, of rurality and urbanism, culture and politics, it is perhaps needed to evoke the tri-logue for a more gruesome task. This is not of nation-building as such. It is an advanced version of that, which could be passingly called nation-sustaining, with rurality and thereof emotional bursts in the wake.

The social spaces and sociability associated with the dreams of mega-cities can seldom cancel out villages. It is manifest with farmers from villages coming to the national highways leading to the cities in protest[45]. The people of villages who still rely on socio-economic structure that a village provides assert through occasional protests and mobilisation. This is adequate to underline that village matters. More ghastly is the assertion of the farmers who decide to end their lives under severe and unsurmountable economic distress[46]. The National Crime Records Bureau reported that farmers' suicides is 7.4 per cent of the total suicides in India in 2019. Each case of farmers' suicide for a variety of reasons has the potential to awaken the Indian conscience, and willing to return to the intellectual posterity on the idea of the village. The utopianism of the village ought to be revisited in such a crying time when the idea of the village has been either reduced into certain categories, or heard through the restive farmers' expressions of helplessness. It was the same helplessness that spilled all over the roads, bus and railway stations, during the pandemic, when the teeming number of migrants traversed to the cities across India. This was the desperate migrants trying to return from the 'cities of work' to the 'villages of home'. A statistics-obsessed social scientist may make an effort towards getting evidences from the Indian Railways to vindicate the rural to urban migrations and such a technical exercise may put a bottleneck in front of the idea of the village, once again. The innumerable evidences of socio-cultural presence of rurality in urban spaces are enough to suggest that the city is no longer a marker of colonial self, opposed to the village. Nor is the village, an uncivil other of the colonial self, of the city.

The cultural history, as well as academic approaches, separated the two, city and village. But they coexisted, in each other. In the lustful love for neat classification, we could not see the intimate relations, of spaces, people, their performative practices. The city, indeed, has assumed to be a more complicated entity, where rurality conjectures a sense of the village. And more importantly, the subjective narratives from the ranks and files of migrants, working with a variety of skill-sets, can reveal enriching ambivalence connecting the cities of residence with villages of inheritance. The complex self of India today entails an enmeshed rural and urban.

This is more messed up once ideological politics, along the names such as Gandhi and Ambedkar, are factored in. Different political regimes could subscribe to a different combination of ideological streams. Replacing Gandhi behind the charkha, celebrating anniversaries and showering occasional platitudes cannot suffice for the critical tri-logue and consequent debate that takes us to see merit in the romantic utopianism of the thinkers. Conducive for imagining, and re-imagining, village in its objective and subjective wholeness, the rich argumentative trope of the trinity of modern India ought to be revisited, again and over again.

NOTES

1. See Ramanujan (1989) on the idea of tradition.
2. The French version of Dumont's *Homo Hierarchicus*, a binary opposite of an envisaged Homo Equalis, appeared in 1966.
3. For example, Gupta (2004) draws attention to the implications of economic changes, including the decline of agriculture, that have people leaving villages in search of employment.
4. See, Pathak (2015). There are many other contributions along this line, which need not be exhausted here.
5. An idea that stems from Cohn (1996).
6. This section of the chapter dwells on an informative sketch by Thakur (2014).
7. A reading of Palshikar (2014) enables us to grapple with this issue.
8. Quoted in Mishra (2010: 214).
9. Jodhka (2002: 2).
10. See http://www.epw.in/journal/2014/13/glimpses-past-web-exclusives/gandhi-ambedkar-interface.html (accessed on March 8, 2017).
11. One remembers Beteille (2002) here.
12. Gandhi (1979: 308-09).
13. See Narayan (2009: 41).
14. Gandhi (1979: 296).
15. Gandhi (1974: 409).
16. Mohan (2010).
17. See http://www.gandhiashramsevagram.org/selected-letters-of-

mahatma/gandhi-letter-to-jawaharlal-nehru3.php (accessed on March 8, 2017).

18. Quoted in Bhattacharya (1997: 80).
19. See Nikhil Bhattacharya, Rabindranath Tagore and Mohan Das Karamchand Gandhi, http://www.mkgandhi.org/articles/tagore G.htm (accessed on March 8, 2017).
20. Ibid., 89.
21. See Ananya Mukherjee, Tagore and the Idea of Cooperation, http://www.thehindu.com/opinion/lead/tagore-and-the-idea-of-cooperation/article2151116.ece) (accessed on March 8, 2017).
22. Tagore (1928: 311-312).
23. Tagore (1919: 41).
24. Tagore (1928: 322).
25. See Das Gupta (1993).
26. Ibid., 25.
27. Tagore's (1941: 45).
28. See Nilanjan Banerjee, Discovering Tagore: Some Unpublished Poems, www.india-seminar.com/2011/623/623_nilanjan_banerjee.htm (accessed on March 8, 2017).
29. See http://parliamentofindia.nic.in/ls/debates/vol7p3b.htm (accessed on March 8, 2017).
30. See Ambedkar and Moon (1989:19).
31. Ibid., 25-26.
32. Ambedkar, The Annihilation of Caste, http://ccnmtl.columbia.edu/projects/mmt/ambedkar/web/index.html (accessed on March 8, 2017).
33. Ambedkar quoted in Chakravarty (2006: 104).
34. See http://ccnmtl.columbia.edu/projects/mmt/ambedkar/web/index.html (accessed on March 8, 2017).
35. (http://www.india-seminar.com/2015/674/674_anup_dhar.htm) (accessed on March 8, 2017).
36. Ibid. http://ccnmtl.columbia.edu/projects/mmt/ambedkar/web/index.html (accessed on March 8, 2017).
37. Mishra (2010: 219).
38. See http://www.epw.in/journal/2014/13/glimpses-past-web-exclusives/gandhi-ambedkar-interface.html (accessed on March 8, 2017).

39. B.R Ambedkar, Buddha or Karl Marx, http://www.drambedkar.co.in/books/category1/8buddhaorkarlmarx.pdf (accessed on March 8, 2017).
40. Ambedkar, B.R. The Annihilation of Caste, https://ccnmtl.columbia.edu/projects/mmt/ambedkar/web/index.html (accessed on March 8, 2017).
41. Srinivas (1955: 99).
42. Beteille (1980: 108).
43. For a glance through this rhetoric, it would be pertinent to peruse the ruminations by Radhakamal Mukerjee (1950), D.N. Majumdar (1958), D.P. Mukerji in Madan (2013).
44. This is interesting to read Uberoi (1998) to fathom the correlation of diaspora cultural imagination of roots connecting *pind* (village in Punjabi) and transnational sociability.
45. A report about the protest against the recently passed bill in the parliament by the Government of India, by Saurabh Shukla and Akhilesh Sharma is, https://www.ndtv.com/india-news/farmers-protest-farmers-to-meet-day-after-talks-with-amit-shah-fails-to-end-deadlock-2336148 (accessed on December 10, 2010).
46. A report on this by Ranjit Sengupta informs us that every day twenty-eight farmers commit suicide in India, see https://www.downtoearth.org.in/news/agriculture/every-day-28-people-dependent-on-farming-die-by-suicide-in-india-73194 (accessed on December 10, 2020).

REFERENCES

Ambedkar, B.R. 1945. *What Congress and Gandhi Have Done to the Untouchable*, Bombay: Thacker and Co. Ltd.

Ambedkar, B.R. and Moon, Vasant. 1989. eds. *Dr. Babasaheb Ambedkar: Writings and Speeches,* Mumbai: Education Department, Government of Maharashtra.

Ambedkar, B.R. and Rodrigues, V. 2002. *The Essential Writings of B.R. Ambedkar*, New Delhi: Oxford University Press.

Beteille, Andre. 1980. 'Indian Village: Past and Present', in E.J. Hobsbawm, W. Kula, Ashok Mitra, K.N. Raj and Ignacy Sachs, edited, *Peasants in History: Essays in Honour of Daniel Thorner*, Kolkata: OUP, pp. 107-120.

Bhattacharya, Sabyasachi. 2011. *The Mahatma and the Poet*, New Delhi: National Book Trust.

Chakrabarty, Bidyut. 2006. *Social and Political Thought of Mahatma Gandhi*, New York: Routledge.

Cohn, B.S. 1996. *Colonialism and Its Forms of Knowledge: The British in India*, Princeton: Princeton University Press.

Dasgupta, Tapati. 1993. *Social Thought of Rabindranath Tagore: A Historical Analysis*, Delhi: Abhinav Publications.

Dhar, Anup. 2015. What if One is Already Included, http://www.india-seminar.com/2015/674/674_anup_dhar.htm (accessed on March 20, 2017).

Dumont, L. 1970. *Homo Hierarchicus: An Essay on the Caste System*, Chicago: University of Chicago Press.

Gandhi, M.K. 1979. 'The Voice of Truth', In *Selected Works of Mahatma Gandhi* (edited by Sriman Narayan), Ahmedabad: Navjivan Publishing House), https://www.mkgandhi.org/voiceoftruth/voiceoftruth.htm (accessed on 8 March 2017).

Guha, Ramchandra. 2001. *An Anthropologist Among the Marxists and Other Essays*, New Delhi: Permanent Black.

Gupta, Dipankar. 2004. *Whither the Indian Village? Culture and Agriculture in "Rural India"* (Malcolm Adiseshiah Memorial Lecture), Chennai: Madras Institute of Development Studies.

Jodhka, S.S. 2002. Nation and Village: Images of Rural India in Gandhi, Nehru and Ambedkar, *Economic and Political Weekly*, Vol. 37, No. 32 (August 10-16, 2002), pp. 3343-3353.

Madan, T.N. ed. 2013. *Sociology at the University of Lucknow: The First Half Century (1921-1975)*, Delhi: OUP.

Maine, Sumner Henry. 1871. *Village-Communities in East and West*, London: John Murray.

Majumdar, D.N. 1958. *Caste and Communication in an Indian Village*, Delhi: Asia Publishing House.

Mines, Diane P. and Yazgi, Nicolas. 2010. eds. *Village Matters: Relocating Villages in the Contemporary Anthropology of India*, Oxford University Press, Delhi.

Mishra, S.N. 2010. *Socio-economic and Political Vision of Dr. B.R. Ambedkar*, Delhi: Concept Publishing Company.

Mohan, Anupama. 2012. *Utopia and the Village in South Asian Literatures*, London: Palgrave Macmillan.

Mukerjee, Radhakamal. 1950. *The Social Structure of Values*, Madison: Macmillan.

Nandi, Ashis. 2001. *An Ambiguous Jounrey to the City: The Village and Other Odd Ruins of the Self in Indian Imagination*, Delhi: OUP.

Nehru, Jawaharlal. 1951. *The Discovery of India*, London: Meridian.

Palshikar, Suhas. 2014. Gandhi-Ambedkar Interface: ...when shall the twain meet?, http://www.epw.in/journal/2014/13/glimpses-past-web-exclusives/gandhi-ambedkar-interface.html (accessed on March 9, 2017).

Pathak, Avijit. 2015. *Indian Modernity*, Delhi: Aakar.

Patricia Uberoi. 1998. 'The Diaspora Comes Home: Disciplining Desire in DDLJ,' *Contributions to Indian Sociology*, Vol. 32, No. 2, pp. 305-336.

Ramanujan, A.K. 1989. 'Is There an Indian Way of Thinking?: An Informal Essay', *Contributions to Indian Sociology*, Vol. 23, Issue 1, pp. 41-58.

Srinivas, M.N. 1955. ed. *India's Village*, Delhi: Asia Publishing House.

____. 1976. *The Remembered Village*, London: University of California Press.

Tagore, Rabindranath. 1919. 'The World of Personality', in *Personality*, London: Macmillan, pp. 41-74.

____. 1928. City and Village, *Visva Bharati Bulletin*, Number 10, pp. 24-25.

____. 1941. 'The History and Ideals of Sriniketan', *The Modern Review*, November, Translated by Marjorie Sykes, p. 433.

Tarlo, Emma. 1996. *Clothing Matters: Dress and Identity in India*, London: Hurst and Company.

Thakur, Manish. 2014. Understanding Ruralities: Contemporary Debates. *CAS Working Paper Series*, New Delhi: Centre for the Study of Social Systems, Jawaharlal Nehru University, http://www.jnu.ac.in/sss/csss/images/Manish-thakur/manish-thakur-paper.pdf (accessed on March 17, 2017).

Tiwari, P., Nair, R., Rao, J., Ankinapalli, P., Hingorani, P. and Gulati, M. 2015. *India's Reluctant Urbanization: Thinking Beyond*, Palgrave Macmillan.

2

What If, the 'Rural' is the Future; and Not the Past?

Bhavya Chitranshi and Anup Dhar

This chapter is based on the study of economic qua labour qua class processes in a village, called Emaliguda, in the Rayagada district of South Odisha. Based on the study of class processes in the village among single women farmers the chapter revisits the division 'urban'/'rural' and the capitalist/pre-capitalist, developed/backward, modern/traditional divide that has become paradigmatic for much of our self-description as also a description of the Other[1]; the paper critiques this description of the rural as *lacking/lagging* other (see footnote 1) and the other as *pre*-capitalist or *under*-developed. The tentative hypothesis the paper foregrounds through a close study of the class processes in the village is the following: would it be enabling to move beyond the first world/third world, urban/rural, capitalist/pre-capitalist, developed/backward framework to a new framework 'circuits of global capital'-'world of the third'[2] in a hyphenated (*not* slash) relation of mutual and dynamic constitutivity, which in actuality is not a relationship between two entities, which is not a new dualism, but is an overdetermination[3] amongst a multiplicity of contradictory class processes—some deep inside or within the circuits of global capital, some at the margins but hooked to the circuits forming a kind of dynamic borderline, and some outside—some exploitative, some non-exploitative—in interminable flux and transformation. What however is circuits of global capital and world of the third shall emerge through the study of class processes in the village. The framework of circuits of global capital and world of the third is important because what was hitherto known as rural is now split and splintered in many directions; or perhaps it was always already split in an infinite multiplicity of possibilities; it was we who had rendered the real infinity and the multiplicity hostage to a homogeneously pre-capitalist, underdeveloped, backward and superstitious bloc: *the* rural. This is an attempt to not lapse into the either/or that is currently dominating us: either the rural is a homogeneous presence, somewhat eternal, pure and pristine—a largely post-developmentalist position, risking reduction; or the rural is slowly getting annihilated and erased from existence—representative of unthinking modernist positions. The chapter argues that what was known as rural is now being re-written as the unresolved and unfinished dialectic between the circuits of global capital and world of the third. This is changing the given map of the world. This also helps us redraw our relationship with the rural. Further, this paper argues that the redrawing of the cartograph of the rural (and by default that of the rural-urban divide) creates conditions or ground for the *political*. The rural has hitherto been seen as our *past*; a past to be transcended. The redrawing of the cartograph helps us see the rural as the *future*; not the whole of the rural; not the rural as a homogeneous entity; but a fragment of the rural—a fragment, following Chakrabarti, Dhar and Cullenberg (2012), we call 'world of the third'; or perhaps, not even world of the third, but a fragment of the world of the third; a fragment that is *cocooned* in the rural, but which, however, is also *crypted*. Cocooned designates *presence*; that which is cocooned (is) inside. Crypted points to *absence*; that which is crypted is hidden, veiled, occulted from view, from consideration. The chapter argues that which is cocooned yet crypted *in the rural* constitutes the future. The study of economic qua labour qua class processes in Emaliguda takes us to the doorstep of that which is 'cocooned *yet* crypted'.

The Knowledge of the Rural

It often happens that the standard 'answer' to a particular question only *appears* to be an answer. In fact, such answers at times perhaps, lead to more questions. A similar mishap seems to have occurred with the question that we have been desperately asking with respect to the rural; the question being, 'what *is* rural'? Is it a 'space'; a 'way of life'; is it an 'idea'; is it to be accessed at the level of 'praxis'? We add another dimension to the existing four: is the rural humanity's past? Or is it humanity's future? Is there something cocooned which however is also crypted in the rural that could make it the context for humanity's future; some 'moments of praxis', some 'partial perspective(s)', some 'subject position(s)' that could be the ground for a future? The paper also argues how this moment of/for a future *within* the rural is crypted or presenced as *impossible* by rendering the existence of the entire space of the rural impossible, impossible in general, impossible in the standard teleological dogma: rural *to* urban, pre-capitalist *to* capitalist, tradition *to* modern, backward *to* developed; as if the death certificate or the epitaph of the already 'cancerous' rural is always already written; this paper problematises the representation of the rural as 'terminally ill'.

The genealogy of the term 'rural' shows that one of the origins of the term can be traced to the Latin noun *rus*, meaning an "open area" (Ayto, 1990, as cited in Woods 2011: 14), at times described as a "space that lay *outside* the cities"; in other words, that which was outside[4] the urban. Later, in Roman literature, rural came to be recognised as a place attached to "a series of moral and cultural associations" and propagated through what Woods calls the "pastoral myth"[5]. It looks like a range of, at times, complementary and, at other times, contradictory myths and idylls surrounding the rural have evolved in Western thought and all these renditions beginning from medieval Europe—of rural as wilderness, or a place of danger and threat—to industrialised 20th century—of rural as a place of peace, tranquillity and simple virtue, have seemed to be presenting to us a particular description of the rural that has in turn served as a basket from which one would draw one's own *definition* of the rural. However, this chapter argues that all the above notions—laudatory or derogatory—are simple and *homogeneous* descriptions of the rural, depending largely upon what qualifies as urban and what does not, what urban desires and what it despises, and what urban imagines the 'outside' (rural) to be and hence what it creates/designates the rural as. Alongside these earlier, somewhat simple and homogeneous understandings and constructions of the rural, there have also been recent attempts, at representing the rural in ways and forms that are statistical, demographic and structural[6] (see Woods, 2011). Further, the foregrounding of "village community" as a "myth of colonial ethnography" or history (see Mines and Yazgi, 2011), in a way has foreclosed the *lived experience* of the rural[7]. Even in the early 1970s when the rural came to be recognised as something which is more than just agriculture, it continued to be described as a static land-based economy. Along with an occulting of crucial aspects of conditions of rural life, the above understanding of the rural, also repudiated reflection on processes of exploitation and oppression in place in the rural.

In addition, what remains paradigmatic of rural myths, idylls, descriptions, prescriptions, characteristics, and representations (whether these be imagined, material, social construct, understood through rural practices, or a category of thought[8]), is that rural has always been rendered as that which is *not-urban* or *not-yet*-urban. It is as if rural lacks a self-description (not just a self-definition) and requires a pre-defined urban in order to have its own definition; a definition which it owes to the 'developed' urban but which it cannot own. The rural-urban divide hence is not merely a geographical binary; it is embedded in discourse.

Moreover, this 'not-yet/not-so-urban' description of the rural is not indicative of *difference* but symbolises the logic of *lack*. Thus, the qualifications justifying the which, where and what of the rural are indicative of the politics behind the idea rural; the frame of reference always remaining as urban. In this way, all descriptions of rural come to be recognised as the *lacking/lagging other* of the urban. In other words, the knowledge of the rural is largely determined by the logic of the two where One is central/primary (let's call it 'p') and the other is a lacking/lagging other (let's call it '~p'); which is in actuality not a logic of the two, because there are no two-s; there is One (i.e. p) and a lacking/lagging version of p: ~p. In that sense, there is *no* rural; the rural is the past-of-the-urban. The rural is the lacking other of modernity; the rural is *pre*-modern. The rural is the underside of the developed; the rural is *under*developed. The rural is the lagging other of capital; the rural is *pre*-capitalist[9].

This understanding of rural as the lacking/lagging other of a so called developed, capitalist and modern urban register, not only dictates what the rural *is* or has come *to be* but also determines what rural should/ought to *become*. This line of thought, justifies both 'brown Orientalism' and the 'civilising mission' of the brown. The mission is to tame the rural—to convert it to what the urban today is—to do away with any form/way of *being* that is/was not yet urbanised. Similarly, the contemporary capitalist-developmentalist agenda of the state has rendered the rural as pre-capitalist and this justification becomes ground for capitalist-developmentalist interventions in the rural; transition from pre-capitalist rural societies to capitalist and modern urban societies, remains the desired outcome of these interventions and policies (see Chakrabarti, Dhar and Cullenberg, 2012: 200-242 for a discussion on the New Agricultural Policy [NAP, 2000]). Elsewhere this process has been designated as Capitalocentric-Orientalism[10].

This 'masculine' quest to conquest has repeatedly looked at the rural as feminine[11], passive and tamable; as always already open to change. The objectification of the rural, the threat of feminine excess and the seduction of its assumed wilderness, tranquillity and resourcefulness, has over time justified its domination and exploitation. Thus, the European civilising mission and in present times its manicured version called 'capitalist development', has not been a simple strategy of moving from backward, undeveloped, and pre-capitalist rural to modern, developed, and capitalist urban, it has also been a deeply masculine process of violating, dominating, exploiting, and conquering the rural.

The Knowledge of the Village

In his book titled, *Indian Village* (2014), Manish Thakur explores the historical and contemporary conceptualisations of the Indian village, especially in its ideological interaction with the state. He argues that, "for the larger part of human history, the village has been the most ubiquitous and intelligible human settlement... (containing) the basic societal design in its microcosm. As an institution, the village has been steeped deep in antiquity" (Thakur

2014: 1). However, the idea of the village or what Thakur calls 'villageism' or 'villagisation' began taking shape for the first time in India's history in the 19th century. The Indian village became the object of study in terms of early articulations under British rule[12]. The colonial regime constructed the 'village'[13] ideal through Western historiography and anthropology. The village space was investigated and demarcated not only for administrative control and policy implementation, but "ultimately to create a bipolar constellation—the state and the village (as against and in addition to rural/urban)... Thenceforth, the village was taken to be a mode of understanding the Orient and its institutions" (Thakur 2014: 3). Further, Thakur discusses how the concept of the village has acquired many meanings and has "undergone extraordinary metamorphosis". However, "the colonial construction of the village outlived the colonial state"; the welfarist discourse has continued to understand and represent the Indian village as a traditional unit (i.e. '~p') to be reclaimed and reformed through an inevitable reliance and dependence on the modern capitalist state (i.e. 'p'). The nationalist discourse, on the one hand, constructed an ideal image of the village, as the civilisational essence, repository of tradition, and as a place where 'real' and 'authentic' India resided (also see Jodhka, 2015 for discussions on Gandhian, Nehruvian and Ambedkarite ideas on village and nation). The development discourse, on the other, treats the village as backward (again '~p'), in dire need of development. Thakur also offers an important distinction between the 'village' as a noun and 'rural' as an adjective and argues how in the post-independence developmental discourse the idea of rural (as traditional, backward, underdeveloped and always already open to developmental interventions) takes over the village. This distinction helps us see the transition in the knowledge of the rural; there is as if a movement from a descriptive understanding of the village to a *prescriptive* understanding of the rural (what the village should become or aspire to become).

Tagore remains a lone(ly) point of departure. He saw the village neither as a signpost of ideal Indian-ness nor as idle slumber, neither as endowed nor as lacking; which is also why Tagore would argue for rural *reconstruction* (*punar-nirman*; not rural *development*). Reconstruction meant there was something (cocooned) in *palli samaj* or in *swadeshi samaj* that was worth reconstructing. Reconstruction also meant there was something (crypted) in *palli samaj* or *swadeshi samaj* that required reconstruction. What was it? Where was it? Why is it not visible? Is it cocooned yet crypted? How does one set up a relationship with what is worthy of reconstruction, with what gestures towards *difference*? Is the truth of the rural lodged here, as against the Orientalist (which reduces the rural to the *lacking urban*) and Capitalocentric (which reduces the rural to *lagging in capitalism*, hence *pre*-capitalist, i.e. a *prior* stage or an *earlier* state of capital-logic) knowledge of the rural? More on this in the last section on "Development Practice as Tagorite Rural Reconstruction".

In this chapter, we question this description and the prescription that follows, by offering an angle (one among many) to look at the question of the rural, through a mutually constitutive dialectic, that of the circuits of global capital and world of the third. It is our contention that this new divide offers a more micro, disaggregated, heterogeneous and dynamic understanding of the rural as also of the urban. Is there a rural cocooned inside the rural, but outside of discourse? A rural outside the 18th century European rural, outside not in a spatial sense but outside discursively, a rural outside the hegemonic language or language of the hegemonic—a *rural that gets foreclosed, paradoxically, in the foregrounding of the rural*. In this paper we refer to that rural outside of the rural as 'world of the third'; where world of the third (as against the *third world-ish village*) is that which is outside the circuits of global capital.

So far we have examined rural as an ugly other of urban. Is there an unwanted other of the rural we seem to not know; a rural within rural that we do not know? It is to understand in what *form* does it exist outside the dominant discourses. Has rural been discursively rendered dead, is the question this paper asks? However, we do not see the rural as just a kind of "living dead" (see Chitranshi and Dhar, 2016), but as an 'x' with a "mode of self-understanding and action" (Thakur in Mines and Yazgi, 2011: 11). It is this self-understanding that this paper tracks. It first works through the Capitalocentric and Orientalist understanding (which may not be the self-understanding as Nikita Khanna's work in village Rukrum [in Jharkhand] and on the question of *dehaat* shows) of the rural—which relegates the rural to a pre-capitalist and pre-modern past—and then tries to arrive at an understanding where the rural is seen as ground for a *post*-capitalist (not just anti-capitalist) and post-Orientalist future—for both rural and urban. We have hitherto studied rural transformation. Can the rural be the ground for transformation?

Few theorisations that problematise the rural-urban binary provide perspectives to work through the questions we are raising in the paper. These theories attempt to answer the question of 'what is rural' in a way that takes us to understandings of the rural that are beyond the usual Capitalocentric-Orientalist frameworks. Without falling back on the idea of urban in order to define the rural, these theories move beyond the binaries of abstract/conceived and concrete/perceived, thereby opening up the category 'rural' to a possible/probable self-description and self-definition.

One, the 'relational approach' to understanding the rural and similar theories that lay emphasis on the significance of the socio-political and economic networks and connections that construct and shape the space of the rural become relevant for our work. This approach contends that human and non-human interactions take place in the political, economic, and cultural milieu constituting the rural space, but it is relations, that rather than simply getting created in a space, in fact create the space. Thus, 'space' in this approach is seen as "a product of practices, trajectories, interrelations" (Massey, 2004: 5), as opposed to ideas that foreground space as "fixed entities, constrained within the static and hierarchical architecture of territory and scale" (Marston et al., 2005; as cited in Woods, 2011: 40). Moreover, the relational approach takes into account the 'non-representational' aspects such as "emotions, impulsive bodily actions, affective relations" (Thrift, 2007; as cited in Woods, 2011: 41).

The dynamic understanding of relational space, concerned also with questions of affect and experience, helps us not only to argue for a contingent-emergent understanding of the rural (as against simple, isolated, and static understandings), but also to rethink questions of space in relation to the question of shifting subject positions. The paper builds upon the idea of relational space to argue that the circuits of global capital-world of the third divide is premised not only on the question of space but also on the question of *subject*. In that sense we are not moving from the rural-urban divide to the circuits of global capital-world of the third divide, but also from conventional understandings of space to an interrelated understanding of space and subject. Thus, 'world of the third' can be approached as a perspective (Chakrabarti, Dhar and Cullenberg, 2016), as also a possible interaction between 'relational space' and shifting subject positions. This new analytic helps us move out of the urban-centric description of the rural, or the rural described as either static space or relations (i.e. kinship, bereft of attention to affect and [split] subject positions).

In addition, Keith Halfacree (2006, 2007) relying upon Lefebvre's (1991) idea of 'space'[14], urges us to examine the rural as a space marked by three overdetermined facets that together constitute rural totality. However, even in their congruence, these three facets simultaneously remain incoherent and chaotic in producing contradictory and fragmented rural reality. The rural space in the three-fold model is understood as,

> (a) rural localities inscribed through relatively distinctive spatial practices, linked to production and/or consumption activities,
> (b) formal representations of the rural such as those expressed by capitalist interests, cultural arbiters, planners or politicians (referring to how rural comes to be constructed through processes of capitalist production and exchange), and,
> (c) everyday lives of the rural, which are inevitably subjective and diverse, and with varying levels of coherence/fracture. (Halfacree, 2007: 127)

Working through these three components of the rural, Halfacree (2007) opens up the dimension of possible/potential rural futures, what he calls "radical ruralities"; this idea is in tune with the argument of this paper where we see rural as not the past, but as the future of humanity. Although Halfacree in his work presents ideas that can re-imagine the rural space as radical, his concept also allows for other ways in which rural can be *radicalised* from within; this chapter is in search for the extant resistant/resisting fragments of the rural (what we call the world of the third) that can become the ground for *post*-capitalist (as also *post*-developmentalist) futures.

In other words, if hitherto rural has been described as that which needs to be tamed, that which can be tamed, through colonialism, capitalism and now through the developmental state, what remains *outside* this tame-able rural is what this paper is searching for; the outside which at times is also the resisting rural cocooned within the rural. We would call this *the truth of the rural*; as against the knowledge of the rural. The truth of the rural makes the rural or a fragment of the rural the condition for a future, the ground for a possible future[15]. The rural is thus no more the past of the now-urban or the present-of the-would-be-urban. But future; generic future; universalisable future.

The 'Truth' of the Rural

This section sharply distinguishes between the hegemonic *knowledge* of the rural and the cocooned-crypted *truth* of the rural. *What* is the truth of the rural? *Where* is the truth of the rural? This section shall explore the possible arrival at two contingent truths of the rural in a *Kondha Adivasi* dominated village named Emaliguda in the Rayagada district of South Odisha between 2013 and 2017; one, the (secret) truth of *singleness*[16] (not singlehood); and two, the (impossible) truth of *world of the third* (not third world).

Our study of the *processes* of labour (not labourers *essentially*; not an essentialised identity: labourer), and more particularly of processes pertaining to the performance and appropriation of surplus labour in village Emaliguda threw up a picture that was complex, disaggregated and decentred (this is of course not to suggest that this is the only way to render complex, disaggregate or decentre the experience the rural; it could be done through political and cultural processes, i.e. through processes of power and processes of meaning; it could be done through processes of gender or processes of caste; in this paper, we have done it through processes pertaining to surplus labour). In other words, what it showed was that there was no One rural (and by default no One urban either). But then this is not a simple argument for multiplicity. It is instead to *find* and *found* with some fidelity a *future* (with)in the rural and not just a *past*.

Our experiences with the 40 landless single women (in *Eka Nari Sanghathan*) showed that they at times cultivated family land as unpaid labourers, encroached and farmed upon undulated government land at other times, and, worked also as daily wage labourers on other people's lands. Only some women who are either very old or those who have enough family land to sustain themselves do not work as wage labourers. Depending on access to land holdings, processes of production, consumption and distribution, there are thus broadly three kinds of structures within which single women live. They can be classified as: (a) women who live alone after being abandoned by their husbands and the natal family, (b) women who live with their sisters and mother (all single women households), and (c) women who live with their parents and/or their brother's family.

Those women who live alone (largely separated women) mainly cultivate encroached land to produce paddy, ragi, beans, pigeon peas, tomatoes, chillies, brinjals, etc. for largely self-consumption. They also grow cotton which they sell to the Telugu middlemen in exchange for cash. Upon working on other people's land they either earn wages in cash or in kind (mostly in the form of paddy or at times vegetables). The cash they earn from selling cotton and as daily wages is largely kept by them. However, at times they may have to contribute to their brothers' household.

Single women's households are common in Emaliguda. The average number of women in such households (drawing from the data of the study conducted) is usually three, with two sisters (the elder sister being mostly unmarried, and the younger being separated or widowed) and a widowed mother. The widowed mother largely looks after the household work given her incapacity to work in the fields in old age. The younger sister mainly works in the factories as a wage labourer, and the older sister works on either the family land that has been left behind in the name of the father (this happens in situations where there are no brothers to lay claim over the land) or cultivate encroached land and/or leased land. During the peak of agriculture, however, all the members of the family come together to cultivate land. At times when the produce of food crops is good, the excess (that remains after calculating for the entire year's consumption) is sold in the local market in return for other food crops or for cash depending on the need of the household and availability of products in the local market. The women collectively appropriate the produce and the cash that comes from sale and wage earning. The money however is mostly kept with the elder sister or the mother.

In families with single women living with parents and/or brothers (and their wives and children), all women (single or not, including young girls in the family) cultivate family land and look after the household. They work in the fields as unpaid household labour with men doing the minimal work of ploughing, that too with tractors, nowadays, and grazing cattle; women thus work both within the perimeters of the home and in the public sphere. Since single women have a marginal position in the family, they are often kept away from decision-making processes. In most families, single women are exploited and oppressed by other women in the household. Some single women single-handedly cultivate small encroached landholdings, but the produce and money earned from that land is to be shared with the family. Single women in these families have minimal control over the produce or their earnings. Unlike in households where women live alone or with other single women, male members in these families can travel far to sell the produce. Apart from the crops mentioned above, some families also cultivate sunflower. Food crops are kept for self consumption, and the excess is sold in the market, both local market (village level) as well as local-global market (district and block level; see Chakrabarti, Dhar and Cullenberg, 2012: 156-160, for the distinction between local markets and local-global markets). The produce from the land, cash earned from the sale of cotton and wage earnings from working in other people's land or encroached land are largely appropriated by the male head(s) of the household.

The cotton produced by these women is sold to the Telegu non-*Adivasi Sahukars* (middlemen who offer seeds, fertilisers and pesticides to the women and buy the produced cotton after deducting the price of seeds, fertilisers and pesticides). This cotton is then taken to Andhra Pradesh and is sold to manufacturers of cotton products—both local and global, who would then sell it either in the local market or in the local-global market; thus some manufacturers would be tied to what we have designated the 'circuits of global capital' (see Chakrabarti, Dhar and Cullenberg,

2012: 149-153) and some would not be. In Emaliguda, with respect to cotton, the single women farmers who appropriate the surplus value (mostly women who live alone or with other single women) generated after deductions for means of production and for the necessary labour equivalent (or to put it simply wage equivalent; i.e. the amount necessary for the survival and reproduction of labour power of the woman farmer) occupy self-appropriative processes (surplus was appropriated by self) but the market they are part of is the local-global market; price fluctuations in the global market would overdetermine processes in the life of the women in Emaliguda. Whereas the price of vegetables sold in the village market would be locally determined. The vegetables are also consumed locally. The cotton that is produced and sold in Rayagada travels well beyond Odisha and even India. However, that does not in any way preclude the possibility of some local mattress manufacturer buying the cotton from the women and producing mattress for local use in and around Rayagada; the price of cotton would then be locally determined, including the overdetermination of economic, political and cultural processes. Though, given the current situation in Rayagada and the hegemony of the Telugu non-*Adivasi Sahukars* and their hold over *Adivasi* life worlds, much of the cotton travels through the value chain set up by the *Sahukars*.

Thus the study has helped us see the decentred and disaggregated nature of the economy as also the "thousand plateaus" of labouring/production processes, and processes of exchange. It has also given us a sense of the processes of performance, appropriation, distribution of surplus labour in Emaliguda and the overdetermination of gender and labour (see Dhar and Dasgupta, 2013). It has shown how economic processes in Emaliguda range from non-capitalist (for example, independent class processes, where surplus is exchanged in the local market and appropriated by the single woman farmer) to capitalist class processes (for example, capitalist forms of production and exchange in the local-global market, for instance for cash crops such as cotton), from non-exploitative to exploitative class positions, from market exchanges to barter. The chapter argues that it is the non-capitalist non-exploitative processes cocooned within the rural that could be the ground for a future.

This possible future however remains crypted in the universal language of *lack* and *lag* (i.e. in the presencing of the rural or the village as generally *pre*-capitalist) that operates as a veil over the experience of the villagers themselves.

We thus see at least two processes at work in Emaliguda, among just the members of the *Eka Nari Sanghthan*, who are single women farmers. One, a need-based economy. Two, a surplus-based or surplus-producing economy. We shall discuss the need-based economy first. Surplus-based or surplus-producing economy shall first be sub-divided into six class processes of which three are exploitative (designated as CA, AB, CB in Table 1 below) and three are non-exploitative (designated as AA, AC, CC in Table 1 below). The six class processes are further disaggregated into 24 class sets (see Table 2 below).

One, need economy. What is a need-based economy? Need-based thinking around economy and development probematises the "commodity fetishism and surplus fetishism" of "Western Marxists". It also shows how the experiences of single women in Emaliguda are marked by a "complex web of overdetermined relations between the realms of market and non-market phenomena, and between what goes on in the surplus economy and its left-outs": *need economy* (Chaudhury, 2001: 181). We define need-based economy or "socially determined subsistence economy" as a "space of production and distribution" understood from a "consumption standpoint" where performance, appropriation and distribution of surplus, i.e. class-based economic activities are ruled out" (see Chakrabarti, 2001: 227). For example, the single women in Emaliguda gather mangoes from the edge of the forest; they consume mangoes; mango (derived from nature) satisfies human need. The same women at times convert mango to mango pickle (so there is production) and again consume it (but production is geared to consumption), at times singly, at times collectively.

Need-based processes, where entities (say, forest products) are consumed directly or where production is geared to just consumption—individually or collectively—slowly make way for surplus-based processes; but without the mediation of market; the process is still consumption-focused and not exchange-focused. For example, mango, gathered from the forest is, at times, converted to mango pickle through human labour. Labour time is expended in the conversion of mango to mango pickle. It is possible that the producer of mango pickle will consume all the pickle herself. It is possible that the producer of mango pickle will keep some pickle for herself and gift the rest to *Sanghathan* members (here the surplus produce is distributed; *not* sold). It is also possible that the producer of mango pickle—by virtue of being a single woman—will get to consume only a part of the mango pickle (in other words, even if she is the sole producer of mango pickle she is getting a part, i.e. a kind of 'necessary labour equivalent'' or to put it simply 'wage equivalent' [not wage though]) and the other members of her extended family—who are non-performers (i.e. they haven't participated in the production of pickle) consume (i.e. appropriate) the rest of the pickle. In other words, they just don't consume pickle, they—the non-performers by virtue of being members of the extended family—live out of the single woman's labour—and appropriate the surplus produced by the single woman. The surplus in this instance is the quantum of pickle produced over and above the quantum consumed by the single woman as necessary labour or wage equivalent. Building on Marx (1954 [1967]: 217) Fraad, Resnick and Wolff (1994) and Spivak (1994) have designated this kind of household/familial process as exploitative and have designated it as a "feudal" class process.

The *Eka Nari Sanghathan* members, in 2016 and in 2017, have come together as a collective of producers/performers of surplus (value) and have produced mango pickle. They first retained some of the produced pickle for their own consumption; they sold the rest; the appropriated surplus (value), appropriated collectively was retained for production of mango pickle again in the next year/cycle. Building on Chakrabarti (2001) and Chakrabarti and Cullenberg (2003) we would call this *production surplus*; it is the quantum of surplus that is looped back into the next cycle of production. Whereas when surplus pickle is not sold and instead gifted/distributed to the community of single women or when surplus value generated by selling pickle is not looped back into the next cycle of production but is used to support older single women, we call it *social surplus*; i.e. surplus used for social purposes and not for production purposes.

Emaliguda sees all of it; what is Emaliguda then as a village? Backward? Lacking? Lagging? Feudal? Capitalist? Would-be-urban? Would-be-capitalist? Local? Global? Difficult to tell. No one description suffices for Emaliguda; and our argument would be that no one description suffices for any village; especially the descriptions that come under the section "The Knowledge of the Rural" look pale and narrow in the face of the complexity that just the space of need-based economy and its borderline with a surplus-based economy offers. Single women farmers thus occupy a host of subject positions with respect to the economic praxis they embody; none of the subject positions can be branded securely in the capitalist/pre-capitalist, that is in the p/~p axis. The presence of women in the need-based economy would be seen as 'backward' in the 'p/~p' logic of thinking; we however see the above two experiences as the *cultural* ground for a future—a future of (a) consuming without the mediation of market, (b) producing surplus and distributing surplus, but not in the value or money form, as also of (c) *sharing* and (d) *gifting*—a future beyond the logic of the p/~p axis. We have designated forms of life outside the circuits of global capital, *world of the third*. In that sense, (a), (b), (c) and (d) are constitutive components of world of the third.

Two, surplus producing economy. Surplus producing economy could be

(i) Self-appropriative (designated as AA in Table 1 below, where A is the individual performer of surplus and the same A is the appropriator) when a single woman produces alone (pickle, cotton, vegetables, or rice), keeps a part of the produce for herself as wage or necessary labor equivalent (for reproducing her own labour power) and either gifts/distributes the surplus produce or takes the surplus produce to the market. Self-appropriative processes could thus take at least two forms in Emaliguda:

(a) Self-appropriative processes without the mediation of market; where the surplus produce is either gifted or bartered.

(b) Self-appropriative processes with the mediation of market; where the produce (usually cotton, at times vegetables) is sold in the local or local-global market and the surplus value appropriated by the single woman farmer herself. Self-appropriative processes are non-exploitative because the performer of surplus has control over the surplus produce/value.

(ii) Communitic where

(a) Single women farmers produce/perform surplus singly but appropriate surplus collectively, with or without the mediation of market—local or local-global, with or without remuneration in the wage form. Communitic processes are non-exploitative when the appropriation of surplus is collective (designated as AC in Table 1 below, where individual performers of surplus [designated as A] appropriate surplus collectively [designated as C]).

(b) A group of producers (designated as C) produce/perform surplus collectively but one (designated as A) among the group appropriates the surplus produce/value; offering in turn just the necessary labour or wage equivalent to the performers of surplus. Communitic processes are exploitative when the appropriation of surplus is individual (designated as CA in Table 1 below). For instance, the single women farmers working in family farms as a member of the family; however, while the performers of surplus are a family collective (designated as C) the surplus that is produced is appropriated by the male head of the family alone (designated as A); who incidentally is also one of the performers of surplus labour/value.

(iii) Communist, where surplus is performed collectively (designated as C) and appropriated by the same collective (designated as C). Communist class processes (designated as CC) are non-exploitative; because the same performers appropriate the surplus. The performers of surplus may or may not give themselves wage. The final product/produce may or may not be sold in the market. In that sense, communist class processes could be in the wage form; and the final product/produce could be in the commodity form. The *Eka Nari Sanghathan* members' initiative, in

2017, to lease 3 acres of low-lying land and cultivate paddy collectively, can be seen as an example of the communist class process. The plan is that 36 women shall, after putting aside a particular quantum of rice as necessary labor or wage equivalent, would also appropriate the surplus rice that would get produced; the surplus rice shall serve as food for the single women for another 10 months; thus taking care of their yearly rice requirement. This is a contingent emergent communist class process in village Emaliguda; the 36 women plan to consume the rice and not sell it; had they sold the final produce, in this case, rice would be in the commodity form.

(iv) Exploitative, where surplus is performed by someone/some (either in the individual [designated as A] or in the collective form [designated as C]) and appropriated by someone else or some others (designated as B) who is also a non-performer (i.e. who has not participated in the performance of surplus). Such a class process (designated as AB or CB in Table 1 below) could be a

(a) Slave class process (where the performer of surplus, the 'labourer' is sold and bought like a commodity); an example in the context of the rural would be bonded labour; one is reminded of Mahasweta Devi's Douloti.

(b) Capitalist class process (where labour power [not the labourer] is sold and bought; i.e. where labour power is a commodity; and where the final product/produce is also a commodity, exchanged in the market through what Marx calls the 'money form').

(c) Feudal class process (where the performer of surplus is not sold or bought nor is labour power a commodity; where the performer [usually a peasant] is tied to land and hands over a part of the produce to the appropriator [usually a landlord]).

A single woman farmer thus occupies a host of (classed) subject-positions with respect to simply the performance (whether it is A or C in Table 1 below) and appropriation (whether it is A, C or B in Table 1 below) of surplus. However, what happens in the obsessive foregrounding of the woman farmer in the rural development discourse, as a lacking/lagging subject of capitalism alone, these noncapitalist economic practices, processes and experiences—which also give rise to and shape subject-positions—that exist *outside* the circuits of global capital and are part of diverse and distinct socio-economies are rendered pre-capitalist in nature (as the lacking other of capitalism; the *yet not* capitalist processes rather than non-capitalist processes). The rural hence has to be understood in terms of a multiplicity of mutually constitutive and even contradictory (contradictory because the same woman may occupy CA, AC, AA, AB, CB and CC class positions, of which AA, AC and CC are non-exploitative and CA, AB and CB are exploitative) subject positions/forms of life or praxis (in this case practices of laboring); and not in terms of the paradigmatic framework 'p/ ~ p' (developed/underdeveloped, modern/traditional, capitalist/feudal, progressive/backward, scientific/superstitious). Table 1 gives us a sense of the subject positions a woman could occupy with respect to just performance and appropriation of surplus:

Table 1

Appropriation of Surplus Labour			
Performance of Surplus Labour	**Direct Labour (A)**	**Non-labour (B)**	**Collective Labour (C)**
	AA	AB	AC
	CA	CB	CC

We shall now disaggregate the six class processes (in Table 1 above) into 24 class sets. Building on Chakrabarti, Dhar, and Cullenberg (2012: 138-42) class sets are understood in terms of the performance and appropriation of surplus labor (performed and/or appropriated by A, B, and C) *and* its relation to the (a) remuneration of workers—wage and non-wage and (b) distribution of output—commodity ("com.") and non-commodity ("non-com."). An institutional configuration of performance and appropriation of surplus labour, output distribution, and labour remuneration is what constitutes a *class set* as distinct from a *class process*.

Table 2

No.	Performance	Appropriation	Distribution	Workers' Remuneration
1	A	A	COM	WAGE
2	A	A	NON-COM	WAGE
3	A	A	COM	NON-WAGE
4	A	A	NON-COM	NON-WAGE
5	A	B	COM	WAGE
6	A	B	NON-COM	WAGE
7	A	B	COM	NON-WAGE
8	A	B	NON-COM	NON-WAGE
9	C	A	COM	WAGE
10	C	A	NON-COM	WAGE
11	C	A	COM	NON-WAGE
12	C	A	NON-COM	NON-WAGE
13	A	C	COM	WAGE
14	A	C	NON-COM	WAGE
15	A	C	COM	NON-WAGE
16	A	C	NON-COM	NON-WAGE
17	C	B	COM	WAGE
18	C	B	NON-COM	WAGE
19	C	B	COM	NON-WAGE
20	C	B	NON-COM	NON-WAGE
21	C	C	COM	WAGE
22	C	C	NON-COM	WAGE
23	C	C	COM	NON-WAGE
24	C	C	NON-COM	NON-WAGE
A = all, B= none, C = shared, com: market commodity, non-com: non-market commodity and non-commodity				

While in Table 1, the disaggregation was in terms of *exploitative* and *non-exploitative* (one can see through Table 1 how the rural is not all exploitative, that is, not all 'victim' [in need of rescue/ development] or 'evil' [in need of annihilation], but a space of also non-exploitative praxis), in Table 2, the disaggregation is in terms of capitalist and non-capitalist (not *pre*-capitalist). In Table 2, class sets 5 and 17 are consistent with the capitalist class set. The rest (i.e. the twenty-two class sets from 1-4, 6-16, and 18-24) are non-capitalist class sets. Of the 22 "what are not capitalist class sets," at least twelve (i.e. class sets 2, 4, 6, 8, 10, 12, 14, 16, 18, 20, 22, and 24) are *outside* the circuits of global capital by virtue of their output distribution being of the non-commodity form. The other ten non-capitalist class sets—even if they are non-capitalist, could be either inside (i.e., hooked to) or outside the circuits of global capital, depending on whether their produce is exchanged in the local-global market, local market or non-market sites. Class sets 5 and 17, if they are not global, could also be inside (i.e. hooked to) or outside the circuits of global capital. Depending on a host of mutually constitutive and contradictory contexts, the odd-numbered class sets in the above matrix can be inside or outside the circuits of global capital. The even-numbered ones are, however, outside. Thus, an outside to the circuits of global capital, marked by the even-numbered class sets and a few of the odd-numbered class sets, including (interestingly) even capitalist class sets, can be conceptualised.

This outside is world of the third, a complex and contradictory ensemble of exploitative and non-exploitative class sets. No kind of *value*—ethical or non-ethical, competitive or shared, violent or tolerant, rich or poor—can be imputed to world of the third a priori. The world of the third can be located in the rural and the urban; it can span across sectors, regions, and nations. World of the third is not located in just the South; even the North is studded with pockets of world of the third, including the metropolis.

What was hitherto known as rural could in terms of Table 2 be inside as also outside the circuits of global capital. When it comes to the cultivation of rice by single women farmers the rural is largely outside the circuits of global capital. When it comes to the cultivation of cotton by single women farmers the rural is largely inside the circuits of global capital. When it comes to need-based economic practices the rural is once again outside the circuits of global capital; however, when it comes to need-based economic practices the rural is not just outside the circuits of global capital;

it is also outside the circuits of local capital; in a word, it is outside market exchanges: local and local-global.. Thus, there is no One rural; there is no One homogeneous rural. There is no One peasant. There is no One rural subject. The same single women farmer is at times inside, at times outside; at times in market exchange; at times, outside it. It would perhaps be better to reconceptualise the rural in terms of contingent emergent subject positions and contingent emergent processes of praxis.

That Which is Cocooned Yet Crypted Within the Rural

However, this chapter is not just an argument for an innocuous multiplicity, or heterogeneity, or decentering. It is an argument for a future; a future cocooned and crypted in the context of the rural. Such that the rural, or more precisely, a fragment of the rural, is not the urban's past; but the future. It is an argument for a possibility where apparently there exits none. It is an argument for a *paradoxical fidelity to a possibility* that has hitherto remained *foreclosed*, that has hitherto remained *rejected*, rejected altogether in the description and self-description of the rural as pre-capitalist, as backward, as superstitious, as traditional, in a word, as pre-modern, as underdeveloped. Herein lies the truth of the rural; the truth that has remained foreclosed in the cacophony around the knowledge of the rural; the truth of a need-based praxis at the heart of what we call the rural; the truth of non-capitalist praxis in the everyday of what we call the rural; the truth of a non-capitalist outside in the womb of what we call the rural; the truth of *being outside*, marking *outsided-ness* to the circuits of global capital, even if partially; further, of the 12 non-capitalist class sets that are outside the circuits of global capital six (class sets 2, 4, 14, 16, 22, and 24) are non-exploitative in addition to being non-capitalist. Those six could the ground and condition for a future. Also, of the 12 class sets (i.e. the odd-numbered ones) hooked to the circuits of global capital (by virtue of output being in the commodity form), once again, six (class sets 1, 3, 13, 15, 21 and 23) are non-exploitative.

The rural is thus not a pre-capitalist past.

It is the ground, context and condition for a future.

'Development Practice' as Tagorite Rural Reconstruction

Tagore calls his work in Sriniketan *rural reconstruction*. Why reconstruction? Why not development? Why *punarnirman*? Why not *vikas*? Because the rural is not just a past to be transcended. It is also the future; a subset of the rural if held on to with "fidelity" could be the ground for a future. However, it is the knowledge of the rural that renders this possibility an impossibility. The knowledge of the rural that renders the rural first homogeneous, and then backward, pre-capitalist and underdeveloped. That defines the rural as we have seen above in terms of the urban. The non-capitalist 'subset' within the womb of what we call the rural could be seen as a past to be transcended. The non-capitalist subset should also be seen as a condition and a possibility for a possible (post-capitalist) future; not naturally; not as a natural corollary; but as the site for the political; the political in turn flanked by the subject and the truth of the non-capitalist outside/Other. In that sense, the rural becomes the text for an uncanny connection between truth-subject-politics; and through such a connection the ground for a possible future.

NOTES

1. The designation of the Other with a capital 'O' is deliberate. It is to hint at the *inassimilable* nature of the Other, whether in the form of the village or the rural. It is to suggest that the Other is not wholly knowable; there is a remainder; and the remainder haunts efforts at knowing, relating, listening and transforming. The *hegemonic function*, however, is to homogenise the Other and reduce the Other to a 'lacking other' (i.e. lacking in urbanity, lacking in modernity, lacking in scientificity, etc.) or a 'lagging other' (i.e. lagging behind in terms of progress, development etc.).
2. World of the third "comprise of the ensemble of class related processes which are *outside* the circuits of global capital" and which are knotted into "local markets as well as into non-market exchanges that transpire *outside* the local-global or the Empire-Nation mode of exchange. The latter signifies that some of the exchanges within world of the third may not be market-oriented at all but could flow simply through informal or formal

arrangements not dictated by the market. Further, even if driven by market considerations, they may not be driven by the considerations of the local-global market; it may well be driven by value-forms other than the money-form (Marx, 1982 [1867]: 19-30)" (see Chakrabarti, Dhar and Cullenberg, 2012: 175-199).

3. Overdetermination "differs sharply from the more conventional methodologies premised on an *essentialist* structure of causality. Instead of *causality*, overdetermination emphasises *constitutivity*. By constitutivity we mean, "being literally brought into existence." Each process is constituted, literally brought into existence, by the combined effects of all the other processes. This means that no process can occur alone. Overdetermination implies that each process operates as both the cause and the effect of other processes, such that each process is *both* cause and effect, such that each process is neither *only* cause nor effect" (see Chakrabarti, Dhar and Cullenberg, 2012: 36-39, italics ours).
4. We shall also argue in this chapter for an experience and concept of *outsided-ness*; an outsided-ness that would be cocooned and crypted in the extant economic experiences and labouring practices of the rural; but that would not be a simple concept of being merely or spatially 'outside the urban'; it would be a concept of *marking* outsided-ness, marking a non-capitalist as also a non-exploitative outsided-ness to what we shall designate as the 'circuits of global capital'. It is this marking of outsided-ness that makes a cocooned part of the rural or a part cocooned *inside* the rural, which however is *also* crypted, a context and ground for the future; more on this in the section on 'The Truth of the Rural'.
5. "Rural life was portrayed as simple, innocent and virtuous, revolving around the honourable profession of agriculture and involving closeness to nature" (Williams, 1973, as cited in Woods, 2011: 17).
6. "Structuralists rejected villages [and village studies] in favor of wider 'social facts', such as caste and kinship" (Mines and Yazgi, 2011: 1).
7. For more on the question of the complex relationship between history and literature, with the former dealing with purportedly 'real' events and the latter with 'imagined' ones, refer to Spivak (2014).

8. "Marc Mormont refers to the 'rural' as a 'category of thought' (1990: 40); the 'rural' is first *imagined*, then *represented*, then takes on material form as places, landscapes and ways of life are made to *conform* to the expectations of the idea of the 'rural'. Experiences of these 'rural' places and lifestyles are fed back into the collective imagination, refining and modifying the idea and thus contributing to a dynamic process through which the 'rural' is produced and reproduced" (Woods, 2011: 16).
9. We show through a detailed class analysis how the rural is not a homogeneous pre-capitalist space; but a disaggregated and decentred combination of capitalist, non-capitalist, exploitative, and non-exploitative experiences.
10. Capitalocentric-Orientalism "relegates *non*-capital to *pre*-capital, to the *lacking other* of capital. Subsequently non-capital itself internalises this constructed identity of pre-capital. Internalization is thus a pernicious phenomenon, which complicates non-capital's othering even further. To come out of such incarcerated conditions one needs to replace the One of 'Capital/pre-capital' with the two of 'capital/non-capital' and to further disaggregate non-capital, and why not, even capital" (Chakrabarti, Dhar and Cullenberg, 2012: 174).
11. "As Kolodny (1975) pointed out, the patriarchal discourse of 'land-as-woman' contained an inherent conflict of meaning between maternal containment and sexual seduction. On the one hand, land was imagined as a mother, 'whose generosity and abundance were marvellous, Edenic, but which could also overwhelm settlers and corrupt their efforts at self-sufficiency' (Rose, 1993: 105); on the other hand, the land was also represented as a temptress, inviting penetration. ... The dominance of the masculinist gaze over landscape has also been reproduced in the construction of the rural as a place of leisure and consumption. As Rose (1993) has observed, the enjoyment of rural recreation has been equated with sexual pleasure, the aesthetic appreciation of rural landscape with the voyeuristic objectification of female beauty, and the exploration of the countryside by walkers, or cyclists or motorists with sexual discovery" (Woods 2011: 20).
12. See Thakur, 2014 for more on the colonial construction of the Indian village.
13. "...By the 19th century, the village in India acquired a set of normative-ideological connotations for both the colonizers

and the colonised. It was now an archaic and primary nucleus of Indian society. It had historically enjoyed a large degree of politico-administrative autonomy, despite paying taxes to various revenue collectors and sending its able-bodied men to the royal army. Also, the unique blend of subsistence agriculture and low-technology crafts and services had made the village economically self-sufficient. Similarly, the village had become burdened with other meanings such as the timelessness of lifestyles and the immobility of people accompanied by their ideological integration to land" (see Breman, 1997: 16, as cited in Thakur, 2014: 3-4).

14. Lefebvre argues for a three-fold understanding of space as lived in its everyday. He invokes the trialectic play of spatial practices, representations of space, and spaces of representation as diverse yet related notions that make up a 'space' (See Lefebvre, 1991; Halfacree, 2007; Halfacree, 2009). Further, theories of space by Lefebvre "proposes that space is produced and reproduced through capitalism, moulded by the pressures of the market and social reproduction, 'colonised and commodified, bought and sold, created and torn down, used and abused, speculated and fought over'" (Merrifield, 2000: 173, see also Lefebvre, 1991; as cited in Woods, 2011: 11).
15. Though villages are "lost objects" in the anthropology of India and though "village studies" have been pushed to the margins of the anthropological field, the "concept and condition called (in various ways) the village is overdue" (see Mines and Yazgi, 2011: 1-2).
16. Emaliguda becomes between 2013-2017 the context for an encounter with the *truth* of women's near-generic experience of singleness amidst what could be called the developmental *situation*, marked by the nodal point: Self Help Group (SHG); as also amidst the *knowledge* of 'poor' rural women, 'victim' women, knowledge of women in the SHG. What is cocooned, what is crypted in the situation; in the repetitive everyday of the situation, in women sitting in a circle, calculating (micro) credit? It is intriguing how in an area with around 30-35% single women in the *Adivasi* spaces (accounting for widows, separated and never-married women alone), women are collected into groups to promote micro-finance, livelihoods, health, education etc. (i.e. standard "developmental agendas") but the reality of their lived experience such as singleness and tribalness is largely kept outside of these interventions. The historico-contextual

'reality' of *being Adivasi, being single, (being non-capitalist),* as also that of *being woman,* is as if foreclosed in the foregrounding of a poor, backward, (pre-capitalist), and victimized rural subject. Where then is the secret? In the singleness of (some) women. Where is the (foreclosed) truth? In the fact, that in our organised consolidation of the one and the all of women, there are (secret) fractures? Singleness is one such fracture in apparent sisterhood; as also in the apparent homogeneity of women's experiences (of oppression). What is the *Real* of the situation (when we say Real we mean the Lacanian Real, not the real of realism)? The experience of singleness even in married women. The hitherto *unseen* becomes a new *scene*, a new staging of/for the political in the forging of *Eka Nari Sanghathan* (see Chitranshi, 2016; Chitranshi and Dhar, 2016).

REFERENCES

Chakrabarti, A. 2001. Class and Need: Towards a Post-Modern Development Economics, *From the Margins,* 1(2), pp. 200-247.

Chakrabarti, A., Dhar, A. and Cullenberg, S. 2003. *Transition and Development in India*, New York: Routledge.

____. 2012. *World of the Third and Global Capitalism*, New Delhi: Worldview Press.

____. 2016. (Un)doing Marxism from the Outside, *Rethinking Marxism*, 28(2), pp. 276-294.

Chaudhury, A. 2001. Western Marxists' Commodity Fetishism: Looking for an Exit, *From the Margins,* 1(2), pp. 181-199.

Chitranshi, B. 2016. Singleness and the Sanghathan, *CUSP: Journal of Studies in Culture, Subjectivity, Psyche,* 1(2), pp. 1-25.

Chitranshi, B. and Dhar, A. 2016. The Living Dead. In Cuéllar, D.P. and Junior, N.L. (eds.), *From Death Drive to State Repression: Marxism, Psychoanalysis and the Structural Violence of Capitalism (De la pulsión de muerte a la represión de Estado: marxismo y psicoanálisis ante la violencia estructural del capitalism)*, Mexico: Porrúa, pp. 59-77.

Dhar, A. and Dasgupta, B. 2013. When Our Lips Speak Gender Labor Together. In Sen, S. and Chakrabarti, A. (eds.). *Development on Trial: Shrinking Space for the Periphery,* Hyderabad: Orient Blackswan.

Devi, M. 1995. Douloti, the Bountiful. In *Imaginary Maps: Three Stories*, Trans. Gayatri Chakravorty Spivak, London: Routledge.

Fraad, H., Resnick, S.A. and Wolff, R.D. 1994. *Bringing It All Back Home: Class, Gender and Power in the Modern Household*, London: Pluto Press, Colorado: Boulder.

Halfacree, K. 2006. Rural Space: Constructing a Three-Fold Architecture. In Cloke, P., Marsden, T. and Mooney, P. (eds.). *Handbook of Rural Studies*, London: Sage, pp. 44-62.

____. 2007. Trial by Space for a 'Radical Rural': Introducing Alternative Localities, Representations and Lives, *Journal of Rural Studies*, 23, pp. 125-141.

Jodhka, S.S. 2015. Nation and Village. In Jodhka, S.S. (eds.), *Village Society*, New Delhi: Orient Blackswan Private Limited, pp. 44-66.

Khanna, N. 2017. Scripting Dehaat: An Autobiographical Possibility, MPhil Thesis, Unpublished Manuscript.

Lefebvre, H. 1991. *The Production of Space*, (Nicholson-Smith, D., Trans.), Wiley Blackwell.

Marx, Karl. 1867. *Capital*, Moscow: Progress Publishers, 1954. Rev. ed. Trans. B. Fowkes, London: Penguin, 1990.

Massey, D. 2004. The Political Challenge of Relational Space: Introduction to the Vega Symposium, Geografiska Annaler: Series B, *Human Geography*, 86 (1), Blackwell Publishing Ltd.

Mines, D.P. and Yazgi N. 2010. Introduction: Do Villages Matter? In Mines, D.P. and Yazgi, N. (eds.). *Village Matters: Relocating Villages in the Contemporary Anthropology of India*, New Delhi: OUP, pp. 1-30.

Spivak, G.C. 1994. Preface. In Fraad, H., Resnick, S.A. and Wolff, R.D. *Bringing It All Back Home: Class, Gender and Power in the Modern Household*, London: Pluto Press; Colorado: Boulder.

____. 2014. Breast-giver: For Author, Teacher, Subaltern, Historian in Mahasweta Devi's *Breast Stories* (Spivak, G.C., Trans.), Calcutta: Seagull Books.

Thakur, M. 2014. *Indian Village*, New Delhi: Rawat Publications.

Woods, M. 2011. *Rural*, Oxon: Routledge.

3

Rural Frames: Bollywood Imagination of Village India

Priyasha Kaul

Introduction

The village has long been a central feature of the popular Indian imagination about the nation in cinematic representations. Mainstream Hindi cinema, popularly referred to as Bollywood, has consistently used the village as a trope in its discourse regarding the nation. While the representation of the idea of the 'village' has changed considerably over the decades, as I discuss in this chapter, its metaphoric significance has continued as a thematic device in Hindi cinema. For scholars, like Chakravarty (1997) and Virdi (2003), Hindi cinema can be seen as a national popular cultural text in constant dialogue with the ongoing socio-economic and political changes in the country (Dudrah, 2006). As the predominant popular cultural form in India, it has often played a significant role in articulating the popular narratives surrounding Indian society (Ganti, 2004). It is perhaps due to this that the idea of the village has played such a crucial role in Hindi cinema's imaginations of the nation right from its very beginnings.

For the British colonial establishment, understanding the Indian village held the key to dealing with Indian society (Inden, 1990: 131). This view was further reinforced by scholars like Karl Marx who considered the Indian village as 'little republics' (Gupta, 2005). Gandhi, as the leading figure of the Indian independence movement firmly believed that the village was the site of the 'real' India and thus needed to be protected from external influences. Since Gandhi considered films a corrupting influence on the masses, active steps were taken by the government to discourage Hindi films, for instance in 1952, the then Information and Broadcasting Minister B.V. Keskar banned Hindi film songs from being broadcast on the national All India Radio (AIR) as they were considered 'erotic and vulgar' and instead allowing only classical music to be played on the radio station (Khurana, 2016). However, or perhaps because of these factors, Hindi films played a key role in this nation-building process often taking its cues from the political establishment. As we see in this chapter, the representation of the village in Hindi cinema has changed considerably over the decades, from the exotic, to idyllic to most recently, a problematic aspect of Indian society. While certain themes like gender and migration continue to have underlying similarities, the role that the idea of the village occupies in mainstream Hindi cinema's discourse regarding the nation has changed dramatically over the decades.

The Changing Rural Frames

While cinematic technology arrived in India in 1896, within a year of its introduction in Paris by the Lumiere brothers, Indians were barred from the initial screenings of films in places such as Bombay (now Mumbai). Several films such as *Coconut Fair* (1897), *Our Indian Empire* (1897) and *A Panorama of Indian Scenes and Processions* (1898) were shot in India to showcase the exotic value of India as a colony for the empire (Gokulsingh and Dissanayake 1989). Documentaries, such as *Inside India: Village Life in Southern India* by Ellis Dungan (Tilak, 2014), highlighted the Indian village as the exotic location of the colonised natives often involved in strange customs that needed to be explained to the 'Western' audiences. The production of these films in India however unintentionally encouraged the involvement and technological know-how of the Indians in the filmmaking enterprise (Raghvendra 2008). By the turn of the century, several studios were established in different locations such as Bombay, Madras and Calcutta, all of which competed with each other to produce short length films. These films were manually taken from one place to another and exhibited in makeshift tents using projectors. As more Indians became involved in filmmaking, cinema in India increasingly borrowed from folk tales and mythological stories from rural India. Thus, in keeping with the larger political discourse, the village became the source for carving out the narrative of the authentic India as the Indian struggle for independence gathered momentum, ironically by both the colonisers and the colonised Indians themselves.

With the achievement of independence in 1947, however, there was no longer a single 'enemy' against whom nationalism could be employed. Independence came at the cost of the partition of the country, which created massive and unprecedented social, economic and political upheaval and misery. Thus, nation building of the newly independent fledgling country became a primary concern. The discourse around the nation in Hindi cinema during the 1950s and 60s, was heavily invested in representing the village as the authentic site of India following Gandhi's ideas about the pre-eminence of rural India as retaining core 'Indianness' against Western influences. As mentioned earlier, for Gandhi, the 'soul' of India resided in its villages and, much like colonial officers like Charles Metcalfe (see Sethi, 1999), he considered the Indian village to be an autonomous and self-sufficient unit in itself. Thus, there was a strong nationalist current in Hindi films of the time towards portraying the village community as the site of untouched innocence and core Indian values. Films such as *Do Bigha Zameen* [Two Units of Land] (1953), *Mother India* (1957) and *Jis Desh Main Ganga Behti Hai* [The Country Where the River Ganges Flows] (1960), placed the village at the centre of the narrative regarding the problems faced by the newly independent India.

The 'Indianness' of the village was brought out using the insider versus outsider framework whereby the village was the microcosm which needed to protect the Indian values under attack from both social evils endemic to Indian society like caste and poverty, as well as, corruption from external influences and modernisation. Poverty was the fundamental evil that plagued the otherwise idyllic village and the main villains in the rural scenarios were either the cruel *zamindar* [landlord] or the dacoits. The dacoits, unlike the landlord, however were invariably treated as characters who had gone astray but could be reformed to return to the fold of the mainstream society. In keeping with the political climate of the time, there was a strong emphasis on redistributive and restorative justice, perhaps best represented in Raj Kapoor's films such as, *Jis Desh Main Ganga Behti Hai*, where the ambiguous vagabond protagonist Raju, whose religious or caste affiliations remained unknown, played the conscience of village India capable of bringing the wayward back into the fold of the nation. In one of the scenes in the film, Raju persuades the gang of dacoits to surrender to the police by saying how the times had changed, and the people had their own government after independence, things were different now, and everyone could participate now in building the new India. The emphasis was on Gandhian notions of the village possessing the spirit and capability to lead the newly independent nation towards the path of righteousness.

The character of landlords such as *Sukhi lala* in Mother India, on the other hand, represented centuries of exploitation of the villagers in the caste-ridden feudal system. The films represented the village as an idyllic but divided space where the poor and the landless were constantly vulnerable against the landed aristocracy and the moneylenders. The film narrative presented a critique of the cruelty of the feudal structure where the petty farmers and the landless had for centuries been victimised due to their naivete and illiteracy. These films often evoked the deep nexus between feudalism with the patriarchal and caste-based structures of exploitation. The quintessential village belle, stereotypically clad in *lehenga-choli* and chunky silver jewellery, symbolised not just the gendered notion of Indianness divided into the inner feminine domain of the private sphere versus the masculine public realm, but also the symbolic equivalence of the women of the village with the land (Kaul 2016). The innocence and 'purity' of the village belle was constantly under attack from the perverse eyes of the landlord, just as he eyed the villagers' land, both being the repositories of honour and social and physical reproduction for the community (Yuval-Davis 1997) .

The village belle, symbolic of the innate core of Indian values represented the village which in turn was the soul of India, was a figure of innocence and sacrifice vulnerable to exploitation and thus had to be protected for her own sake. Just as she was under threat from forces within the village scenario, she was also under constant threat of being swayed and led astray by the suave city dweller. Films such as *Barsaat* [Rainfall] (1949) and *Bandini* [Prisoner Woman] (1963), portray the city dweller as selfish and utilitarian with scant regard for the ways of the village, betraying and abandoning the innocent village woman in search for his own pleasure. It is significant that the city dweller is referred to as '*pardesi*', literally meaning from another land and not just an *ajnabi* or stranger, to place the village as the core or innate realm in the insider versus outsider dichotomy used in framing Indianness.

The idea of modernisation played a pivotal role in this cinematic discourse framing the insider versus outsider dichotomy. Mainstream Hindi cinema provided a layered account of the dichotomies of poor versus rich, landless versus landed, righteousness versus debauchery, rural versus urban. Modernisation was represented either in terms of adoption of 'Western' technology in the external public domain or 'Westernised' values leading to moral corruption in the inner private realm. The adoption of Westernised technology was often associated with the assault on the traditional way of life in the village, and thus an imposition and threat to the village as the heart of Indian society. In films such as *Naya Daur* [New Era] (1957) and *Do Bigha Zameen*, the introduction of technology into the village in the form of construction of a mill or motorised transportation system is seen to bring about a disturbance to the village microcosm leading to resistance. The agents responsible for introducing technology into the village, the landlord or the city dweller, are often doing so for selfish utilitarian purposes in the pursuit for amassing more wealth. The introduction of modern technology and those associated with it, therefore, are negatively portrayed as exploiting the village and village folk for their own benefit. The cinema of this time-period portrays a sense of suspicion against the idea of 'modernisation' which is both implictly and explicitly associated with technology and moral corruption. The ideal typical village was pitted as the real India while cities had become modernised and corrupted by impersonal values and moral ambiguities like cheating, gambling and alcoholism. Raj Kapoor's films, perhaps exemplified this narrative whereby the innocent village native, invariably the male protagonist, is forced to migrate to the city due to various economic hardships in the village in search for a better life and to save money for rescuing his family back in the village. On reaching the city, however, he is soon led astray and lured into the 'evils' of city life typified by lying, cheating and leading a morally ambiguous lifestyle at best. It is only towards the end of the narrative that an appeal is once again made to his innate morality and true 'Indian' values that still lie buried inside him, enabling him to once again recover his true Indianness and return to the village. The narrative often therefore concludes with the return of the village native back to the rural environment as the 'home'. The nostalgia for the lost homeland is played out in the context of the village versus the city. The narrative device therefore uses the push-pull migration perspective (Peterson, 1958), by combining the economic and affective aspects of migration with the development narrative. The mainstream cinematic discourse regarding the status of the village in the newly independent India of the 1950s and 60s, revolves around questions of the socio-cultural price that the Indian society is willing to pay for the technological and industrial development of the nation. As the lyrics from the title song from *Jis Desh Mai Ganga Behti Hai* state:

> Hoton par sacchai rehti hai
> [we always speak the truth]
> Jahan dil mai safai rehti hai..
> [our hearts are without any malice]
> Zyaada ki nahin lalach humko
> [we have never been greedy for much]
> Thode mai guzara hota hai
> [we have been content with whatever little we have]
> Matlab ke liye andhe hokar
> [we have never been blinded by greed and selfishness]
> Roti ko nahin Pooja hamne
> [we have never pursued material gains]
> Hum to kya sari duniya yeh kehti hai
> [not only us, the whole world recognises this]
> Hum us desh ke waasi hai, Jis desh mai ganga behti hai
> [we come from the land which is as pure and sacred as the river Ganges which flows here]

As these words express, the narrative tension revolves around the issue of what would modernisation and development mean for the fabric of Indian social formation. Is development at the cost of losing out on 'Indianness' and the distinctiveness of what makes the idea of 'India', something desirable for the new nation grappling to find its feet? Within this nationalist cinematic discourse, therefore, the village forms the essentialised core of India and its easily abstractable and idealised sense of Indianness. It is not a surprise therefore that the village as an abstract entity becomes the conceptual space which needs to be protected from any onslaught of external influences and the emphasis is on measured change cautioning against too rapid a socio-cultural impact on society leading to chaos and anomie in society.

As against this backdrop, the village as a theme receded into the background in Hindi cinema of the 1970s and 80s, rarely figuring in the narrative, and dealt with superficially even when it did. With the rapid spread of urbanisation and socio-economic problems associated with it and an unstable political environment in the country leading to growing social unrest among the populace, the focus of mainstream cinematic narratives, moved to the urban poor and their problems. Thus while migration from rural to urban continued as an important theme in the cinema of this phase as well, the frame of the lens moved from the rural end of the continuum towards unplanned unleashing of urbanisation in a society undergoing socio-economic and political transition and instability.

The films which engaged with the idea of rural space in this phase therefore, at least conceptually, could be divided into two broad categories: the first, which are not really about the village but figure the village as a scenic backdrop for the narrative to play out, while the second, whereby the village space forms only a conceptual foil against which the struggles of city life are experienced and expressed. Thus, in the first category, one finds a series of films such as the iconic *Sholay* [Embers] (1975) where the village forms the exotic background as a narrative device. Unlike the films of the earlier decades, the films of this time-period did not engage with the idea of the village in terms of the socio-economic conditions. The films represented the village as a static picture frozen in time, symbolised by certain stereotypical symbols such as women fetching water from the well and communal celebrations such as village fairs where everyone from the village gathers together to sing and dance. Two themes which however continued to remain constant were the depiction of gender and migration. Women continued to be represented as the repositories/holders of the honour and values of the village, something that has continued even in contemporary cinema of the time. The theme of migration from rural to urban, however became much more pronounced in the cinema of this time period that witnessed rapid urbanisation and political turmoil. This brings us to the second significant category of films in this time-period whereby the village space forms only a conceptual foil against which the struggles of city life are highlighted in the narrative. Gupta (2005) has argued that migration has been not just due to the attraction of the city but due to the problems in the village. This can be seen in various Hindi films over the years where the village dweller upon migrating to the city finds a completely alien world with unfamiliar ways and values. Films such as *Gaman* [Departure] (1978) and *Piya Ka Ghar* [Marital Home] (1972) showcased the struggles of the migrants forced to move from a peaceful and community-driven life in the village to a fast paced and anonymous urban life. The focus here was on the existential and survival issues, such as finding a living space and employment, commonly faced by the new migrants in big cities such as Mumbai. The narrative captured the process of adjustment and adaptation that the migrants had to go through whether in terms of leaving their loved ones behind in the village or coming to terms with the demands of the urban environment. While this theme of rural to urban migration can be seen as a continuation from the Hindi cinema of the 1950s and 60s, unlike the earlier films where the representation of the experience of migration was in terms of the dangers of moral degradation and corruption, here the emphasis was more on issues of everyday survival and existential anxiety in the urban space. With the change in the larger economic environment, the protagonists whose migration experience became central to the cinematic narrative were broadly drawn from the lower middle class strata rather than those such as farmers or manual labourers.

From the 1990s onwards, however, even this representation of the village rapidly receded from the mainstream cinematic discourse regarding Indian society. The fact that the village no longer occupies a significant place in the popular cinematic imagination regarding the nation in itself becomes poignant through its blatant omission. In a post-liberalisation India, the focus has firmly shifted to the urban as the defining feature of India. The public versus private frame which was earlier articulated through the village versus city lens to elucidate the idea of Indianness, is now framed in terms of India versus abroad. The discourse firmly shifting in favour of the upper class as the section of the population dominating the mainstream idea of India. In terms of the overarching Hindi cinematic discourse on India, the city dweller changes from being the *pardesi* or stranger from another land, versus the villager as the authentic Indian in the initial decades, to completely taking over the idea of Indianness in post-liberalisation India. The village in this process has been invisiblised and ultimately abandoned from the larger rhetoric regarding the desirable future of the nation. While a handful of films like *Pardes* [Foreign Land] (1997), *Taal* [Rhythm] (1999) or *Mela* [Village Fair] (2000) have featured the village as an insignificant backdrop to set up the character of the quintessential innocent village belle as the damsel in distress, post-liberalisation mainstream Bollywood cinema has rarely depicted the village as a significant part of the narrative. Perhaps the only two rare mainstream and commercially successful films of this time which have dealt with the question of the significance of the rural in contemporary India have been *Swades* [Homeland] (2004) and *Peepli Live* (2010). *Swades*, a commercially well received film, starring Shahrukh Khan, revolves around the character of Mohan as the central male protagonist who returns to India and encounters the realities of village India. Mohan is a successful scientist working at NASA who comes to India to find his childhood nanny *Kaveri Amma* who raised him, only to find out that she now lives in a village called Charanpur with his childhood friend Gita. In the attempt to persuade Kaveri Amma to move to the United States of America with him, Mohan goes to *Charanpur* and finds himself faced with the realities of rural India. Over the course of the narrative, he is moved by the lack of basic infrastructure and social and economic development that the villagers are still forced to live with. He falls in love with Gita and tries to convince both her and Kaveri Amma to move to the US with him which both of them refuse to as they believe the village needs their help. Mohan therefore returns to his job at NASA but is overtaken by an overwhelming sense of guilt that he could do more meaningful work in India to alleviate the plight of the village left behind for the overall development of his homeland. At the end of the film, Mohan moves back to India with the belief that it is his responsibility to contribute to the development of the village which has been left behind in the race for development and a better life.

As the narrative shows, Kaveri Amma represents the metaphoric motherland which resides in the villages of India and has been abandoned by the young upwardly mobile, educated professional India. Mohan's search for his roots that takes him to Charanpur is symbolic of village India as perhaps still being the soul of the real India but one that has been left behind and does not fit into the frame of the shining Indian superpower success story that is firmly focused on the urbane Indian narrative. The village therefore has much catching up to do if it hopes to continue to stay relevant to the contemporary India's image of itself.

Peepli Live, six years later on the other hand, presents an even starker image of rural India trying to come to terms with a struggling agricultural system and growing apathy of the political establishment and mainstream media. Set in a fictitious village called Peepli in *Mukhya Pradesh*, literally meaning the prominent state, it deals with the issue of farmers' suicide and the plight of the ordinary rural life. The story revolves around Natha, a poor alcoholic farmer who is unable to repay the loan that he has incurred. He hears that the government might waiver the loan of a farmer's family if he has committed suicide. Natha is contemplating this idea, when Rakesh, a local news reporter overhears this and reports it in the media which soon snowballs into a sensational national news headline of a farmer about to commit suicide in the Peepli village. In the meantime, as the elections are approaching, the ruling and opposition political parties both try to use the issue of Natha's impending suicide for their own benefit in order to win elections. Hounded by the media and goons from the political parties, he finds himself in a barn which is accidentally set on fire. Natha however manages to escape from the fire which instead kills Rakesh. The local officials mistake Rakesh's body for that of Natha, and refuse to pay any compensation to his family as it is an accidental death rather than a suicide. At the end, Natha escapes from the village and starts an anonymous new life working as a manual labourer at a construction site in the city.

In a country where, twelve thousand farmers committed suicide each year between 2013 and 2017 (Mahapatral, 2017) and there is one farmer suicide every half an hour (Sardesai, 2017), *Peepli Live* presents a satirical yet hard-hitting cinematic narrative of a village India caught in the quagmire of poverty, economic uncertainty and political apathy. It represents the ongoing agricultural crisis and the abandonment of the village as a conceptual category from the mainstream Indian discourse regarding the nation and its developmental trajectory.

In both these commercially successful mainstream Bollywood films, the village symbolises the dark reality of the Indian development story where the rural has not only lagged behind but has become a shameful aspect of the Indian growth story ridden with crippling poverty and backwardness. It is the aspect of the Indian success narrative that rarely ever finds itself to be worthy of the national news media or celebration in contemporary India. Sainath (2016) has argued that for the young middle class urban India, the complex reality of rural India has become limited to only a set anecdotes featuring keywords such as poverty and farming. This is not a surprise considering that over a period of five years, only 0.67 per cent of the national dailies were found to have stories regarding rural India featured on their front pages (Media Neglecting Issues of Rural India: Sainath, 2017). The vast complexity of rural India finds a momentary space in the national mainstream media frame only when a crisis, such as the farmers' suicides or agricultural protests, becomes sensational breaking news. For the educated upwardly mobile cosmopolitan urban India, represented by Mohan in *Swades*, this aspect of India is deeply upsetting and out of sync with the shining India growth narrative that is the mainstay of the mainstream political and media discourse regarding the nation in contemporary India.

In terms of the insider versus outsider paradigm, therefore, the depiction of the rural becomes symbolic of the problematic aspect of the current discourse regarding the nation, riddled with backwardness, while the urban, in spite of the problems associated with it, represents the 'real' picture of a rapidly developing and progressing India. It is the urban India, of which the diaspora is seen to be a seamless extension, which has taken over as the representatives of Indianness in post-liberalisation mainstream Hindi cinema. The mainstream cinema of this time-period has mainly focused on the affluent, geographically mobile urban population. The focus of migration has shifted from the rural-urban movement to migration from India to abroad, particularly the Anglophone countries in the West. In post-liberalisation India, the focus of mainstream Bollywood cinema has firmly moved towards the depiction of the urban middle class aspirational dream of luxury and affluence in a globalised world. The rural as a conceptual space stands at odds with this cinematic image of India's new modernity. While in the earlier decades, the village was depicted as fearing too much modernisation and technology and was valorised as the pride of the nation where the true Indian values reside, in post-liberalisation mainstream Bollywood cinema, the village has come to be represented as almost a shameful aspect of modern India. The rural can now be seen as having lagged behind in the vision of the new shining India as a result of failing to become modernised or technologically savvy enough to partake in the vision of the 21st century India which sees itself as a rising superpower in the world.

Reflecting Frames

Over the decades, the representation of the rural as both a concept and an empirical reality has gone through considerable change in mainstream Hindi cinema. In this chapter, I have argued that the idea of Indianness forms the central axis around which this representation revolves. The fulcrum of this axis comprises the internal versus external dichotomy in the form of poverty versus development, moral righteousness versus corruption, backwardness versus modernity. The framing of the idea of Indianness, in this process therefore, has moved from one opposite end of the spectrum to another along the rural-urban continuum. Mainstream

Hindi cinema of the initial decades depicted the village as the core of Indian society and thus needed to be protected from external influences. The urban was the space of corruption and deception where wealth and luxury represented the evils of 'modernisation'. The mainstream cinema of this time-period represented the rural as the idyllic domain of moral and self-righteousness where the desire for material success and technological development was seen with suspicion and wariness. With rapid urbanisation and modernisation of society, however, the focus of the mainstream cinematic lens began to shift from the rural towards the urban and the urbanisation process. Rural-urban migration became a significant theme in mainstream cinema where the migrant experience was typified by the survival issues faced by the rural poor migrating to the urban areas in search of better life prospects for themselves and the village left behind. This involved a conceptual shift from the rural being an empirical reality to a background presence against which the narrative of a rapidly changing India was being played out. The idea of the village has further receded in post-liberalisation mainstream Hindi cinema, with only a rare few engaging with the rural scenario in any significant manner. In a complete reversal of the initial portrayal, however, the village in post-liberalisation mainstream cinema is the shameful aspect of the Indian growth success story that the urban professional India would rather ignore. From being the core protector of Indian values within the Gandhian paradigm, it becomes the outsider in the contemporary mainstream cinematic Indian discourse regarding the nation firmly located in English-speaking, professional and upwardly mobile urban India.

REFERENCES

Bose, M. 2007. *Bollywood: A History*, New Delhi: Roli Books.

Chakravarti, S. 1993. *National Identity in Indian Popular Cinema, 1947-87*, Austin: University of Texas Press.

Dudrah, R. 2006. *Bollywood: Sociology Goes to the Movies*, London: Sage.

Dudrah, R. and Desai, J. (eds.) 2008. *The Bollywood Reader*, Maidenhead: Open University Press.

Gokulsingh, K.M. and Dissanayake, W. 1998. *Indian Popular Cinema: A Narrative of Cultural Change*, London: Trentham Books Limited.

Gupta, D. 2005. 'Whither the Indian Village: Culture and Agriculture in 'Rural' India', *Economic and Political Weekly*, Vol. 40(8), pp. 751-58.

Inden, R. 1990. *Imagining India*, Oxford: Basil Blackwell.

Kaul, P. 2016. 'Gender in Post-Liberalisation India: The Complex Trajectories of Gender and (Postcolonial) Nationalism in Hindi Cinema' in Shaminder Takhar (ed.) *Gender and Race Matter: Global Perspectives on Being a Woman (Advances in Gender Research Series)*, London: Emerald Publishers.

Khurana, S. 2016. 'Breath of Fresh Air: From Agriculture to Cricket and Language, AIR Shaped a New Nation in Many Ways'. Available Online at *http://indianexpress.com/article/lifestyle/art-and-culture/breath-of-fresh-air-2889916/* (January 31, 2018).

Mahapatral, D. 2017. 'Over 12000 Farmer Suicides Per Year, Centre Tells Supreme Court'. Available Online at *https://timesofindia.indiatimes.com/india/over-12000-farmer-suicides-per-year-centre-tells-supreme-court/articleshow/58486441.cms* (December 15, 2017).

'Media Neglecting Issues of Rural India: Sainath' 2017. Available Online at *http://www.thehindu.com/news/cities/Mangalore/media-neglecting-issues-of-rural-india-sainath/article19530616.ece* (December 3, 2017).

Mishra, V. 2002. *Bollywood Cinema: Temples of Desire*, New York: Routledge.

Peterson, W. 1958. 'A General Typology of Migration', *American Sociological Review*, Vol. 23(3), pp. 256-66.

Prasad, M. 1998. *Ideology of the Hindi Film: A Historical Construction*, Oxford: Oxford University Press.

Raghavendra, M.K. 2008. *Seduced by the Familiar: Narration and Meaning in Indian Popular Cinema*, New Delhi: Oxford University Press.

Sainath, P. 2016. 'Rural Reporting: Opening Spaces for the People's Voices', *Media Asia*, Vol. 43(3-4), pp. 127-37.

Sardesai, R. 2017. "Why is the Indian Farmer Angry?" Available Online at *https://www.youtube.com/watch?v=9J1isnYbguA* (December 15, 2017).

Sethi, R. 1999. *Myths of the Nation: National Identity and Literary Representation*, Oxford: Clarendon Press.

Tilak, V. 2014. "An American in Madras Traces Career of Unlikely Pioneer in Tamil-Language Films'. Available Online at *https://india.blogs.nytimes.com/2014/02/06/an-american-in-madras-traces-career-of-unlikely-pioneer-in-tamil-language-films/* (November 30, 2017).

Virdi, J. 2003. *The Cinematic ImagiNation: Indian Popular Films as Social History*, New Brunswick, NJ: Rutgers University Press.

Yuval-Davis, N. 1997. *Gender and Nation*, London: Sage.

FILMOGRAPHY

Bandini [Prisoner Woman] (1963), Dir Bimal Roy, India.

Barsaat [Rainfall] (1949), Dir Raj Kapoor, India.

Do Bigha Zameen [Two Units of Land] (1953), Dir Bimal Roy, India.

Gaman [Departure] (1978), Dir Muzaffar Ali, India.

Jis Desh Main Ganga Behti Hai [The Country Where the River Ganges Flows] (1960), Dir Radhu Karmarkar, India.

Mela [Village Fair] (2000), Dir Dharmesh Darshan, India.

Mother India (1957), Dir Mehboob Khan, India.

Naya Daur [New Era] (1957), Dir B.R. Chopra, India.

Pardes [Foreign Land] (1997), Dir Subhash Ghai, India.

Peepli Live (2010), Dir Anusha Rizvi, India.

Piya Ka Ghar [Marital Home] (1972), Dir Basu Chatterjee, India.

Sholay [Embers] (1975), Dir Ramesh Sippy, India.

Swades [Homeland] (2004), Dir Ashutosh Gowarikar, India.

Taal [Rhythm] (1999), Dir Subhash Ghai, India.

4

Village Studies and Possibilities of 'Multispecies' Ethnography

Ishita Dey

Introduction

One of the oft cited reasons for a loss of anthropological interest on village studies is attributed to the critique of structural functional methods associated with studying villages. Structural functional methods failed to move beyond representing villages as self-sustained communities and this assumption according to Mines and Yazgi (2010) is a residue of the colonial administrative reading of the village (2010: 3).[1] The authors point to the critique of Cohn (1977) who thought that the structural functionalists provided a template to study villages and understand villages. In the words of Cohn (1977) it was a charter myth that was handed down to British officials that was used to represent, govern and understand 'village republics'. The works of S.C. Dube, McKim Marriot, D.N. Majumdar constantly tried to explain the wider networks of social relations and anthropologists never tried to argue for exclusive status of villages. Rather, there was a constant attempt to make macro linkages. However most of these studies remained confined to studying villages where the human was at the centre that shaped caste, class, religious and clan identities. There has been practically no attempt to make sense of the village from the perspective of non-human. Is a non-human reading of the village life-world possible? In this chapter I argue for a methodological shift in village studies within anthropological knowledge in India. I show that our understanding of the village has to encompass other lives—the non-human. A study of the non-human as I demonstrate in the chapter requires a nuanced reading of multispecies. Before we dwell on the discussion of multispecies ethnography in a village in Mayurbhanj district Odisha, it is important to highlight what we mean by multispecies.

Donna Haraway (2007) in her work argued for a species turn in anthropology. Her seminal work *When Species Meet* shows the mutual adaptation between and across species and the becoming of 'companion species' (Haraway, 2003). In the manifesto Haraway outlines what she means by companion species. She makes a clear separation from companion animal and feels the term 'companion species' is heterogeneous. According to Haraway, companion species embodies four ideas: 'co-constitution, finitude, impurity, historicity and complexity' as it unfolds in the everydayness of nature-culture (2003: 15). She outlines four tones that are equally important to stay true to a multitude of meanings she wants to propose through this term. Firstly, an evolutionary framework inspired by Darwin. The very term species requires a biological reading and specifically so in a post cyborg world. Post-cyborg, the question of the biological remains central and 'machinic and textual are internal to the organic' (2003: 14). Secondly, the term species is also about defining 'difference'—philosophically. Thirdly, it is a combination of corporeality and semiotics. Fourthly, drawing from Marx and Freud she feels species is 'filthy', 'gold' and 'wealth'—in other words complex. The species turn in anthropology has been instrumental to take into cognisance formation of natureculture. In other words, it has been instrumental for following biographies of things in formation which has been marginal either as landsape, food has been at the forefront of anthropological work (Kirksey and Helmreich, 2010). Some of the seminal works of recent times that can qualify as multispecies ethnography can also be classified as food items. In this context it would be important to highlight the works of Anna Tsing on Matsutake mushrooms and Heather Paxson's work on American artisanal cheese and locate it in the geographical catalogue of anthropological works. I borrow the term geographical catalogue from Yasmeen Arif who demonstrates how as anthropologists we are situated in a geographical catalogue where we have been mapped into specific 'geographical localised specialisations'. Mostly these geographical localised specialisations have also shaped the way in which we understand spaces and sites located 'here' and 'there' and how the knowledge about here is constantly negotiated within dominant 'knowledge production practices' and we face a challenge of how do we anthropologise the world from our location and secondly, and the most important and relevant question I wish to reiterate is 'what is the imagination of a geographical world for a located anthropologist'? These questions are relevant in the methodological shifts I want to draw here. If we were to revisit village studies, and I speak here as an anthropologist who taught a class of development practice students in Ambedkar University Delhi, India. I feel the imagination of the village has to be rethought beyond the three axis that it has revolved around so far: 1) village as a fixed site rather than a dynamic space shaped by human and non-humans 2) the synonymous use of village and rural in our understanding of the village studies 3) need to reimagine the global locatedness of the village. If I were to take a cue from Arif (2016), I would revisit the question what is the imagination of a village in today's geographical world for a located anthropologist teaching in an interdisciplinary course that encourages students to undertake action research. How do shifting contours of anthropology, particularly the species turn is relevant for an understanding of the village as a concept rather than as a site?

This chapter is divided into three main sections. In the first section I try and situate the geographical landscape of Jamposi to argue that the village is not merely a fixed site that enjoys the benefits of the state welfare schemes to make it self-sufficient be it through administrative functioning of panchayats or a revenue arm of the state. Is there a way of studying the village beyond the humans? Is there a way in which ethnography can give visibility to other things that resides, interact and shape social relations between humans?

In the second section, I move on to a discussion of the forest produce to understand how different items like sal flowers, mushrooms shape the life worlds of Jamposi. Drawing from narratives on collection, rearing and rituals observed, I show how the world of non-humans intersect with humans. I argue that a study to understand dependence of people on forests needs to be approached from the perspective of interspecies.

In the final section, I draw on three related studies of privileging of single species to show that multispecies ethnography needs to reimagine the global locatedness of the village. In trying to draw a global locatedness, I do not follow the commodity chain framework and try and establish the global markets of the forest produce. Instead I draw upon a man-animal conflict and depletion of a forest produce to argue that a biotic life of Jamposi is shaped by the conflict between species and any study of non-human lifeworld needs to address constitutive nature as well as conflict between and across species.

Studying the Village

This chapter is based on field work which was done in intermittent phases in the course of 2015-16 in neighbouring villages around the Simlipal Biosphere reserve. For the purposes of this chapter, I focus on one site—Jamposi which is part of the Mayurbhanj distict. At the very outset it would be important to separate the village as an administrative unit and an anthropological conceptualisation of the village. Schlesinger (2010) in his study points to the semantic planes of meanings that the word village can evoke in its usage. For Schlesinger, the village is a place, space and a world and the spatiality it evokes in its reference in everyday speech is a significant point to note. According to Schlesinger (2010) 'as a place, the village can be definite—a point with a certain location. It can also be definite like an area, an expanse with a certain boundary' (2010: 202). Drawing from Schlesinger, Jamposi like Apshinghe, a village in Maharashtra is a revenue village that comes under the Saleibada Panchayat and Thakurmonda Block of Mayurbhanj district.

Mayurbhanj district as official records suggest is named after two medieval ruling families—Mayuras and the Bhanjas. There were close cultural ties between these families. It is believed that the headquarters was at Khijjinga Kotta and was destroyed by Sultan Firoz Shah Tughlaq in 1361. The capital was transferred to Haripur and with this shift the kingdom was referred to as Mayurbhanj to commemorate the traditional relations between the two families. Amidst the two ruling families, the Bhanja rulers remained influential. The significant years in the history of Mayurbhanj are 1751, 1803, 1830-1834 and November 9, 1948 and January 1, 1949. These years are significant to understand the history of Mayurbhanj during fracticidal war, relationship with the coloniser and how it was incorporated within the folds of the post-independent Indian state in general and Odisha in particular. According to Nilamani Senapati (1967), Mayurbhanj was semi-independent till 1751 following which it came under the Maratha regime. By 1803, it became part of the colonial regime and the period from 1830-34 witnessed rebellions by Kol which led to handing over of parts of the Kolhan region to the British government. By November 9, 1948 Mayurbhanj came within the folds of the Indian state. On January 1, 1949 Mayurbhanj merged with Odisha because of cultural and linguistic links. In this official record, Mayurbhanj is described as 'well wooded' and the role of forests in the economy is emphasised time and again (1967: 223). In this context, it is important to note that the Simlipal forest is referred to as a semi-evergreen forest and Sal is the chief tree of the forest.

Today Simlipal is a biosphere reserve[2] and according to the official webportal of the reserve it has made special efforts to conserve the tiger. The wildlife in Simlipal primarily catered to the interests of the royal family and their guests. The forest was initially managed by the Kings of Mayurbhanj in 1885. C.C. Hart prepared a working plan in 1896-97 till 1946, through lease and contract. The forest became an important source of timber extraction till the change of its administration first with merger of the ex-state in the Union of India on November 6, 1948 and part of Odisha on January 1, 1949. Post-independence, liberal shooting permits were a hindrance to wildlife protection. In 1973, Simlipal was declared as a tiger reserve and this single species approach has been later a subject of criticism. There are 64 villages located inside the sanctuary and about 1200 villages on the periphery[3]. Jamposi, the site of our study is one of the many villages on the periphery of Simlipal.

An understanding of the village as I indicate needs to be located against the localised geographical context of Jamposi that revolves around the life forms of Simlipal Biosphere reserve, socio-economic activities of the Mayurbhanj district, emergence of Jamposi, the life forms of Jamposi and the engagement of human with non-human forms. In other words, a multispecies ethnography of Jamposi village would involve a close reading of life forms that has shaped the life-worlds of Jamposi village. How do we understand the non-human life worlds in sites such as Jamposi?

Ho is the most common spoken language in Jamposi. Out of 97 households in Jamposi a few speak Oriya and a few speak Hindi. The conversations, chats and walks were mediated by translators who were development professionals as well as local villagers. While this was challenging, this allowed me to traverse to closely look at language critically. While slowly I started acquainting myself with Ho it remained a challenge. This provided me a scope to think about representation and how language plays a crucial role in the politics of representation. The role of language in naming things and processes associated with the forest has a long history and across these two sites and several other sites that I explored allowed me a way to situate the problematic. I tried to study the forest from the perspective of the humans, their sense of its use, rather than mapping the social life in itself. Is mapping of a social life of forest produce independent of humans? Not necessarily so. However is there a way of representation that is not synonymous with language that separates humans from non-humans. Kohn in his work shows the possibility of 'representational forms that go beyond language'. He demonstrates that it is possible 'by stepping beyond the human' and 'non-human life-forms too represent the world' (2013: 8). He adds a note of caution of not to conflate representation with language instead to widen the horizon and here he engages with Peirce to argue that signs are both 'iconic' and 'indexical' and 'non-symbolic representational qualities pervade both human and non-human' (Ibid). Kohn urges us to a reading of signs outside the human framework. This framework widens the scope and method of anthropology and redefines the object of what has been studied so far. Anthropological monographs documented the 'other' through 'language, culture, society and history' (Kohn 2013: 5).

Drawing upon conversations, group discussions, surveys and social mapping, I propose to mark a paradigmatic shift in village studies through a mapping of forest produce that connect the life worlds of humans and non-humans. This paradigmatic shift is fuelled by an emerging body of literature where the insects, plants, fungi and microbes appear alongside humans, in the realm of the bios (Helmreich and Kirkskey, 2010: 545). Is there a possibility to think of village studies from the lens of multi-species? Multispecies ethnographic works on microbial life of cheese (Paxson, 2008), matsutake mushrooms (Tsing 2016) has shown possibilities of working with organisms and how they impact social lifeworlds. In fact, Paxson's microbial world of cheese making is a product of the post-pastoral landscape where artisanal cheesemakers are working with a post-pastoral ethos. Here, there is no separation or opposition of nature and culture. Instead, cheese making is cultured nature. In other words it is a journey of how the life worlds of bacteria, yeasts, ruminant animals come into contact with human skill. Similarly, this paper proposes for a methodological shift to understand villages that are dependent on forests from the lens of multispecies ethnography. Through a multispecies ethnography of non-timber forest produce in Jamposi, a village in Mayurbhanj district of Odisha, I argue that a mapping of village life worlds has to be rethought beyond the human and the relationships that are shaped by insects, plants and fungi. An attempt will be made to reconstruct the biography of the village through how the non-humans shape the life worlds of the humans and the sociality that emerges in the politics of non-timber forest produce.

What is a Forest Produce and Where is the Forest?

As I entered a house in Jamposi village, the family members were busy attending to at least three kinds of forest produce. An old woman sat with piles of leaves. I asked her if it was Sal leaf. She nodded. A heap of sal leaves was stacked neatly in the corner of the courtyard. It was a sunny afternoon. She shared that many women from the village are engaged in leaf collection at least for five days. Dry leaf or patra collection is one of the common tasks undertaken by women. Mostly women collect the leaves and use them for stitching sal leaf plates which are sold in local haats. Sometimes these plates are also used for household purposes. Apart from dry Sal leaves, women also collect wood from forests. I am alerted to the seasonal nature of the produce. She shares that apart from leaves and wood, women also collect sticks for brushing teeth. Pointing to the seasonality of the produce, women and men explain to me the seasons and months in which these items are found. One of the family members joined the conversation and commented that since it was a sunny winter afternoon, I can spot many families painting houses. When I asked about the correlation between painting houses and forest produce, I was pointed to a pot that was being set for boiling. I was asked to check and told to identify the wood chips that were boiling. I failed. I was told that it was bark of the asan tree. I recollected what Srimati from Mandam had told me about this colour preparation. Asan bark is boiled with soda and the purpose of this laborious colouring process is to reduce damage during the rainy season. Cowdung and mud are mixed and spread over an area and left to dry. Then the area is rubbed with a rock/stone followed by the asan bark mix which adds a wonderful richness. Asan bark I was told can be found in forests or from old trees in the village. When I asked where they go to collect these things, someone raised a finger pointing to the mountains with a green cover. Interestingly, many villagers synonymously used words for mountain and forests. In Ho, the mountain is called Buru and the forest is referred to as Bir. There is no separate word for the sky. I was told that they go to collect wood, leaves and other things from Merda Buru.

Merda Buru will not find a space in the official mapping of Jamposi's forest. If one stands near the school opening to the vast area, one will spot the mountains with green cover. It seems like the village is located against the backdrop of the mountains. Whenever one asks about the name, usually people respond Simlipal. However, a little prodding about rituals associated with collection of various forest produce will reveal names of forests and also rituals associated with Jaharai. During my first visit to the village, as we discussed the prohibitions associated with rearing of tasar, one of the villagers mentioned that villagers offer prayers at the Jaharai or sacred grove. Jaharai is an enclosed space with different kinds of trees. There is a ritual head known as the Rauriya who presides over the rituals. Mrityunjay and I take a walk with S, who also works as an extension worker. Commenting on festivities, we are told that there are four festivals that are crucial to the life of Jamposi. Apart from personal offerings, villagers offer puja through the Rauria on four occasions. They are: Maghiporob, Bahaporob, Heroporob and Jam Nama. Maghiporob is celebrated around the first and second week of February. Each house carries a kukuda (hen) to the Jaharia. Kukudas are sacrificed and the meat is distributed throughout the village. I ask if there is any brew they make from forest produce. To which I am told, 'Handiya na karole puja hobo na' (There cannot be any puja without the local rice brew). She adds, to mark this occasion villagers buy new clay pots to cook rice. During Bahaporob, the sal flower is worshipped. There were reels of laughter as I asked where is the forest? Pointing to the sky, mountain and stretch of greens I was told, 'that is our buru (forest) and bir' (mountain). The ritual calendar and ritual roles play an important role in understanding gendered sociality around produce such as adu (potato), sago (greens), udd (mushrooms), tubers that enter the kitchen space and the commercialised NTFP that of lac and tasar where social restrictions prohibit women from engaging in rearing practices. In Jamposhi too, there is a goddess who protects the forest. She is known as Maburu (goddess of the forest). Maburu is worshipped around February. As part of Bahaporob's festivities animals are sacrificed. Goats or hens are sacrificed and consumed every alternate year. The third festival is Heroporob which is celebrated in August. It is mandatory to buy new clay pots. During this festival, steamed rice cakes or pitha is eaten. Rice powder is mixed with salt and wrapped in a sal leaf and steamed. The fourth and final festival is Jam Nama or a festival to celebrate new food. Jam is food and Nama is new. It is observed in September. New rice from the upland is worshipped. The sal tree, therefore is one of the most important trees and it is not a coincidence that Jamposi is known for tasar rearing. The sal tree is used for several purposes—the flower is worshipped in March, followed by collection of sal tree seeds or Saromanj from May-June, Jungle tasar is reared/collected mostly between August and September and finally a kind of resin called Jhuna is collected from the sal tree from October. Other than that dried sal leaves are collected throughout the year to prepare leaf plates. Mostly sal trees are found in the forests and villagers have to access forests for sal-related produce. However, one of the respondents alerted us that it is very easy to find mahua, jackfruit, kusum and asan trees. As soon as I heard kusum tree I asked if they cultivate En or lac since Mayurbhanj was known for lac production. We met one family who made a living from lac cultivation. However, many women also shared how they clean the kusum seeds and take them to local mills to extract oil. Another oil that is used across the villages is the oil extracted from the Mahua fruit. While kusum oil if used for applying on body and hair, mahua oil is used for cooking and as a repellent to keep away snakes. Jamposi is known for its jackfruits and in the course of the fieldwork almost every respondent shared the record sales in 2016. The Mahua tree was found to be most lucrative as the

Table 1: Forest Produce Available in Jamposi Village

Forest Produce	Month
Wood	January-February; June-July
Stick for brushing	Throughout the year
Dried leaves	January-February
Haritaki	December-February
Amla	January-February
Bahra/Harida	January-February
Mahua flower	March-April
Tamarind	February-March
Tiril/Charo seed (Chironjee)	April-May
Sal tree seed	May-June
Mahua seed	June-July
Kusum seed	June-July
Jackfruit	June-July
Mango	June-July
Junglee tasar	August-September
Edible mushrooms (Boda chatu, patra chatu, katha chatu, bali chatu, rootka, tumba)	July-August
Potatoes found in forest Adu (pitaadu, petesangha)	October-November

seeds, flowers and fruits could be used for various purposes. What was interesting in the course of the discussions that the moment the nomenclature of non-timber forest produce was used, the male members of the village shared forest produce that could be sold in the local markets. Women talked about forest produce used for domestic purposes. One such forest produce is the mushrooms or udd (Ho)/chatu (Oriya). In Jamposi, women identified six kinds of mushrooms that they collect, cook and consume. They were: Bora chatu, Patra chatu (mushrooms found on leaves), Katha chatu (mushrooms found on wood), Bali chatu (mushrooms found in sandy soil), Rootha chatu (mushrooms found under the soil) and Tumba chatu (mushrooms found in upland paddy fields). There are mushrooms as well. Apart from mushrooms two kinds of potato (Pita Adu) and Petesangha are eaten and consumed.

The cycle of forest produce is seasonal and requires a deepened knowledge of the forest eco-system as most of these items require collection rather than rearing. In other words, the collector has to assess its biotic value.

Biotic Life and Inter-Species Conflict

Biotic life and its preservation has mostly revolved around celebration of uniqueness and creating enclosures to ensure its survival. Attempts to classify areas as reserve forests, sanctuary, biosphere are many such ways to preserve other species around 'single' species. I argue such preservation techniques dampen the co-constitutive relationship of the non-human world. I will draw upon two examples to elaborate on this. In the case of the Simlipal biosphere reserve, the government has encouraged Hill Kharias to engage in rice cultivation in the hope that they will depend less on forests while the Hill Kharias do not want to accept rice cultivation or rice as a staple food. The introduction of paddy cultivation goes against the practice of food gathering. While the government views food gathering as a source of over exploitation, the forest is a source of food across many other villages and this practice holds true for Jamposhi. Savyasaachi (2016) asks us to revisit the governmental efforts and such programmes. He adds a cautionary note. If the developmental programmes disrupts the food chains and life cycles this will also impact the forest dwellers' recognition of a 'life-force' (2016: 486). Loss of life-force, as is the case with the Project Tiger Reserve created grounds for deforestation as food chains and lifecycle of plants are disrupted. What leads to disruption of the lifecycle of plants? One immediate cause of disruption of the lifecycle in Simlipal is depletion of honey and tubers according to Hill Kharias (Ibid: 489). Savyasachi shows that the Hilla Kharias are part of a knowledge system and the preservation of the forest cannot be done without incorporating their knowledge about the non-human life world. While the present policies try and maintain the inter-species conflict through segregation of species, a discussion on forest produce and forest dependent spaces like Jamposi reveals an inherent sociality in the seasonality of the produce and its uses. At the same time, by ensuring exclusive spaces, Savyasaachi cautions that forest dependent communities might be forced to collect plants, shoots and fungi before their maturity. The coexistence of human and non-human needs a deeper understanding and this is evident in the disappearance of birds in areas where tasar is reared. Vinisha Singh Basnet follows the case of missing crows from Jamposi in Odisha to its absence in Narayanpur and Tasaria villages in Jharkhand. There has been a conscious attempt to poison crows to save tasar cocoons. Similarly, the forest department in a bid to save tigers, to draw from Savyaasachi might be responsible for depletion of tubers and honey. Depletion of forest-based resources fuels a change in diet and this is equally applicable for humans and non-humans. In Chhattisgarh, lac rearers reported to me that monkeys are fond of the sweet texture of the lac insect. Jamposi, like many other areas under Karanjia division has been witness to Human Elephant conflict (HEC) cases in recent years. According to a study, HEC led to seven human deaths and one injury from 2001 to 2006. Usually elephants raid paddy fields and this leads to heavy loss of crops. Raiding groups varied from a single elephant to a group of 13 elephants. In the non-paddy season, brinjal cultivations were raided by elephants and followed by raids on jackfruit and mango trees in May-June also coinciding with the time when these fruits ripen and are ready to be sold in the market (Sahu and Das, 2012).

The conflicts discussed show how species have been pitted against each other for forest management. Whereas, the adaptability of an intespetial world is evident in the life of Jamposi village be its economic dependence on forests or in its rituals. It is at this cusp of interspecies that we need to understand villages as sites in formation. Inter-special contradiction as we[4] try and make sense of the naming of Jamposi. Jamposi was previously called Matalasahi. A person named Matala was the first inhabitant of this place. The place always had dense forests and Matala was scared to live all by himself. He invited people from the Munduri clan from the nearby village—Dandapani to stay here. People from neighbouring villages also joined in. Since Matala was the first inhabitant and also the discoverer, the village was named after him. Gradually, the land was cleared and the village came under the attention of the revenue department. Once a revenue inspector visited the village and was startled to find that the village is called Matalasahi. He and his co-workers suggested finding an alternative name. Since there were many Jamun trees, the official from the revenue department suggested that the village could be named after the Jamun tree. Hereafter the village was called Jamposi. Most of the families who stay here have migrated from areas which would today come under Jharkhand.

Jamposi, as some family members recall was a safe place to hide from the forest officials. Some families tried to resettle in Bhadrak but were forced to return to Jamposi as they did not have money to pay the revenue. When British officials came to Jamposi a person used to beat a drum and alert the villagers and they would hide in the forests. This was done as the villagers never had sufficient money to pay taxes. The history of the naming of Jamposi shows a privileging of a species, a tree—an idea that remains inherent to preservation techniques adopted by the Indian state to preserve birds, animals and trees as well. It is also evident in the way in which forest produce has been conceptualised around timber. The very categorisation of non-timber privileges timber.

Conclusion

In this chapter I have tried to argue for a multispecies ethnography within village studies. Through the vignette of forest produce I show that without a holistic understanding of multispecies, an understanding of village lifeworld remains incomplete. Village lifeworld and its readings needs to move beyond the macro social processes and a deeper understanding of entrenched identities can also come from the sociality that human beings enjoy with the non-human world. In trying to argue for a multispecies ethnography, I map the forest produce and its seasonality. The seasonality of the produce shows the seasonal nature of the ecological landscape that Jamposi shares with Simlipal. A reading of Jamposi or any other neighbouring villages has to be understood in the global local politics of single species conservation, taxonomies of classification and its bearings on the everyday life. This requires attention to the non-human, attention to the microbes, shoots and fungi. The village, in other words has to be imagined at the intersection of human and non-human—a methodological shift shaped by a multispecies turn in world anthropology.

NOTES

1. Pointing to Dumont and Pocock's (1957, 1957b) criticism of William Wiser, Diane P. Mines and Nicholas Yazgi (2010) argue that William Wiser (an American missionary involved with Indian village service, a colonial development agency) presented a romantic view of the village Karimpur as a closed and autonomous unit bound by the harmonious and self-reproducing ties of the 'jajmani system'.
2. 'Biosphere reserve is an international designation assigned by UNESCO for representative parts of natural and cultural landscapes extending over large areas of terrestrial or coastal/ marine ecosystems...' (Source: http://odishawildlife.org/ simlipalbiosphere.html); Accessed on February 5, 2017.
3. http://simlipal.org/history.php; Accessed on May 24, 2017.
4. Sweetleena Panda from PRADAN helped me to explore the legend behind the naming of Jamposi.

REFERENCES

Arif, Yasmeen. 2016. 'Anthropologizing the World and Worlding the Anthropologist', *American Anthropologist,* 118: 848-851. doi:10.1111/aman.12697, Accessed on February 1, 2017.

Cohn, Bernard S. 1977. 'African Models and Indian Histories', in Richard G. Fox (ed.), *Realm and Region in Traditional India*, New Delhi: Vikas, pp. 90-113.

Dumont, Louis and David Pocock. 1957a. 'Village Studies', *Contributions to Indian Sociology*, 1(1): 23-41.

____ . 1957b. 'For a Sociology of India', *Contributions to Indian Sociology*, 1(1): 7-22.

Haraway, Donna J. 2003. *The Companion Species Manifesto. Dogs, Peoples and Significant Otherness*, Chicago: Prickly Paradigm Press.

____ a. 2007. *When Species Meet*, Minnesota: University of Minnesota Press.

Kirksey, Eben and Helmreich, Stefan. 2010. 'The Emergence of Multispecies Ethnography', *Cultural Anthropology*, June 14, 2010, https://culanth.org/fieldsights/277-the-emergence-of-multispecies-ethnography, Accessed on May 11, 2017.

Kohn, Eduardo. 2013. *How Forests Think? Towards an Anthropology of Non-Human*, Berkeley: University of California Press.

Mines, Diane P. and Yazgi, Nicholas. 2010. 'Introduction: Do Villages Matter?' In Diana P. Mines and Nicholas Yazgi (eds.), *Village Matters: Relocating Villages in the Contemporary Anthropology of India*, Delhi: Oxford University Press, pp. 1-28.

Savyasaachi. 2016. 'Tiger and Honey Bee' in Nandini Sundar (ed.), *The Scheduled Tribes and Their India: Politics, Identities, Policies and Work*, Delhi: Oxford University Press.

Schlesinger, Lee I. 2010. 'Arms and the World. Village Apshine (Maharashtra) Bounding and Extending Where'. In Diana P. Mines and Nicholas Yazgi (eds.), *Village Matters: Relocating Villages in the Contemporary Anthropology of India*, Delhi: Oxford University Press, pp. 199-237.

Senapati, Nilamani. 1967. *Orissa District Gazeteers, Mayurbhanj*, Cuttack: Orissa Government Press.

5

Violence on Dalits in Village India: Metaphors, Marginalities and the 'Problem of Exit'

Bidhan Chandra Dash

While the collective conscience in India has always been nostalgic about the "Indian village" life as natural, innocent and therefore authentic, the Dalit leadership has shunned the village as 'a sink of localism, den of ignorance, narrow-mindedness and communalism'. Although, Ambedkar supported movements and policies against landlordism, he was less optimistic about any transformative potential of Indian villages. He viewed the 'Dalit labour' in rural India as essentially a "problem of exit", so much so that, he never had any political agenda or campaigns for the Dalit agricultural labourers (Omvedt, 1994: 157). However, contrary to Ambedkar's wishes, the Dalits, even today, are overwhelmingly located in rural areas, predominantly work as agricultural labourers, lead a wretched life; and face socio-economic and political suppression, as well as, cultural mutilation. What is more appalling is the fact that despite centuries of collective action, the Dalits are increasingly subjected to systematic and brutal violence very often resulting in mass murders. This chapter seeks a different entry point to the popular debate on the 'violence of Dalits'. It attempts to deconstruct the often assumed, commonsensical, understanding of space and practice conjectures. Examining some of the exceptional and everyday incidences of violence against Dalits in contemporary rural India, this chapter advocates a discursive engagement with the metaphor of the village itself, as a site for potential emancipatory politics. The chapter argues that such engagement within the 'Dalit Discourse' is not only urgent but also emergent, particularly in the context of globalisation, in which, the metaphor of the village returns as an ultimate antidote to the evils of modernity—a new synthesis of social life in 'late-modernity'.

The Dalit Conundrum with Village India

Many years later, sitting under the shade of a tree near his wretched home in the scorching summer heat, old Arjuna Doma, would recall his "(mis)adventures. Revolting against constant abuses and ill-treatments by the dominant castes, he would cycle to the nearby village Ahmadpur and convert to Islam. However, his revolution would be for a short while. He would be excommunicated by the entire village, including his own caste. Bereft of 'caste-based labour' and 'caste-based entitlements', he would be forced to submit to the village authorities and beg to be 're-converted' back to the Hindu caste fold.

Aju Khan lived the prime of his life in Biranarasinghapur[1], a Brahmin-dominated village located in coastal Odisha His story is typical of everyday suppression and surrender of millions of Dalits to the dominant caste order. His story also reveals a lot about the spatial practices of caste and Dalit oppression. Sociologists have insisted that it is not the 'exclusion' per se, which is the important issue of concern; rather, it is the 'terms of inclusion' of the lower castes and their participation. In addition to this one cannot draw a pan-Indian pattern, rather this 'terms of inclusion' is embedded in the local spatial practices of caste (Srinivas, 2009: 37). Arjuna Doma's story can be listed as another example of such 'terms of inclusion' of the Dalits embedded in the spatial practices of diverse village localities in Indian society. The conundrum of 'being part, yet apart' is the crisis of the Dalit existence in the villages of India. It is not the exclusion, but terms and contexts of inclusion that needs attention. This story of Arjuna Doma/Aju Khan aptly summarises what Ambedkar called the 'problem of exit' while referring to the Dalits of rural India. As if, the Doma community of Biranarsinghapur would realise the ingenuity of Ambedkar's analysis and decide after a decade later to abandon Biranarshingapur and resettle in Biripara[2], a wasteland. Interestingly, this mere distance of geographical space is not a distancing of ecology, economy and habitation, in many ways their caste-based economic relationship of patron client has remained and even continues till today. Etymology of *'pur'* and *'para'* is also interesting to observe for a nuanced sociological discussion of village India. We will elaborate on this point at a later stage.

Arjuna Doma's story is also a story of the Dalit predicament with a tyrannical *'conscience collective'* which leaves no scope for escape. Is it the tyranny of the locality that encourages a pogrom? Pertinent here is to ask, is there a relation of the violence on the Dalits with that of the spatial constitution of locality? Interconnected to these questions is whether the village in India has been a simple expression of a spatial configuration? Is it a local configuration which has been nationally imagined, globally constituted and historically manipulated? How does one make sense of these spatial practices of diverse village landscapes constitutive of Indian society? From a sociological perspective, one may be interested in asking how has sociology as a discipline addressed the violence on Dalits in village society? This chapter ventures into these aspects of the Dalit existence and its intrinsic relationship with what has been called village India and argues that more than the reality of Indian villages, it is the metaphor which has constructed the village in India, and thereby shaping the existence and identity of the Dalits.

This chapter seeks a different entry point and argues that the growing violence on the Dalits in contemporary Indian society is more of a product of the ways the Indian village and rural lifestyle was historically and popularly imagined and constructed by various forces. In this chapter I argue that the leaders and policy makers deliberately ignored the reality of the village. They superimposed a metaphor which became a vital part of the nationalist imagination of 'India' as a nation, thus reconstructing and shaping the spatial practices of rural life. Village and caste became two prominent markers of Indian society, when the orientalists sought for the exclusivity of the Occident by glorifying a narrative of timeless village India. It became the mirror of the ancient past of the Western world. It was a small republic—harmonious, self-sufficient in its own ways that defined the Indian population as cultural religious as opposed to the occident where modernity has brought materialism and secular consciousness.

The Everyday and Exceptional of Violence

Arjuna Doma/Arju Khan's story could be, arguably though, representative of the everyday violence that the Dalits undergo in a village society. His story should not be dismissed as rare or occasional; rather it is rampant and constituted a significant aspect of the everyday life of a Dalit in India. A passing look at the recent data generated by the National Crime Record Bureau (NCRB) gives us a comprehensive idea of the nature and magnitude of the conundrum that the Dalits had to go through. In the year 2013, there was an increase of 17.1 per cent in crimes committed on the Dalits. In the subsequent year, the rate of increase was 19 per cent. The all India crime rate on the Dalits was 22.3 per cent in the year 2015 and in the subsequent year it was 20.3 per cent.[3]

I say this as a conservative estimation because what the official records do are generally conservative in recording the data on violence committed against the Dalits, they capture only the tip of the iceberg. The number of atrocities which are not reported to the police and so remain unnoticed is far greater. Shah et al. (2006) juxtaposed this limited statistical indicator with that of other statistics produced by the Crime Record Bureau, i.e. the number of cases pending in the court by the end of the year 2000. Their findings conclude that 'while a large number of cases of atrocities against the Dalits go unreported, even the registered cases suffer delays in the judicial process and remain unsettled'. A cursory glance at the court statistics 'revealed that the conviction of perpetrators of atrocities are very low, especially compared to the rate of acquittal which is very high (Shah, et al. 2006: 135)'. The official statistics for the decadal period 1990 to 2000 indicate that a total of 285,871 cases of various crimes were registered countrywide by SCs, of which 14,030 were registered under the PCR Act and 81,796 under the POA Act. This means that an average of 28,587 cases of caste discrimination and atrocities were registered by SCs every year during the 1990s. In 2001, the number of cases was higher at 33,500 (Thorat, 2009: 144). The table below shows a three-year comparative account of crimes committed against Scheduled Caste.

Table: Comparative Incidence of Crimes Against Scheduled Castes

Sl. No.	Crime-Head	Year					% Variations in 2013 Over 2012
		2009	2010	2011	2012	2013	
(1)	(2)	(3)	(4)	(5)	(6)	(7)	(8)
1	Murder	624	570	673	651	676	3.84
2	Rape	1,346	1,349	1,557	1,576	2,073	31.54
3	Kidnapping and Abduction	512	511	616	490	628	28.16
4	Dacoity	44	42	36	27	45	66.67
5	Robbery	70	75	51	40	62	55.00
6	Arson	195	150	169	214	189	-11.68
7	Hurt	4,410	4,376	4,247	3,855	4,001	27.13
8	Protection of Civil Rights Act	168	143	67	62	62	0.00
9	SC/ST (Provention of Atrocities) Act	11,143	10,513	11,342	12,576	13,975	11.12
10	Others	15,082	14,983	14,958	14,164	10,797	18.59
	Total	33,594					

Source: NCRB, Annual Report 2013: 110.

The above table is an evidence of the increasing incidences of violence against the Dalits. As shown in the table the total number of incidences of violence keeps increasing every year. In the year 2014 (which this table does not carry), it rose to 47,064, and in the year 2015 it was 45,003. Three types of crimes reported stand out here, first is the increasing number of cases of what has been termed as 'Hurt', which would mean an aggregate of various kinds of incidences where Dalits are hurt, both physically and mentally. Secondly the disproportionately high number of cases of rape, which show the concentration of violence on women of the community. In other words, it is the Dalit women who bear the brunt of the violence unleashed on the community. Murder stands third in the list suggesting how a community is targeted and socially prosecuted.

To understand both the 'everyday' and 'exceptional' of violence what is needed is to move beyond the narrative of 'non-violence' in the making of India as a nation state. Dread, threat and survival were part and parcel of the construction of 'non-violence' and the simultaneous attempts of the nationalist leaderships to control 'violence', in order to confirm to the ideal of 'nonviolence', can be an important entry point to understand the processes of making a nation-state. As Rao (2011: 162) has pointed out that "the latent violence of the crowd and the undisciplined satyagraha volunteers were constant sources of anxiety for Gandhian civil disobedience. Gandhi castigated the violence of the Dalit satyagrahi who broke through police forces to enter temples and expressed fear of a more general Dalit violence. He brought the problem of violence to the forefront when, in 1932, he responded to Prime Minister Ramsay MacDonald's Communal Award allowing the Depressed Classes a double vote". Similarly, Gandhi also believed that the reality of the village was that the economy of village India has gone through processes of mutilation and its technology has remained archaic, the cultural practices embedded in village India had many positives to offer. He had a deliberately constructed utopian understanding of the cultural practices of village India, the realisation of which would create a perfect alternative to the merciless logic of capitalism. Nagraj succinctly explains this thought process when he says in order to 'avoid the pitfalls of utopian thinking, Gandhiji made a futuristic reading of the past and the present (Nagraj, 2010: 137)'.

If Ambedkar conceived the separate electorate as a political weapon that allows the Depressed Classes to reject Hindu Hegemony, by fasting until death, Gandhi used the popularity of his personality and the possibility of his death and a subsequent threat of violence on the Depressed Classes. As he believed that the separate electorate, according to Gandhi would foreclose any possibility of the Hindu repentance. He was of the opinion that a political separation would encourage violence and create a condition of civil war between the Hindus and Harijans, and between the Hindus and Muslims. Gandhi's fasting was a tool for a threat to violence by infliction of self-violence, a violent process of disciplining the self. Gandhi made it clear that "one fasted against a loved one who was to be reformed, not to 'extort rights' from an enemy. The fast was terribly public and deeply private, both a spectacle of suffering and a disciplinary mechanism to vanquish the desire. It is both a penance and a punishment, a penance to the self and a punishment to the public (Rao, 2011: 164)".

Ambedkar noted that such politics of fasting inflicted a violence of its own. First, it fails to recognise the Dalit quest for dignity and social recognition. Secondly, it reconfigures the Dalit quest for political autonomy as perpetuation of social violence, insulating the historicity of Dalit violence (Rao, 2011: 165). The tables turn in a subtle and nuanced manner. The victim of violence is conceived as a perpetuator of violence. However, my point here is well established that violence and victimhood constituted the making of a Dalit political subject and this constitution had a tremendous impact on the 'lifeworld' of the Dalits and their quest to a dignified life in the colonial context.

Social scientists have understood violence in varied ways—"as fact, experience, affection, affliction, trauma, memory rhetoric, philosophy, law and govermentality, and there are layered complexities to each narrative of violence (Kannabiran, 2016: 02)". Obviously, this chapter deals with all these aspects but rather imagines a modest task to look at violence as part and parcel of the historical construction of Dalit identity and subjecthood and its closely knit relationship with the village as a 'space', rural ways of life as a process that constitute the existential world of Dalits. I attempt here to understand 'the absent presence' of violence. 'dread', 'threat' and 'survival' are categories through which the relationship with the everyday and an exploited enslaved subjecthood can be understood. Another important way violence can be understood is by signposting it as an extraordinary or even exceptional event, an aberration or an exceptional moment (Kannabiran, 2016: 03-15). By signposting the exceptional, one can roll out a historicity of violence in the making of Dalit identity. However, both have a close relationship with the 'village as a space' or the spatial practices of the village and, more importantly, how it has been historically constructed in the popular discourse, so much so that the construction overpowered the context.

Everyday Violence and the Dalit Lifeworld

News reports abound with violence of various kinds, regularly jolting the inertia of Indians that caste-based discrimination is still alive and flourishing in Indian society. A rare and comprehensive study was launched by the Action Aid survey in eleven states published in 2006. Apart from many important findings this study delineated a disturbing mindset of the dominant castes with respect to violence. Most of the violence was unleashed with the intention of teaching the Dalits a lesson, so that they realised their place in society (Shah, et al., 2009: 12). Underlying the act of violence is the assumption that 'we will get away' with this. Evaluating the violence on Dalits in *Village India*, Nagraj (2010), identifies two clear patterns. The first is the notion of justice in village society, the second is the assertion of the Dalits to secure new rights which the traditional society refuses to concede. The first form of violence confirms the worst fear of Dalits regarding the true nature of caste Hindu society and creates a kind of consciousness towards their existence in Indian society. The second form of violence is a reaction of traditional Indian society to the beginning a new awareness. "The first pattern of violence shapes a struggle and eventually a movement, while the second one is eventually an expression of a proto-movement (Nagraj, 2010: 125-26)."

A petty theft or a minor stealing committed by the Dalit would be considered as a grave act of offence and the village society transforms itself into a state—with all its judicial and policing powers. The individual act of violations results in punishment to the entire Dalit community. The punishments are quite extraordinary, for example, Nagraj documented an incident where the guilty was forced to eat human excreta (Nagraj, 2010: 128). The incidences of violence occur when the Dalit attempts to assert her rights and appeals for constitutional means for reward of such rights. Many studies conclude that the Dalit assertion of rights breaks the consensus that marks the village and creates a condition of disturbance which in turn culminates in violence. There are also established techniques adopted by the dominant sections of society to reinforce their power and to assert their superior status. Most of the time, the state employees collaborate with the upper castes in the process of violence (Shah et al., 2006: 135-43).

Signposting Violence on the Dalits

By banning 'untouchability' and making it a punishable offence, the new Constitution of India, provided legal and juridical mechanisms to deal with the issue of Dalit equality and dignity. The constitution directed the state to actively participate and intervene with an approach of positive discrimination to counter the historical inequities that the 'Scheduled Castes' suffer and devise mechanisms to counter the violence unleashed on the Dalits. From 1947 to 2016, various laws were enacted and amended, where the legal definition of the Dalits as 'Scheduled Caste' as an 'injured subject, constantly redefined the Dalit subjecthood. Initially, it was channelised with the category of 'civil rights', later on 'atrocity' formed the new definition of the Dalit problem in the Indian context. Rao (2011: 176) makes an interesting observation in this regard. According to her, the growing bureaucratic apparatus to monitor untouchability soon spawned a metamonitoring apparatus for watching over members of the Department of Social Welfare and the Office of the SC/ST Commissioner and to recommend measures to amend the Untouchability Offence Act. This produced an acquired knowledge regarding anti-Dalit violence, which occupied a central discourse in the making of the Indian state as well as Dalit activism as a barometer of social relations.

Paradoxically, however, both the making of the modern Indian state and the Dalit political subjecthood through the legislative mechanisms, simultaneously were accompanied by increase of violence on the Dalits. This time around, large episodes of collective and systematic violence on the Dalits marked the new ways in which domination and subjugation was practised in India as a nation. Kilvenmani, where 44 Dalits were burnt alive in Tamil Nadu in 1968 marked a new era of violence against the Dalits. One can, in fact, signpost many such events and select a few episodes to prove this point. Kannabiran reviews a number of exceptional incidences—Belchi where 14 Dalits were burnt alive in Bihar in 1977, Motichijhanpi where hundreds of Dalits were massacred by the state in Sunderbans in 1978, Karamchedu where 6 Dalits were murdered, women raped in 1991, Melavalavu where an elected Dalit panchayat leader and 5 Dalits were killed in broad daylight and there are also Chinduru and Khairanjalis as well as recently Una (Kanabiran, 2016: 15).

Teltumde (2016: 177) relates the nature of this new violence as part of a new capitalist development. According to him, the class and caste intersected in Kilvenmani, where instead of individual rage, the new genre of caste violence was a consciously planned and organised action executed at the level of the collective, by and on a collective, with the intention of terrorising the latter. Teltumde's interpretation could be read into many such cases of violence where land and right to land becomes one of the important struggles for the Dalits. However, land is one of the central aspects of the violence on Dalits, there are also matters of dignity, flouting the collective conscience as in the case of Chinduru and Karamchedu, where assertion of civil rights and defying the collective conscience marks the starting point of violence. In an attempt to signpost the exceptional nature of violence, I will detail two cases of such a brutal and systematic conscious attempt to teach the Dalits a lesson that took place in the early 1990s in Andhra Pradesh.

The Karamchedu Massacre

Karamchedu in Andhra Pradesh is one of the biggest villages in the whole of Prakasham district and the place is known for its fertile land and better irrigation facilities, provided by two irrigation projects, namely the Krishna canal and the Nagarjuna Sagar canal. The dominant castes in the village are the Kammas who are famous for their wealth. Karamchedu is also the native land of some of the well-known film producers and businessmen of the state. Due to this increasing prosperity and expanding business in other sectors like film and urban business centres, the Kammas of Karamchedu, who were basically 'tenant cultivators', gave up tenant cultivation. This allowed the Dalits to have a better bargain within the tenancy cultivation system, thus saving them from bondage labour, though not enough for a comfortable life.

Another aspect which is significant from the point of view of understanding the Dalit situation is that Karamchedu was a active place of communist mobilization. In the 1950s the small peasants belonging to the Kamma castes along with Dalits and agricultural labourers were the strength of the Communist Party. Even now a major Kamma settlement in the village is called 'Moscow' (Reddy, 1985: 1546). With the marginalisation of the left and the rise of TDP as a major alternative to the Congress, the Kammas of Karamchedu shifted their loyalty to the TDP (Srinivasulu, 2004: 38). The Dalits of the Karamchedu have been loyal to the Congress, despite their masters shifting loyalty. The Kammas understood the resistance of the Dalits, especially the Madigas' not supporting the TDP as an act of violation of the relationship of domination and subordination, something unexpected from powerless Dalits.

On July 17 1985, the Kammas planned to teach the Madigas a lesson for their increasing assertive nature. The pretext was a trivial incident which happened the previous day, when a Madiga boy objected to a Kamma person washing his buffalo in the drinking water tank and thus polluting it. The Kammas' beat the Madiga boy mercilessly. The attack was meticulously planned and nothing was left to chance (Srinvasulu, 2004: 38). As Reddy (1985) shows the number of Kammas who were in thousands, attacked the Madiga households armed with sticks, axes and spears. The Madigas panicked and in a state of shock started fleeing. The womenfolk initially thought they would not be beaten, but to their dismay they were not only beaten but raped and killed (Rao, 1999: 223; Reddy, 1985: 1548). On the afternoon of July 17 a mass of shattered humanity arrived at the Church compound at Chirala, some were dead, many were numbed and dazed. Six Dalits were brutally killed in the attack (Ilaiah, 2004: 239).

The police also started beating the Dalits. This is evidenced by the fact that the first person to be locked up after the incident was a Dalit youth. The Dalits of Karamchedu established a camp at Chirala, which popularly came to be known as the Karamchedu camp. Within a few days the camp became a space for Dalit assertion. Many Dalits from different parts of Andhra Pradesh came and joined the affected people. A state wide mobilisation of

Dalits happened and thus began a new period of Dalit movement in Andhra Pradesh (Ilaiah, 2004: 240).

The Chundur Carnage

On 6th August 1991, another exceptional incidence of mass violence took place in Chundur, which again shows the dominant collective conscience that creates a system where the Dalits have to remain subordinate. The Reddys of the Chundur constitute the majority community. The Malas are the majority Dalit community and the second largest caste next to the Reddys. There has been a relatively equitable distribution of land holding in the Chundur village, as the Malas also owned some amount of land, unlike the Madigas of the Karamchedu village. There was also some level of literacy among the Malas, which was even much higher than the Reddys of the village (Srinivasulu, 2004: 40). The railway station of Chunduru, a town 15 kilometres away from the village is the major provider of employment for the Dalits, which resulted in relative autonomy for them from the bondage of agricultural activities and made them conscious of their political and civil rights. Here also Dalit violence happened from a quarrel arising regarding a trivial incident. This happened in a cinema hall, when an educated Dalit youth decided to buy a 'chair class' ticket, knowing the fact that Dalits are not allowed to sit in the chair class and further put his feet on the seat in front of him, occupied by an upper caste person. A quarrel broke out leading to the beating of the youth and his father, who was a school teacher. This led to tension in the village leading to social boycott of the Dalits. A planned attack on Dalits with the active involvement of the police was made, similar to the one at Karamchedu. The only difference being that in Karamchedu the Dalits were chased to death and in Chundur, the police chased the Dalits away from the village and into the death trap. Men well armed killed the Dalits and threw them into the rivers and canals with unparalleled brutality (Sinvasulu, 2004: 42). The report on the Chundur carnage[4], explained in detail the results of social boycott on Dalits. The killing of the Dalits was planned extensively. Around Rs. 40,000 collected for the Dussehra festival and 1.5 lakhs collected for the construction of a temple were used to buy arms. The survivors took shelter in the church.

The Dalits refused to accept the relief measures till such time as the Chundur criminals and their cohorts had been awarded acceptable punishment[5].

From the massacres of the Karamchedu rose a massive mobilisation of Dalits in the coastal Andhra region, represented by the organisation called the 'Dalit Mahasabha'. The DMS organised rallies, meetings and condemned the killings on Dalits. The DMS is believed to have arisen from the Karamchedu camp. Kathi Padma Rao and Bojja Tarakam were the two new leaders who emerged from the Karamchedu camp. Kathi Padma Rao was a youth who taught in a degree college in Guntur district and was a rationalist and good orator. Tarakam was a government pleader in High Court. The famous Marxist poet Gadder from the People's War Group (PWG) also joined the Dalit Mahasabha. The new movement created a rupture in communist discourse and attempted to bring together both Marxism and Ambedkar as their guiding principles (Ilaiah, 2004: 240-42). This new assertion resulted in a valiant attack on the state and the leaders of all political parties. They neither accepted the sympathies of the government nor the opposition parties. They did not even entertain any of the Dalit political leaders and characterised them as '*Dalit Dalaries*' (Dalit Compradors) (Ilaiah, 2004: 242).

One can draw several conclusions from episodes of violence on Dalits. One commonality that stands out is that most of the violence being discussed is unleashed in some village setup. This conclusion has its own dangers, for example, by locating the Dalit violence specific to the village, one may fall into the trap of 'essentialisation'. However, I am not denying the fact that violence on the Dalits is not taking place in urban and semi-urban localities or even the towns. What I am proposing is to historically understand the metaphor of the village and how the metaphor produced certain kinds of subjecthood that re-established notions of caste in the post-colonial Indian society. My proposition is that the metaphor of the village and its social structure plays a pivotal role in the understanding of violence on the Dalits.

The Idyllic Village and Idealisation of Rural Life

Writing in the late 19th century, Sankritist/Orientalist Sir Monier Williams[6] would applaud the timelessness and permanence of village India. "It has existed almost unaltered since the description of its organisation in Manu's code, two or three centuries before the Christian era. It has survived all the religious, political, and physical convulsions from which India has suffered from time immemorial"[7]. The colonial discourse of the Western world depicted the village as the locale where caste, the essential institution of India, appears in the form of a strange community of collective actors and a peculiar political economy of subsistence exchanges, the so-called 'jamani system'. By the late 19th century, an idealised image of the village as a self-contained community had been firmly established in colonial literature (Inden, 2000: 132-33). This fitted in well with the European description of the peasant community based on the family farm. Sir Charles Metcafe described them as self-contained 'little republics'. These projections of village India was guided by 'an essentialist dichotomy drawn between the 'ancient' and the 'modern', one that was primarily concerned with the constitution of economic agents at home and the deconstitution of political agents abroad (Ibid.: 130-32). The Constitution of India as a land of villages was also due to the efforts of the British to deconstitute the Indian state. By the 19th century the Indian villages were described as quintessentially "Asian", and truly rural in nature.

Madan points out that subsequent studies have attempted to debunk this imagery of Indian village society, for example, Milton Singer and Mckim Marriot introduced the idea of 'rural-urban continuum' into the village studies. These studies showed how the ties that relate the village to the outside world also brought wider society to the village. (Madan, 2002: 08) The participant observation method and ethnography provided systematic and in-depth understanding of the village life (Thorner, 1976: 08). While attempting to move away from the essentialist dichotomy, scholarship on village India fell into the trap of anticipating the villagers as rational actors, and denying the traditionality attached to the village. Inden (2000) argued that, fundamental to this essentialism is a persisting 'dichotomy of 'inner' and 'outer', with the insistence that the village was economically self-contained, the view that relations inside it were organic and hierarchic, while those outside it were antagonistic and anarchic. I argue here that this particular essentialism contributed to the colonial forms of knowledge rather than interrogating it. This essentialism also contributed to the understanding that villages are everywhere in India and that structurally and culturally they are all the same. Combined with the assumption of homogeneity, that villages are everywhere in India pretty much the same, we are given our picture of a cellular rural society". This diverse and large landscape of villages in India was camouflaged with the metaphysical homogenising construct unfortunately called the 'Indian village' (Ibid.: 157-58). He argues that this metaphor provided a moralistic exclusivity to the village that needs protection from the modern state—that realm of politics where there is deceit and exploitation. "Because they are so opposed, the one is a realm of aimless, non-developmental flux, while the other is a timeless, self-contained world of solidarities and reciprocities. The former is, so to speak, the level of meaningless change in Indian civilisation. The latter is, on the contrary the level of changeless meaning (Ibid.: 157-59)."

This moralistic metaphor, I argue is not just a political construct, it is the way of being Indian. It has produced a middle class modernist self that loves a village but lives in cities. This self is a split self which is at the same time deeply traditional, yet works in the most advanced economy of the era. After Weber, it would be a fallacy to call it a dichotomy as there can be innumerable causal relationships that a researcher can develop from this contradiction of society. It produces a personality which is oriented towards a legal-rational action in the cities, yet easily inserts itself to the traditions of the village society. This self willingly does not want to change the village because one aspect of its inner self adores and longs for it. It is the longing for that metaphoric construction of a pristine world. This self also carries a portion of rural to the cities, constructing a parasitic middle class that is deeply hierarchical as well as, optimistically rational. Education, particularly science education which has been mandated to achieve a blend of traditional glory with modern practices plays a very important role.

Sociological Construction of a Metaphor

Scientific knowledge being modernist in its inception could only see the diverse village societies and rural ways of life as figments of the bygone era, almost an afterthought. Western Sociology has remained preoccupied with the study of social life in urban and industrial societies (Jodhka, 2004: 367). At best the transition to the urban and industrial fascinated the classical sociological writings. The distinction of rurality has been significantly vested in its oppositional positioning to the urban, where the other-than-urban meets the multifarious conditions of vastly differing scales and lifestyles (Cloke, 2006: 18).

Rural has been frequently regarded as residual and less fashionable to the sociological study. "There has been an ultimately futile search for a sociological definition of 'rural', a reluctance to recognise that the term 'rural' is an empirical category rather than a sociological one, that it is merely a 'geographical expression'. As such it can be used as a convenient short-hand label, but in itself it has no sociological meaning (Newby, 1980: 3, quoted in Hiliyard, 2007: 01)." Ferdinand Tonnies, would almost mourn the rise of urban industrialism as involving a loss of community. Weber would resent the 'disenchantment of the world' and 'iron caging' of human imagination. Inherent in such conceptualisation would be a critique to industrialisation. However, this mourning of the village life formed a basis of sociological theorisations on the village as a geographical and social space which is in the process of decay and evaporation hence does not need much attention.

Sociological writings of the village in India, always considered the village as a simple geographical entity, although an integral part of Indian society but it is rather a civilisational concept about to be drowned in the deep sea of history. It could not deconstruct the homogeneity constructed in a diverse village landscape. It could not make a differentiation between a '*purí*' and a 'para' and the relation of conflict, contraction and of dominance and subordination in these simple differentiations of naming. The location of each landscape in the larger picture of an agrarian landscape did not matter to the sociologists. The adoption of participant observation and ethnographic methods by anthropologists always treated the village as a kind of sociological reality. For Dumont (1957), the village solidarity is nothing but the solidarity of the dominant castes, since he believed that the village is only a dwelling place of various castes. Caste, instead is a social reality (Dumont, 1966: 70-71). While somewhat agreeing to this idea of the village, Srinivas (2009) on the other hand, attempts to infuse existential agency to this imagined geographical location. He argues that the village is a social reality as it has its own productive unit dominated by patron-client relationships. This typical 'bond' between the master and the labourer is not only a product of the caste-based hierarchy, but also an offshoot of the scarcity of labour in the agrarian society of India. Hence, the village was stratified both on the lines of caste and land, but this stratification had an underlying solidarity which accepted the caste hierarchy, yet these caste hierarchies contribute to the notion of interdependence for the sake of survival (Srinivas, 2009: 37-38).

Srinivas believed that the pre-British era of Indian society had a consensus or acceptance to the notion of caste. However, such acceptance was not devoid of conflict and violence. "Violence was an integral element in the tradition of the dominant castes, and political conditions of pre-British India provided ample opportunities for violence. Further successful exercise of violence resulted in a caste, or a section of it, being able to claim Kshatriya status (Srinivas, 2009: 15). Although, Srinivas recognises the crucial role played by violence in the caste hierarchy, he could not integrate it into his framework of understanding caste hierarchy. However, perhaps what he missed out in his analysis is the violence that has been unleashed by the dominant castes of a particular village or locality to establish a hierarchical order of the social system. The collective conscience of the village has been by and large the conscience of the dominant castes.

The Nationalist Construction of the Indian Village

This imagery of the village as an innocent, infant social system, harmoniously arranged little republic played a key role both in the rational claim of the colonisers and the initiation of what we know today as the Indian nationalism. The European past and its metaphor of the village became the present of the colonial and therefore adorned considerable attention and significance. From the Orientalists, through the Sanskritists to the Colonial Census Commissioners and the anthropologists, all of them treated the village as the marker of colonial difference (Srinivas, 2009: 05). Nationalism in India also conveniently accepted this difference and went further to imagine a sovereign domain of the spiritual and cultural that needed to be guarded against the colonial rule (Chatterjee, 1993: 09). However, this domain and the language that constructed it were both products of the colonial imagery. Gandhi, Nehru and Ambedkar, the three most important figures and ideologues of the nationalist movement were city dwellers. Most of their political action was performed in the cities. None of them looked at the village as a concrete reality with regional variations or with historical specificities having internal dynamics of change. All of them understood the village as a civilisational entity and seemed to have assumed some kind of a similarity of it across space and time (Jodhka, 2002: 3345). The village for Gandhi, in particular was not merely a place where people lived, it was the very essence of Indian civilisation and represented a way of life which potentially critiqued the city-based technologically-driven West (Ibid., 3346). The nationalists were nostalgic about village India, this nostalgia was echoed by Gandhi who famously declared that the real India lives in villages. This metaphor of the village as opposed to its reality gradually became a commonsense discourse in Indian society. The village became a metaphor which constituted the sacred, untamed Indian self (Nandy, 2001: 28).

Almost a century later, a famous intellectual and activist would interrogate the statement made by Gandhi. She would retort that India dies in villages, India gets kicked around in villages, India lives in cities (Roy, 2004). For the Dalits it has been a kind of 'total institution' where violence and killing has been the order of the day. This metaphor of the village was woven into the nationalist imagining to the extent that the self-sufficiency and autonomy of the village became one of the important aspects of the policy making process. Panchayati Raj, became the instrument through which this autonomy could be preserved, thus preserving one of the essential elements of the village India constructed by the colonial discourse with the willing active participation of the nationalists (Thakur, 2005: 28).

The Metaphor of the Village and the Dalit Discourse

"Without knowledge, intelligence was lost, without intelligence morality was lost and without morality was lost all dynamism. Without dynamism money was lost and without money the Shudras sank. All this misery was caused by the lack of knowledge.[8]"

Mahatma Jyotirao Phule located the misery of the lower castes and peasants to their lack of access to education. Like many social reformers, he also thought that education is the most effective weapon to fight caste exploitation.

In the book titled as *Cultivators Whipcord*, Phule describes multiple layers of exploitation and oppression structurally unleashed on the peasants. In his writings he always treated the Dalits as peasants. In this particular book, he explains at least three layers of oppression. First is the oppression emerging out of Brahminic religious dogmatism which is unquestioningly accepted by the lower castes as they are 'letter-less', they are exploited by the 'Brahmins under the pretext of religion that it would be hard to find a parallel example anywhere in the world (Deshpande, 2002: 121)'. Phule also observed the modernisation of Brahminism, He indicated how Brahmins have appropriated and populated themselves in the British administration, thus deliberately keeping opportunities closed for the lower castes and peasant. The British government has also devised new forms of administrative reform that crippled the lower castes to improve their lot. Phule cites the policies initiated by the newly established forest department, ceasing access of the poor peasants and lower caste to natural products and grazing lands for their sheep and goats, as well as, unused land on which many of the lower castes depended for their livelihood. "Thus the Brahmans employed in government jobs, and the mythologists, storytellers, teachers in schools strive day and night, using all their cunning, to prevent the breakdown of these distinctions and hierarchies (Despande, 2002: 179)".

Ambedkar in many of his interventions would disagree with the nationalist conception of the village as a self-sufficient independent unit. He would argue against the Panchayati Raj as an institution and doubt over the "five good men" administering and delivering justice to the depressed classes. He would shun the village society and mock the intellectuals of India for the nostalgia for village society.

'The love of the intellectual Indians for the village community is of course infinite if not pathetic. It is largely due to the fulsome praise bestowed upon it by Metcalfe who described them as little republics having nearly everything that they want within themselves, and almost independent of any foreign relations. The existence of these village communities each one forming a separate little State in itself has according to Metcalfe contributed more than any other cause to the preservation of the people of India ... I hold that these village republics have been the ruination of India. I am therefore surprised that those who condemn provincialism and communalism should come forward as champions of the village. What is the village but a sink of localism, a den of ignorance, narrow-mindedness and communalism? (Ambedkar, 2014: 61-62)".

In many of his speeches and interventions, Ambedkar emphasised the extreme form of atrocities and oppressions carried out against the Dalits in the villages of India. Issues such as bonded labour, landlessness, ineffectiveness of the governance structure in providing opportunities and justice to the Dalits as labourers was a constant theme of his interventions. He understood this as the tyranny of the majority.

"In the villages they were without land and were virtually the slaves of the caste Hindus. ... when some untouchables had escaped from their villages to take up well-paid work under the military authorities, the caste Hindus had managed to force them back to work for them. Owing to the preponderance of caste Hindus in the Subordinate Police and Revenue Services the government was already, from the point of view of the untouchables, not a British but a Hindu one (Ambedkar, 2014: 484)."

Although Ambedkar was concerned about the Dalits in rural India, particularly the Dalits who are agricultural labourers, he considered the problem of the Dalit agricultural labourer as the 'problem of exit'. "Throughout his political career, Ambedkar adopted almost no programme or campaign for the agricultural labourers as such. His main concern was that Dalits should cease being agricultural labourers, that they should escape from their landlessness either by securing industrial or white colar employment or by obtaining land for cultivation (Omvedt, 1994: 157). Although, Ambedkar supported various movements against landlordism and land ceiling, further he also fought against bonded labour. But the thrust of his concern was the 'problem of entry of rural Dalits to the industrial workforce. Ambedkar saw no possibility of emancipation for Dalits in the social structure of village India. The 'problem of exit', empathetically denies any possibility of existence, let alone, the initiation of any project for emancipation for Dalits in rural India. At a time when the nationalists and rights alike were celebrating a village society and rural ways of living, consciously and metaphysically constructed by them to represent the cardinal values of Indian society, and thus the fundamental metaframe on the basis of which modern/future India can be imagined, Ambedkar, in his retaliatory temper, would deny everything that is attached to the 'metaphor' of the village and rural life in general.

Unlike Ambedkar, Phule would locate his politics of emancipation in the village itself. He would attempt to forge a movement of all the lower castes at both the cultural and material level that could help the Shudratishudras a dignified life in the village society. His writings and its forms, his conception of the peasant, farmer and appeal for education for them makes him a scholar who looked at a complete cultural and material transformation of village society. One can find a significant difference in the politics of Phule and Ambedkar. While Phule strove for a politics of majoritarianism, devising a politics that attempts to build solidarity among the lower castes and Dalits, Ambedkar's major concern was the Dalits as minorities in the geopolitical entity, as he could see the tyrannies unleashed by the landholding Shudra caste groups on the Dalits.

The Village and the Narratives of Violence on Dalits

There are deep-rooted relationships between violence and the making of Dalit subjecthood in the post-independent and postcolonial conditions in Indian society. According to Nagraj (2010), the Gandhian notion of the village had important implications for the predicament of Dalits in village India. Gandhi found in the narrative of the village, either utopian or realistic there can be a lot of positivity to offer for the future of India. Ambedkar, on the other hand, did not believe in such an idealistic existence of the village. I argue that despite all the efforts of Ambedkar, the Dalits remain in the village society and despite increasing assertive politics, they are brutally killed in village India. The question is what is the way out? How can one conceive of an emancipatory politics in this context? One significant attempt can be to change the collective consciousness, the identity demands a deep-rooted investment in social construction of village India. This requires a collective mobilisation and formation of solidarity. However, looking at the genealogy of the Dalit movement in India, one finds no project for the village. No plan of action to intervene in the power dynamics of the village as a social landscape. There is no emancipatory construction of the Dalits in village India and no attempt to overhaul the social structure in village society in India. Therefore, the Dalit movement needs to re-imagine the village as a space for a potential counter-hegemonic politics, which requires a discourse that rejects the homogenization of village as an innocent geographical landscape. Similarly, any sociological studies on 'village India' needs to address the complexities of hierarchies and geopolitical processes of exclusion and inclusion, in order to provide meaningful answers to the emerging questions of rural life in India.

NOTES

1. Biranarasinghapur, is one among the three villages set up by the King of Puri by bringing Brahmins from Kanauj, Uttar Pradesh. The Brahmins of these villages were involved in the regular affairs of the king and his court. There were about ten Doma families along with a few barber families in the village.
2. Biripara is a wetland declared by the Government of Odisha, which would become the settlement of the Dalits of Biranarasinghapur, after they abandoned their original village because of constant caste atrocities.
3. Data mentioned above are collective from the Annual Reports of the National Crime Report Bureau, published by NCRB.
4. A fact finding report was prepared by the Samata Sanghatana, an organisation of academics, activists, feminists and other professionals. The report was based on information gathered by a

team consisting of K. Ilaiah, John Wesley, K. Sajaya, K. Uma, R. Srivatsan and M. Shatrugna, which visited the site on August 10, 4 days after the incident.

5. *Economic and Political Weekly*, special correspondence (1991), 'Upper Caste Violence: Study of Chundur Carnage', September 7, 1991.
6. Williams, M. 1891. *Brahminism and Hinduism*, London: John Murray.
7. Ibid., 455.
8. Jyotirao Phule writing the Prologue of his treatise on farmers called it "Cultivators Whipcord" in 1883, Despande, 2002, *Selected Writings of Jyotirao Phule*, New Delhi: Leftword Books, p. 117.

REFERENCES

Ambedkar, B.R. 2014. *Ambedkar: Writings and Speeches*, Vol. 13, Bombay.

____ . 2014. *Ambedkar: Writing and Speeches*, Vol. 10, Bombay.

Borroah, V.K. et al. 2015. *Caste, Discrimination and Exclusion in Modern India*, New Delhi: Sage.

Chatterjee, P. *Nation and its Fragments*, New Delhi: Oxford University Press.

Cloke, P., Marsden, T. and Mooney P. 2006. *The Handbook of Rural Studies*, London: Sage Publications.

Deshpande, G.P. 2002. *Selected Writings of Jyotirao Phule*, New Delhi: Leftword Publications.

Dumont, L. 1966, 'The Village Community from Munro to Maine', *Contribution to Indian Sociology*, No. 09, December, pp. 67-89.

Hillyard, S, 2007. *Sociology of Rural Life*, New York: Berg Publication.

Inden, R. 2000. *Imagining India*, Bloomington: Indiana University Press.

Jodhka, S.S. 2002. The Nation and the Village: Images of Rural India in Gandhi, Nehru and Ambedkar, *Economic and Political Weekly*, Vol. 37, No. 32, August 10.

Kannabiran, K. (ed.) 2016. *Violence Studies*, New Delhi: Oxford University Press.

Madan, V. 2002. *The Village in India*, New Delhi: Oxford University Press.

Monier-Williams, M. 1891. *Brahminism and Hinduism or Religious Thoughts and Life in India*, London: John Murray.

Nagraj, D.R. 2010. *Flaming the Feet and Other Essays: The Dalit Movement in India*, New Delhi: Permanent Black.

Nandy, A. 2001. *An Ambiguous Journey to the City*, New Delhi: Oxford University Press.

Nerula, S. 1999. *Broken People: Caste Violence Against India's "Untouchables"*, Bangalore: Books for Change.

Omvedt, Gail. 1998. *Dalit Movement and Democratic Revolution in India*, New Delhi, Oxford University Press.

Rao, A. 2010. *The Caste Question: Dalits and the Politics of Modern India*, Ranikhet: Permanent Black.

Reddy, D. Narasimha. 1985. Karamchedu: Dialectic without Development, *Economic and Political Weekly*, 20(37): 1546-1549.

Roy, A, 2004, *The Greater Common Good*, Bombay: India Book Distributor.

Srinivas, M.N. 2009. The Indian Village: Myth and Reality, in *Oxford India Srinivas*, New Delhi: Oxford University Press.

Srinivasulu, K. and P. Sarangi. 1999. Political Realignments in Post-NTR Andhra Pradesh, *Economic and Political Weekly*, 34 (34 and 35): 21-28.

Thakur, M. 2005. Vision in Conflict: The Village in the Nationalist Discourse, *Social Change*, Vol. 35, No. 3.

Thorner, D., 1976. *The Agrarian Prospects in India: Five Lectures on Land Reform*, New Delhi: Allied Publishers.

6

Traditional Modernity: Class, Caste and Gender in Occupational Patterns in Rural Uttar Pradesh

Ishita Mehrotra

This chapter is primarily an exercise in mapping the occupational profiles of select caste groups from three villages in eastern Uttar Pradesh. In so doing, emphasis is on how caste, class and gender underscore these profiles. In other words, the traditional and the modern are not dichotomous. Traditional structures and norms are deliberately deployed and exploited to ensure modern capitalist accumulation. This discussion also serves to bring out the continued relevance of village studies. The chapter is organised in the following manner. Section 1 emphasises the importance and utility of village studies. Section 2 details the occupation mapping and weaves this description with emerging analytical contentions. Section 3 concludes this chapter by positing the argument that the village is definitely changing. But, it is more the case regarding men as they pursue capital aggrandisement or seek to secure livelihoods in the larger context of neoliberal modernity. Where women are concerned, this has meant a reinforcement of traditional structures, relations and processes. In fact, men are able to do so precisely because of women's unfreedom. I propose that India's pursuit of capitalist modernity is based on the exploitation of traditional hierarchies, where women and especially Dalit women from labouring households fare the worst.

Section 1: Continued Relevance of Village Studies

The very idea of 'village'—as a spatial, socio-cultural, economic and a political unit—has undergone tremendous change. Initially, the village was seen as a microcosm of India. India lived in the village and to modernise, the village had to be studied and decoded for only then could appropriate development planning be initiated to put India on the path to prosperity and modernity. The village was seen as a counterpoint to the city, to urbanisation, to industrialisation, to western education, to equality—in a nutshell, modernity. Today, the village does not feature in the national imagination, not in any substantive political, social or economic sense. It is invoked only in times of crises—abject poverty, starvation deaths, communal violence, droughts and farmer suicides. Methodologically also, village studies have lost their charm and utility—apparently so. It would be worthwhile to explore how much of this has to do with the changing discourse of development theory and therefore a reordering of priorities of donor governments and their development agencies. I will nonetheless argue that the tradition of village studies continues to be as relevant as ever—a fact, borne by some seminal village studies in the Indian context (M.N. Srinivas' monographs on a Mysore village from the late 1940s to the mid-1960s, Andre Beteille's works on a Thanjavur village from the 1960s through the 1980s, various works of Jan Breman from the 1950s till now and of course, the Palanpur Studies between 1957 and 2010, and most recently, the Project on Agrarian Relations in India since 2006).

It is true that rural India occupies political centre-stage only in times of elections. In the economic domain it is seen as a 'waiting room' to be escaped. In the social domain, it is the den of caste and religious discrimination (as are the cities). It is also true that issues of poverty, employment and discrimination need to be studied in the urban milieu as well given the scale and nature of migration (amongst other things) which has made the rural-urban dichotomy fallacious. However, the village and the tradition of village studies continue to be very relevant. Village studies, longitudinal and otherwise, facilitate close and continuous observations and participation. They are particularly useful when working with the marginalised and vulnerable who might be intimidated by formal, structured large-scale surveys with minimal scope for first building relationships of trust, recognition and friendship. This is especially true for those 'stuck' in the village for reasons of caste, gender, age, disability, lack of social capital, etc. Longitudinal village studies serve as a yardstick against which to map socio-cultural, political and economic changes not just in the villages, but also with respect to how the increasingly mobile villagers identify themselves and relate to these in rural and urban settings.[1] Village studies enable in-depth descriptive mapping exercises which can then become the basis for a critical analysis of changes and continuities—in areas of occupational profile, power dynamics, social mobility, politics, cultural and religious practices, etc. Since village level research maximises opportunities to capture these dimensions comprehensively, relationally and to extend a comparative picture across villages (and hamlets even), the same reasons also make village level research conducive to unearthing 'new knowledge' which make for an interesting picture when juxtaposed with 'received wisdom'. The advantages of village studies have been documented by several scholars including Janakarajan (1997), Breman (1985), Harriss-White and Harriss (2007).

Section 2: Intersecting Class and Gender

In this section, I will describe the occupational patterns of various caste groups. As far as possible, class and gender aspects will be nuanced. But first, some limitations of this study. The material discussed here was collected as a part of my doctoral research on rural labour relations of Dalit women belonging to classes of labour households. Occupational profiling was not the focus of study but this information was necessary to gain an understanding of the local labour market. As such, there might be instances where the discussion comes as sketchy, as reading too much into one example or as lacking in adequate explanation. Nonetheless, I believe that this is an important discussion for it provides a grounded understanding of how class, caste and gender intersect in labour markets. This is a particularly under researched area in the context of eastern UP. There are examples which make for interesting stories but since these are isolated examples, they cannot be understood as general trends. But still they need to be told because figuring out the why behind them adds to our substantive knowledge. I have deliberately stayed away from using theoretical conceptualisations in discussing various classes simply to keep this study accessible for all. The purpose is to just lay out how class, caste and gender are lived and experienced in everyday working lives.

2.1 Upper Castes: Continued Accumulation and Dominance at the Top; Increasing Penury at the Bottom

While caste and class overlap to a great extent, there is some internal differentiation. While most of the Brahmins are an accumulating class, there are also some households which are able to reproduce themselves only on a simple basis. There are an even smaller number of Brahmin households struggling to ensure their sustenance on an everyday basis.

The rich or accumulating Brahmin households are mostly semi-medium, medium and large landowners engaged in mechanised commercial farming organised on hired labour. It is notable that land is no longer the only or even the main source of accumulation and power. To the extent that family labour is engaged in agriculture, the men supervise work on their farms and in the absence of male relatives, either the elderly women of the household or daughters (note not daughters-in-law) organise work through a lead labourer and distribute wages on the completion of work. These Brahmin households are asset rich—they own tractors, trucks, diesel pump-sets, tube-wells and other agricultural machinery such as trolleys, tillers, cultivators, chaff cutters etc. These assets are a source of income when rented out and a means of sustaining dominance when the poorer villagers are 'allowed' to use these 'free' or at 'concessional' rates under the garb of patronage. But obviously, the poorer are also more often than not the labouring Dalits and the underlying political-economy of 'discounted' rates is that the men and women of these indebted households work for these upper caste-class employers on a priority basis on wages below the prevailing market rates or for no remuneration at all (for details see Mehrotra, 2013). Brahmin households are also into livestock rearing (cows and buffaloes mainly) but less so for commercial purposes and more for religious reasons.

Non-agricultural self-employment is very limited but where it exists, it is indicative of a substantive asset base and income generation, employment creation and connections to local bureaucracy and public resources. Examples of some self-employed Brahmins include the owner of a medical store, a taxi service owner, owner-operator of a JCB (earth moving heavy machinery), owner cum principal of a school, flour mill owners, contractors dealing in wood, contract work with the PWD (Public Works Department), etc.

Outside self-employment, whether agricultural or non-agricultural, there are isolated cases of Brahmin men working as teachers and one was a journalist. Regarding women, there was a sole example of a nursery teacher.

To the extent that migration was seen amongst this caste group in the wealthy Brahmin households, it was either tied with public employment or lucrative private employment opportunities. For example, one worked as a reader and his family was based with him. One owned a medical store in the state capital. Another was engaged in steel business, two others worked for a private security company and one was employed in a medicine shop—odd jobs in the urban informal economy. It should be noted here that these indicate a basic level of education, social capital, some level of experience and are 'clean' and not onerous jobs. These jobs are relatively secure and better paid and as such can be taken as indicative of economic progress. Such casual work is not the same as those at the bottom of the urban informal economy—unskilled construction work, peddlers, etc.

Public employment is one source of respectable, regular and comparatively well paid work. There were isolated cases of some such Brahmin men employed in police, army, paramilitary, for instance. The only example of regular female employment with comparatively better pay was that of an *anganwadi* worker. Technically, *anganwadi* workers are not regular formal employees of the state, but locally they are perceived as such compared to the vulnerability, exploitation and humiliation experienced in other local jobs.

A small section of the Brahmin households is not so affluent. That these are semi-medium and medium landowners, reiterates the point made earlier that the link between land and poverty or prosperity is not absolute any longer. These households are neither into extensive cash cropping nor do they have any other regular income source. In fact, most of these households have mortgaged substantial land areas to meet household, health, wedding, etc. expenditures. They see farming has becoming too expensive while returns continue to be low—they give high labour costs, low yields and crop diseases as examples. On part of the remaining land that they still cultivate, sugarcane is grown as a cash crop. Compared to the rich Brahmin households, farming here is labour and not capital intensive. Tractors are used, production is organised on the basis of family labour and a few labourers may be hired for paddy transplantation or weeding. In addition to supervising labourers, men of these households may themselves undertake farming and even the elderly or middle-aged women contribute manual labour. Livestock rearing is undertaken as a commercial activity.

It would be fair to say that these households are not into local agricultural or non-agricultural wage labour or even self-employment. A tractor mechanic who worked out of his home was the sole example of non-agricultural self-employment. A petrol pump attendant and a teacher were examples of non-agricultural employment.

There were only two instances of formal public employment. The male member of one household was employed in the army and another man worked in the district development office.

One would assume migrant work to feature significantly amongst these households who are not rich but not so poor either, so as to be able to make ends meet. But this is not the case. Men from only some households do migrant work, for example, as welders, shop assistants, casual workers in factories, as a dye master, etc. Barring one case, migration is not family based. The question that comes to mind here is that why don't these households resort to migration?

Amongst the Brahmins, there were a few households that could best be understood as labouring households in the sense that ensuring daily survival was a struggle. These households either did not own any land to begin with or their entire landholding had been mortgaged over the years and so were in effect landless—

again, one might own land on paper, but might actually be living an impoverished life. Just to flag off here, there is clearly a mismatch between official definitions of poverty derived on the basis of income, assets or calorie intake and the complex picture that these households present. Who is poor, as per the state definitions? Who is poorer? A Brahmin family living in a concrete though crumbling two-room house, owning land but which has partly or entirely been mortgaged, a family with no running source of income? Or a Chamar or Mosahar family living in part concrete and part mud one room structure—where human beings and animals jostle for space and where people can barely stand to their full height? Households with some land were into own cultivation, drawing on family labour of men and women. If at all, one or two labourers might be hired during the peak agricultural season. Livestock rearing was another income source.

These labouring Brahmin households, dependent as they are on the sale of their labour power to survive, are not to be seen in the local labour market. There was only one contrary example, that of a woman who did agricultural wage labour. And her participation was 'justified' on the ground that she had no other option to support her mentally unstable husband and their six children. It is not surprising that upper castes, irrespective of their class position, do not engage in local wage labour. Locally, there is only agriculture and related wage labour available or lowly odd seasonal jobs such as that of construction work—where one usually sees middle and lower caste labourers. Construction work, manual labour jobs such as loading trucks, assisting in shops—labour opportunities that are seen in villages, are also dominated by men. In other words, these are the preserve of lower caste men from labouring households.

What is surprising though is that these labouring Brahmin households do not turn to self-employment as income opportunities. There could be possible reasons for this—lack of education and skills, no asset base, unwillingness to come into contact with other middle and lower castes who would constitute the bulk of the customer base, or because this is not their caste's traditional occupation? The only example of self-employment was a home-based general store run by a widow.

Migrant work is an important source of income in most of these households. Again, it is temporary, undertaken by young men. They work as skilled construction labourers, as security guards, brick kiln workers and as casual labourers. What sets these migrant workers apart is that whenever they are back in the village they do casual labour. This is unlike migrant workers from even slightly better off households who would not undertake local wage labour while they were in the village.

These labouring Brahmin households also rely on *'Brahmin ka dhanda'*, i.e. their caste occupations for their survival—in this sense there is a continuing link between castes and their traditional occupations in the village system. They conduct marriage ceremonies and other religious functions. They also go from village to village, asking for *'bhiksha'* (grains, food, clothes, etc.). These Brahmins, materially as deprived as Dalits from labouring households, are nonetheless not subjected to the contempt, humiliation and exploitation that Dalits are. Caste, of course is one factor. But, the absence of Brahmins in the local labour markets also means that their labour cannot be exploited. Amongst the poor, there appears a clear difference between attitudes and self-perception along the lines of caste. Poor Brahmins project an air of helplessness and pity. Poor Dalits do not bear any grudges, they are aware of their oppression, they are critical of their exploiters, they do not seek handouts but rely on their power to labour.

Overall, Brahmins as a caste group provide interesting insights on how caste, class and gender intersect in economy, society and in the political domain.

Where Brahmins are an accumulating class, they are definitely a dominant caste (Srinivas, 1987). But in this dominant caste-class category, who is actually accumulating, who is dominating who? It is Brahmin men who are accumulating, who are controlling their women, who own and/or effectively control the productive resources; it is Brahmin men who oppress the labourers. This is evident in the above description. Brahmin men have successfully managed to diversify out of agriculture into more prestigious and lucrative businesses. The asset base or capital—land, agricultural equipment or property in a more general sense—is either directly in the name of men or is effectively controlled by them. In terms of educational or professional skills too, men are more qualified than women. As was traditionally the case, the political domain continues to be the bastion of men. It is men who are either directly in positions of power or control access to corridors of power. If not themselves serving in the panchayat, they seek to nevertheless control its functioning by putting up proxy figures. To cite an example, in one village where the pradhan's seat was reserved for Scheduled Castes, the most prominent Brahmin family of the village had successfully propped their Chamar servant as the pradhan. The head of this household had previously served as a pradhan. It was common for serving panchayat members or block level administrative officials to 'consult' the most prominent households of the villages on important matters such as elections, construction of roads or schools, allotment of development funds, access to various loan schemes, etc. Not only do Brahmin men have direct or indirect access to private and public resources, but they are also very well networked with the local administration. It is precisely this access to resources and powers which allows these Brahmin men to, in turn, control labourers by way of prudently 'distributing patronage' amongst their 'loyalists'. Caste, class, education, political power—these are the markers of social status. So, in a manner of speaking, the notion of social status too is attached to the man. Social standing is ascribed to men and it is men who enjoy this position. This is also the case because it is men who are visible in the public sphere, who are perceived as and actually are the breadwinners (this in contrast to the Dalit labouring households where we will see that while it is women who ensure daily household survival, their migrant husbands are seen as the breadwinners) and it is men who are into esteemed (regular, more remunerative and clean) jobs.

The caste-class relationship is more complex in the case of Brahmin households dependent on wage labour, migrant work, etc. for their survival. They are able to ensure their daily survival but without accumulating. They also lack assets and political connections. Unlike the rich Brahmin households, members of these households are directly engaged in their own cultivation—class differentiation within the same caste group. For these households, migration is as much a social as an economic phenomenon. Migrant work is an important source of income; migration is a way out of exploitative socio-economic relations typical of the village economy; and it saves them the humiliation of doing wage labour for middle castes or Dalits. Humiliation works both ways. Capitalist Brahmins mentioned that they would not hire poor Brahmins as wage labourers, that it would be embarrassing to do so. What lies behind this embarrassment? Possibly, capitalist and labouring Brahmin households might be related leading to awkwardness or jealousy. Delayed and/or wage payments, partial wage payments, serving tea and food in plastic ware to Dalit labourers, hollering at labourers—such means of labour control vis-a-via *apni biradri* would be difficult to impose. To a limited extent, migration also reflects a failure to turn education into productive employment and this is true of the richer Brahmins as well. I was told by a Brahmin man that his son had an MA degree but could not find any respectable and productive employment and consequently took to migration. Migrant work appears as an alternative to degrading local wage labour.

Caste consciousness strongly influences economic behaviour of these households. So much so, that they would rather mortgage their land and live on it. A woman from a labouring Brahmin household in fact told me that being a Brahmin she cannot do wage labour and the only reason why she worked in her field was that they could not afford to hire labourers. She felt ashamed to be labouring, even in her own field.

Breman (1985), in his fieldwork on rural labour relations in Gujarat, had observed that though upper caste-class members engage in political and economic rivalry with each other, they closed ranks when it came to labourers. This is true even in my field villages. Brahmins and Rajputs close ranks in matters of elections or in setting wage rates—but this solidarity of course comes across most clearly, where class position is also shared. This solidarity is not witnessed between rich and poor Brahmins, this is especially so in the case of economics where the capital-labour antagonism is the predominant narrative. In the political and social sphere, one can see the rich and poor Brahmins or Rajputs intermingling in celebration of festivals, or the poor Brahmins expressing political support for candidates from their *biradri* in the hope that once they win, these Brahmins would help them access public schemes and resources, would help them with credit, etc. So, in a manner of speaking, the caste blurs the capital-labour contradiction in the social and political domains. Caste is also an important basis of labour solidarity. Labourers' work groups and in fact even labour struggles are shaped by ties of caste, village, hamlet and street. Amongst the capitalists, a shared caste and class position becomes the basis for further consolidating accumulation strategies. Amongst the labourers, their economic precariousness is manipulated by these very upper caste-class capitalists to keep them divided and subjugated.

A Brahmin woman lamented that she was given such a caste by God that she cannot do *banihari* (wage labour) for others. She was embarrassed doing her own agriculture but it had to be done and there was no other option. If a needy person comes to her for old clothes, she gives her own clothes so that the *'izzat'* (honour and respect) of a Brahmin is not violated. When another woman was asked about wage labour, she felt insulted and asserted that a Tewari (Brahmin) will ask for *'bhiksha'* (food, grain, etc. obtained by asking for alms, charity) but not do *banihari.* Such statements are clearly emblematic of the many complex ways in which caste and class interact—coming from an upper caste does not automatically translate into dominant class position. Likewise, the labouring poor comprise disproportionately the Dalits but also certain upper castes like the above households. Among the class of labourers, Brahmins will always be perceived as being better off than Dalits. A labouring Brahmin household would make economic and social choices in keeping with their caste—giving away clothes and food when the household itself is in such a precarious position, not doing agricultural wage labour in the village, etc.

In the case of other upper castes as well—notably the Rajputs and the Baniyas, similar caste, class and gender linkages are seen in their employment relations. Most of the Rajput households are accumulating households owning large plots of land, are into commercial agriculture organised on the basis of hired labour. Men of these households are into highly skilled employment as an engineer, doctor, lawyer, into public employment (police, CPWD, electricity department, *Krishi Adhikari,* etc.). Whether these households migrate or still have some family members residing in the village, they enjoy the benefits of salaried public employment and all the non-monetary benefits as well, these households are accorded a high social status by virtue of their socio-economic position and they are politically influential as well. Women from these households, however, continue to be excluded from the productive domain and restricted to leading their lives behind *purdah*—to be mostly seen only inside the walls of their house and not be heard at all. Of course, there is also economic differentiation between these castes as well, but this does not mean that women from poorer Rajput and Baniya households do wage labour or not observe other socio-cultural restrictions—just like among the Brahmins.

While the Baniyas are not as rich (as the Rajput households), they are nevertheless able to sustain themselves. As a caste group, Baniyas show a very strong linkage with their traditional occupation of business. In addition to agriculture, male members of most of these households are into petty business owning general stores, cycle repair shops, and omelette stalls or operating as peddlers. The products they sell include vegetables and fruits, snacks and sweets, utensils, tobacco products, stationery, clothes, cosmetics, medicines, etc. Income from business might not be much and it fluctuates, depending on where shops are located, what is stocked, or what kind of customer base they attract. Nevertheless, these households manage to sustain themselves on a daily basis, own assets (cycles on which they peddle their wares, stores, stoves, etc.) and this is not dirty and menial work like agricultural labour. This work is also considered respectable because it is their caste occupation. To some extent their women are visible in the productive domain—middle-aged and elderly women help men in home-based shops, a few women who owned sewing machines worked as tailors from their homes. Is this a progressive phenomenon, empowerment? On the one hand, visibility in the public domain, access to productive resources, being an earning member of the family—these are of course good but not necessarily posing a challenge to established structures of patriarchal authority and power. This does not translate into effective control over assets and resources or control over even one's income. Women are not included in decision-making matters, especially those concerning property. Moreover, home-based work tends to be very exploitative, in the case of both men and women, but more so for women. Operating from home, the customer base for these women tailors primarily comprised families from the nearby hamlets. The close socio-cultural ties between these families means that payments are below the market rates and are often delayed. And whoever, can afford the tailor (who will be male) in the main village market, will go to these to avail of better quality service and more design choices. While self-employment was the mainstay of most Baniya households, very few also engaged in local agricultural wage labour. Men did agricultural wage labour, moulded bricks in brick kilns, etc. Where women did agricultural wage labour, they undertook work only within their hamlet or in nearby areas. This is so because for a Baniya and more so for a woman Baniya, to go out in search for work is shameful. Only in situations where a woman is the sole earner or if the household is in a very precarious economic position, will these women do agricultural wage labour. While socio-cultural restrictions continue to operate here too to control women's agency and their mobility, to the extent that these women participate in wage labour and even inside the households, they do not practise seclusion like the Brahmin and Rajput women. Young men migrated to work as casual labourers in the urban informal economy.

2.2 OBCs: The Late Joiners

Ahirs, Koeiris and Ansaris are numerically the most significant other backward classes. Broadly, these castes are able to provide for themselves and ensure their daily survival. There is little economic differentiation. There are a few surplus generating and accumulating households, which have a good asset, education and skill base. Similarly, there are some households which struggle to even secure their daily livelihood. These 'outlier' households are not typical of other backward classes as a whole. All households are engaged in agriculture which is mechanised, a mix of commercial and subsistence farming depending on landholding size, organised largely on the basis of family labour (including younger married women, especially in the poorer and nuclear households) but also drawing on hired and exchange labour, especially during peak season time (harvesting, transplantation), especially where land has been leased in. Pursuit of traditional caste-based occupation (*gvalas*) comes across very strongly in the case of Ahirs. Sale of milk and curd is one source of income for these households. It is the women of the household who take care of the livestock, sell milk and curd to other households of the village or to shops in the vicinity (in the latter case, male members of the households deliver milk to the shops or the shopkeepers collect milk from the house). Agricultural wage labour is done by both men and women. Women's participation in the local economy, however, is circumscribed by considerations of caste, class and gender. Several Ahir women, for instance, mentioned that they did wage labour only in their own hamlet because of *sharm* and *laaj*, because agricultural wage labour is not their caste occupation but that of *majoora jaat,* i.e. labouring castes. Women's engagement in local wage labour is also influenced by the wider socio-political and economic relations. For instance, a few Ansari households located adjacent to the *pradhan*'s house earlier did wage labour primarily for him. This because these households were dependent on him for accessing public schemes, for credit and for access to his fields to graze their cattle or even to access their own fields and in general, they did not want to anger or upset the pradhan who is a power figure in that position and as one of the main employers in the village. Now, with upward mobility resulting from migration, these women have stopped doing wage labour but even then they sometimes do wage labour or provide unpaid or tied labour services for the pradhan if called upon. An interesting point made by one of these Ansari women was that their 'untouchable' status meant that they could not be hired to do domestic work inside the houses of upper caste-class people. Here, untouchability is expressed in terms of religion. Not only this example, but I also noticed that even Dalits avoid drinking water from hand-pipes located outside Muslim households. Villages are characterised not only by caste and religion-based spatial segregation, but village-based socio-cultural and economic relations are also built on caste and religion.

With the exception of a few *anganwadi* workers, occupational diversification outside agriculture, whether in the village or as migrant workers, is seen in the case of men only. Unlike the upper caste-class, migrant work here appears as a coping and risk spreading mechanism. Where more than one young man from the same household has migrated, it is common to find them in the same place and work-site. The kind of odd jobs that village-based men or these migrants do in cities and when in the village (returning migrants seldom do local wage labour for the duration of their stay in the village)—as brick kiln workers, in construction—as skilled workers and unskilled labourers, as drivers, scrap dealers, factory workers, welders, weavers, teachers, as carpenters, insurance agents, operating the village PDS store, etc.—is indicative of minimal or no education (with the exception of teachers) or employment and income security. Those working in brick kilns around the village are more likely than not indebted to their kiln owner or manager since they live on money borrowed from them in the off-season. In isolated cases, where men worked at kilns, their wives too worked as unpaid attached family labour. Migration has a long history among the Ansaris particularly. In one village, the Ansaris had started migrating as far back as the 1970s. If caste and religion-based segregation are a reality even today, one can well imagine what it would have been like four dacades ago. It will not be wrong to say that, faced with socio-cultural exclusion and a precarious economic situation, Ansaris started migrating out much earlier in search of productive employment. Today, Ansari migrants reflect stable migration patterns—in terms of destination, type of work and in the case of a few households remittances are significant and regular.

In the case of OBCs as well, where migration is linked to public employment, it is family-based. But this migration is different from the type of public employment linked migration seen in the case of upper class-castes. Here, public employment refers to manual labour such as in government coal mines or in agriculture where the job description given was that of spraying pesticide. Here, the work is harsh and dangerous, not considered a prestigious job and not indicative of a strong education, asset base. A few men worked in the police, but more than this there is no information. But what is greatly valued is employment security and a decent and regular income. Being in 'service' (formal, regular employment) is considered very prestigious.

Non-agricultural self-employment is a male domain—for instance, owning and operating grocery stores, a dancer cum singer who performed at weddings, working as taxi drivers, running a tobacco shop, a mobile repairing shop, motorcycle or cycle repair shop, shops selling electronic goods, clothing, footwear, medicines, etc. In two instances, start-up money was taken from a SHG. Where business if located in the main market, shop-owners benefit from a broader clientele and timely payments at market rates. Where business is home-based or located inside the village (usually the case with poorer households), as in the case of a flour mill and some general stores (*kirane ki dukaan*), senior women of the household may help out. Very few women (all Ansari) worked as tailors—in a few cases, they only occasionally took on work and mostly used their sewing machines for personal use and in other cases, women spoke of a small customer base, of social relations determining economic relations. Overall, the self-employment activities show that these castes have to some extent managed to diversify away from agriculture, are able to access credit through sources like SHG and own productive assets (shops, sewing machines, etc.).

Unlike the upper class-castes, women belonging to the other backward classes, irrespective of their caste, do not observe socio-cultural restrictions like purdah—newly married women being an exception. This is true of Ansari women as well. They do not veil and move freely within their hamlet. With respect to women, upward economic mobility is usually associated with withdrawal from the public sphere and practice of seclusion. But not so among the Ansari women. While they continue to be anchored in care and reproductive economy, they do occasional wage labour, take cattle for grazing, collect firewood, interact with their neighbours, etc.

Some important points emerge from this occupational mapping of OBCs. First, the breakdown between caste and occupation is not absolute, especially where women are concerned. Second, while women continue to bear the daily responsibility of household reproduction, they do not have decision-making powers. In fact, in the absence of migrating male relatives, it is those left behind in the village—women—who bear the burden of overlapping socio-economic relations of dominance and subjugation. Men experience social and economic liberation through migration and occupational diversification, this is made possible by women's unfreedom. It is women who perform exchange labour, provide tied and unpaid labour services to the creditors who belong to the dominant caste-class. Third, men belonging to the other backward class enjoy social capital which they use to secure migrant work.

2.3 SCs: Fallen Behind the Race

Chamars and Mosahars are numerically the most preponderant Dalits. Overall, Dalits constitute the labouring class, a class which finds everyday survival a huge struggle. There is hardly any economic differentiation among the Dalits. The few 'outlier' households (all Chamar households) are those where a family member was or is in public employment—these households clearly bring out the importance of regular formal employment in poverty reduction. I also noticed that in these households, children attended private schools, stayed in schools for a longer time and these households had invested in assets, notably land, house, vehicle, etc. Education and secure employment also means a greater sense of self-worth. Members of these households take great pride in the fact that they do not have to work for anyone else. Clearly then, employment creation—one that gives a decent and regular income—is important given the spill-over it has for education, building an asset base and social justice. What of the role of affirmative action—unfortunately this was not investigated. On the downside, these handful of households possibly indicate two other significant things. One, formal/public/secure employment is a male preserve. Second, caste is unable to break class barriers. In the caste based spatial organisation of villages, even the better-off Dalit households live in their 'caste hamlets/street' albeit slightly away from the labouring households. These 'outlier' households and the dominant Brahmin and Rajput households might have similar class interests (for example, keeping wages depressed), but this does not mean that there is any economic, political or social interaction across these caste groups. For instance, *badkas* deliberate amongst themselves on issues of wage hikes, labour strikes, *panchayat* issues, accessing political power and they are not seen visiting each other's homes. In terms of power and status then, clearly the upper castes are dominant and command more subservience. Though, it should also be noted that similar class interests does not mean exactly the same class position—Brahmins and Rajputs are bigger landowners, are more into commercial agriculture and related activities. The class position of these 'outliers' also makes them 'apart' from their own caste people. An interesting example is that of a Chamar household where the man was actually the then serving *pradhan*, but in name only. He was a proxy figure for the village's most dominant Brahmin household, the male head of which was the previous *pradhan*. In fact, the former used to work for this influential Brahmin household and while he may now be the village head, he does not actually do anything in that capacity, he is not even identified as a *pradhan*. He is a peddler selling bananas and his wife does agricultural wage labour.

As far as the labouring Dalit households are concerned, they practise subsistence oriented agriculture and a few households grow sugarcane on a very small scale. The Mosahars, being landless, are an exception—no Mosahar household was engaged in their own cultivation and in fact, they had been settled on government land. They do not lease in land also because they can hardly afford farming costs and even if they can the uncertainty of lease is a big drawback. In case of all other Dalit labouring households, their own agriculture was organised on the basis of family and exchange labour (to a lesser extent probably because of the very small holdings and the trend of nuclear families). What was different here was that even young married women participated in their own cultivation and livestock rearing (for commercial purposes). What stands out is that Dalits do not even own livestock often, these are taken on *batiya*. This was especially true of the Mosahars. Here too, caste plays a role. Apparently, milk from Dalit households fetches a lower price—it is not of good quality, it comes from 'untouchable' households.

It has been suggested that patriarchy is not as defining a feature of Dalits as it is of upper castes. This is certainly true where female labour participation is concerned in own cultivation. Women from these households also do not practise *purdah*. They provide unpaid labour services to upper caste-classes. However, where non-agricultural earnings are concerned, whether from self-employment, local wage labour or migrant work, men rule the roost. In other words, women are restricted to the private sphere, to unpaid work which is crucial to household survival. Better economic opportunities—which are also clean work opportunities and devoid of socio-economic oppression typical of villages—and the social worth that can be derived from doing such work are not available to women.

Non-agricultural self-employment is rare among Dalits and there can be several probable reasons for this—they do not have assets, capital to invest in inventory, skills which would attract a wide customer base, social capital, non-Dalits do not like entering Dalit hamlets to purchase goods and services. The few examples found in the field were that of a rickshaw puller, cobbler, tailor, ploughman, fruit-seller (cycle peddler), a fisherman selling his catch alongside the road in the local market and a small general store. There was one instance of a disabled man (a Mosahar), who learned stitching in a local market, was provided a sewing machine by the district administration as a part of Mosahar development efforts. Though he has to pay for it in future, he earns more than he did at the shop. However, payments are often delayed and lower than market rates. Labour struggles of Mosahars (see Mehrotra, 2013 for details) indicates two things—one that collective organisation, awareness and political consciousness (as is the case with Mosahars) are important to accessing entitlements and second, ultimately the government is indeed the '*mai-baap*', i.e. citizens will hold the state responsible and accountable. This raises important questions for the increasing outsourcing of even primary state responsibilities in the larger context of informality.

Very evident is also the sharp disjuncture between caste and traditional occupation. Only a few older Chamar women continued with their caste work of *dais,* assisting in child birth. Since these are older women and doing their traditional jobs (in other words, not challenging boundaries), socio-cultural restrictions limiting mobility are not seen here. In fact, these women travel great distances for work. They are compensated with clothes, money, grains, livestock or a small piece of jewellery. On special occasions like weddings, some Chamar women are called upon to sing at functions and they may be paid a token amount and/or are served food and sweets. They are not only important sources of income and food, but an integrated part of the fabric of village life. Women pointed out that they undertake these activities because of '*vyvhar*' (literally meaning behaviour and implying general social relations here), i.e. referring to the common community bond and as wage labourers. This '*vyvhar*', of course also serves to buttress their exploitation as wage labourers.

Wage labour and migrant work are crucial components in the livelihoods of Chamar households, while Mosahars are completely dependent on local wage labour for their survival. In the context of local wage labour, agriculture, even with its seasonality, is the most common source of income. And as in other cases, there is a sexual division of labour with women doing weeding and paddy transplantation and the men doing all sorts of spade work. Male tasks, but of course, pay more. Compared to other Dalit women labourers, Mosahar women interestingly travel great distances for agricultural work, they undertake work on a contractual basis and are able to negotiate for a better wage. They are also able to corner MGNREGA work. This is attributed to their organisational strength and politicisation—something to be understood with reference to Mosahars as a collective and not just with reference to Mosahar women (for details see Mehrotra, 2017; Singh, 2013). Households seek to maximise wage-earners and income sources. Even young married women and older women are engaged in wage labour, despite there being other productive family members available. There are a few households that do not undertake wage labour due to old age or health reasons. In addition to agricultural wage labour, there are examples of men working as rickshaw pullers, tractor drivers, skilled and unskilled construction workers, etc. In addition to such casual work, Mosahar men also work at nearby brick kilns. Brick kiln work is seen as the worst form of work, even though local men only mould bricks. This is because kilns are sites of alcohol making and consumption and of sexual misdemeanours. Attached unpaid family labour is common. Despite this, brick kiln work is fundamental to the survival of landless Moshars because of the line of credit that is extended to them in the off-season. At the same time, this also ends up perpetuating their exploitation as bonded labour.

In the case of Chamars, only men migrate for work and they are largely found in brick kilns, construction and other forms of casual labour. Unlike some of the upper and middle castes who have managed to secure prosperity through the route of migration, for Chamars this is an unstable, survival activity with all its attendant exploitation—involves low paid overtime work, living with many others in small accommodation, long work shifts, etc. What is distinctive here is that these migrants engage in agricultural work as well (in sugarcane farms, tending to livestock)—something not seen in the case of other migrants. Agricultural work is something to be avoided as far as possible—it is dirty work, it does not pay much and is not respectable. One Chamar migrant even worked as a cobbler. For men doing caste jobs is not a done thing and that too as a migrant when migration serves as an economic and a social escape. This just brings out the extreme vulnerability that Dalits live with on a daily basis. In fact, unlike other migrants, returning Dalit men are extensively engaged in local work. They cannot afford to sit idle, to be exploited is better than not to be exploited at all.

Why don't most Mosahars migrate? Mosahars explained this with reference to their landlessness and the absence of even a minimum buffer against food security. This means that they have to be resident in the village to provide for the household on a daily basis. More so because, men undertake non-agricultural labour which is more readily available and pays more. This has to be read in conjunction with the trend of family nuclearisation. Another reason is that there is perhaps enough work for them to survive on, owing to a relatively large number of landowners dependent on hired labour, in the village and locally. An important reason for low migration is that many of these households are also indebted to the area kilns and cannot migrate in the dry season. In the wet season, agricultural work is available in the village. Poor networking is another handicap. There is a contractor, from nearby, who recruits some Mosahars for tomato farming in Nainital. A few other male migrant workers work as casual labourers elsewhere. Unlike other returning male migrant workers, Mosahar migrants extensively undertake local wage labour when in the village.

The above description also points out that within Dalits, there is another layer of hierarchy and discrimination, along the lines of degrees of purity and pollution. Mosahars are clearly the worst off. Mosahar classes of labour depend directly or indirectly on the sale of their labour power for their daily reproduction and are engaged in most demeaning and debt-based oppressive forms of wage labour. They are castigated as rat-eaters. Other Dalits do not want to visit their hamlets, drink water from their hand-pipes, they are very jealous of their ability to organise and agitate successfully. The living conditions of Mosahars are the worst. The hamlet is located on a low lying ground and in the monsoon certain areas are flooded causing damage to crops and houses. Their huts are tiny and low. Other than agricultural implements, productive assets are hardly seen (also see, Dhuru, 2008).

Section 3: Same Yet Different: Interrogating Rural India

Drawing on the above description, it is definitely the case that rural India shows signs of change and continuity. Scholarly engagement with village studies is necessary to bring out the transformation of village India. This is important for large segments of vulnerable sections who still reside here or reflect strong attachments to village life. Village studies are no longer confined to disciplines of Sociology or Anthropology. The village has emerged as a site of fieldwork for economists, development scholars, political geographers. The village today is imagined not as a nation incarnate but as a multidimensional space—economic, political, socio-cultural, ecological—and this multidimensionality is not bound by the physical borders of the village.

India's pursuit of capitalist modernity is based on the exploitation of traditional hierarchies, where women and especially Dalit women from labouring households fare the worst. This finds resonance in Lerche (2010) work. According to him, in wage labour, formal occupations are at the top and casual agricultural labourers and bonded labour at the bottom. Self-employment activities that show a substantive asset base and/or employ workers are at the top and those indicative of survival mode or draw on unpaid family labour are at the bottom. These occupations correspond with low income and power base. Dalits and Scheduled Tribes are concentrated in these. Though Lerche does not comment on the gender aspect, he cites and draws on Chen (2008) who argued that women are generally preponderant at the bottom of the informal economy (including agriculture) in low waged work.

NOTES

1. How villagers relate to these changes is something which is refracted through their life-cycle changes, through their identity of gender, caste, class, through local value systems, through family structures, etc. Other than these positionalities, what also makes a difference is the geographical setting in which one is embedded. For example, in villages caste is still sacrosanct to a great extent. So, a poor Brahmin will not work for an upwardly mobile Dalit. But in an urban setting, the caste of the employer is irrelevant. Across caste groups, socio-cultural restrictions on women operate much more stringently inside villages than in cities, at least in North India. For example, restrictions on mobility, in terms of dress code or 'caste norms' which dictate social interactions vis-a-vis eating, socialising on festivals and religious occasions, etc.

REFERENCES

Breman, Jan. 1985. *Of Peasants, Migrants and Paupers: Rural Labour Circulation and Capitalist Production in West India,* New Delhi: Oxford University Press.

Chen, Martha. 2008. Informality and social protection: theories and realities. *IDS Bulletin*, 39(2), 18-27.

Dhuru, Arundhati. 2008. *Musahars: Bonded to Poverty*. Available at: http://www.thesouthasian.org/archives/2008/musahars_bonded_to_poverty_1.html [Accessed: November 16, 2009].

Harriss-White, Barbara and Harriss, John. 2007. *Green Revolution and After: The 'North Arcot Papers' and Long-Term Studies of the Political Economy of Rural Development in South India.* QEH Working Paper Series-QEHWPS146, Working Paper Number 146.

Janakarajan, S. 1997. Village Resurveys: Issues and Results. In: Breman, J., Kloos, P. and Saith, A. (eds.), *The Village in Asia Revisited*, New Delhi: Oxford University Press, Ch. 10, pp. 397-428.

Lerche, Jens. 2010. From 'rural labour' to 'classes of labour': Class fragmentation, caste and class struggle at the bottom of the Indian labour hierarchy. In: Harriss-White, Barbara and Heyer, Judith. (eds.), 2010. *The Comparative Political Economy of Development: Africa and South Asia*, Oxon: Routledge, Ch. 4, pp. 64-85.

Mehrotra, Ishita. 2012. 'Political Economy of Rural Female Labour: A Study of Labour Relations in East Uttar Pradesh (UP), India'. Unpublished PhD Thesis, SOAS, University of London.

____. 2017. 'Subsidising Capital and Male Labour: The Scandal of Unfree Dalit Female Labour Relations'. In: Anandi, S. and Kapadia, Karin (eds.), *Dalit Women: Vanguard of an Alternative Politics in India*, New Delhi: Routledge.

Singh, S.S. 2013. 'Intervention, Identity and Marginality: An Ethnographic Account of the Musahars', *Economic and Political Weekly*, 48 (20): 52-59.

7

Beyond *Sadak*, *Bijli* and *Pani*: Discourses of Infrastructural Power in Today's Rural India

Anjana John

Introduction

Infrastructure provides the basis of modern societies in both developed and developing countries (Larkin, 2013: 328). Infrastructure is argued to be one of the means in which states acquire and centralise power (i.e. infrastructural state in Mann, 2008). The present chapter analyses the role of infrastructural states in providing *sadak* 'road', *bijli* 'electricity', and *pani* 'water', and how social inequalities influence and impact the distribution of energy in rural India. This chapter is based on an action research of electrifying the 15 households of a Baiga hamlet in Pindrukhi village in Madhya Pradesh during the year 2015-16.

The chapter shows the importance of the state as one of the main actors in connecting the notions of development and energy, which is also evident in its political discourse. Electricity is one of the important fruits of India's statist development discourse. However, in this context it is also important to highlight that the relationship between energy and development is extremely violent, as the history of development of this country is also the history of displacement and dispossession—a history dotted with development induced displacement. Protests and conflicts surround these issues even today, thousands of people are losing their lives, livelihoods, land and culture in the name of infrastructural development. In other words, the role of the state is double-edged. The state aims to fulfil its duties towards its citizens (i.e. the common good), but its implementation has time and again collapsed into violent tactics. This chapter's analysis is duality in the context of a delayed electrification, which contains two registers: the romanticised idea of bringing *bijli* 'electricity', on one hand; and the inequalities in energy distribution, on the other hand. The latter is framed in terms of 'energy poverty' and 'energy inequality'.

Exploring the 'Darkness'

Like most villages, the hamlets in Pindrukhi are organised along caste and or tribe. In the village, caste or tribe-based settlements are known as Tolas. There are seven Tolas. If one is travelling from Amarpur (the Block in which Pindrukhi village comes under), Pindrukhi is nestled along the left side of the Amarpur-Sakka road. Out of the seven Tolas two hamlets are visible from the road. Like most villages in Madhya Pradesh the distance between the Tolas can vary from 1-2 kilometres. The two hamlets visible from the road are Bajrangad Tola (named after a temple where Bajrangbali is revered) and Sadak Tola (named after the main road). In other words, to access other Tolas one has to cross either of these two Tolas. There is no proper road to connect the Tolas and most often one is crossing private lands or wastelands to reach other Tolas. Therefore during the monsoon, only the pathway from Bajrangad Tola is accessed by villagers to reach other hamlets. During the summer and winter months, other Tolas of Pindrukhi can be accessed through Bajrangad Tola and Sadak Tola. Incidentally, infrastructural access to the village is marked by a bus stop[1] which shifts according to the needs of the season. In the months of summer and winter the bus-stop is closer to Sadak Tola and it shifts near Bajrangad Tola during the monsoon. Both pathways from Bajrangad Tola meet in a vast open space near Sati Tola. During my first day of arrival in the village, I was driven on a motorcycle and was directly taken through Sadak Tola, followed by a bumpy ride over a rocky uphill stretch near Sahu Tola. Later as I walked around, I discovered that there is a pathway connecting Sati Tola, Sahu Tola, Mukaddam Tola and Baiga Tola. The Baiga hamlet marks the boundary between the village and forest. Each of these

Tolas has a ward member who is an elected representative and all the wards are reserved for candidates from the Scheduled Tribe background.

Though there is a reservation policy for the Scheduled Tribes in ward elections, socially the dominant caste group in Pindrukhi are the Sahus (OBC). Most of the shops in the area are owned by members from the Sahu community and they are even related to each other through endogamy. Despite their social dominance, Sahus are spread across four Tolas—Sahu Tola, Sati Tola, Bajrangad Tola and Sadak Tola. Mukaddam Tola is primarily a Gond hamlet. In Pindrukhi, Sahus are the dominant caste group and Gonds are the dominant tribe. The other communities in the village are Das, Pardhi and Baiga tribes. Members of the Gond community also reside in Sadak Tola and Bajrangad Tola. Members of the Baiga tribe reside in Baiga Tola and Pardhi Tola is inhabited by the Pardhi tribe (one of the tribal groups listed as a criminal tribe by the British administration)[2].

The 15 Baiga families in Pindrukhi follow a settled agricultural style for the past four generations. They depend on the surrounding forest for firewood, wild vegetables, bamboo, etc. The distribution of landholdings among the Baigas reveals that only fifty per cent of the families have lands of their own. Four families own three acres, three families own less than half an acre and one family has no land. Members from ten families work as agricultural labourers in the fields of others (i.e. in fields owned by Sahus). Younger male members often migrate (male members of 13 families have gone to work more than once) to the nearby cities looking for jobs (as construction labourers and agricultural labourers) whenever they are short of money. Another source of income comes from selling bamboo products in the local market. The Sahu neighbours are the emergency moneylenders and agricultural labour providers for the Baigas. While the Baigas see them as their well-wishers and role models, the Sahus of Pindrukhi perceive the Baiga community as 'unclean', 'alcoholics' and 'wild people'.

Whenever I was in conversations with the Baiga Tola residents about the absence of electricity in the hamlet, someone always raised his/her frustration against the authorities for alienating them along with the Pardhis, since the rest of the village's electrification process was already completed and comes under the same central government scheme. They were also upset about the fact that there was no positive response from the Gram Sabha whenever this concern was raised by them.

It was evident that the "darkness" in Baiga Tola and Pardhi Tola not only symbolised the institutional negligence towards a marginalised community but also the impact of the prevailing social inequalities and discrimination towards the Baiga and the Pardhi tribes of Pindrukhi. My conversations with various institutional authorities (Panchayat Office, Block Office and the Electricity Board) regarding the delayed electrification of these two hamlets also substantiated the above observation as many of them stated that there is no need of electricity for these "SC/ST people" as they are wasting government's money by availing free of cost benefits.

State, Power and Infrastructure

In my action research, initially the inquiry of electricity access started with both Baiga Tola and Pardhi Tola which did not have access to electricity. However, in the Dindori Electricity Board documents; Pardhi Tola does not come under the village Pindrukhi and belongs to the neighbouring village Nanda. Though the oral narratives of the villagers and records of the panchayat office list Pardhi Tola as part of Pindrukhi, this ambiguity remained as a hindrance for my further action. Therefore, officially, Baiga Tola was the only hamlet which did not have electricity access in Pindrukhi but was entitled to receive electrification. Whether or not the Pardhi Tola belongs to Pindrukhi, it is important as the relationship between infrastructure, state and energy are interlinked. Also, the identity of Baigas and Pardhis and the nature of their relationship with the state play a pivotal role in this scenario. The Baiga tribe is one of the primitive tribal communities living in central India and for several decades thy have been discriminated against and often evicted from forest areas by government agencies.[3] However in the government documents they have been seen as a "protected community". According to the official website of Dindori district, the Baigas have been declared as "National Humans".[4] At the same time, there are ambiguities in the existence of Pardhi Tola in the official documents.

It is important to note that Pardhi is one of the 200 tribal groups who were categorised as the Criminal Tribes by the colonial state of India. Today, they are known as the Ex-Criminal Tribes or the Denotified Tribes. The term "criminal tribes" was coined by the British government and it entered the official vocabulary when the Criminal Tribes Act was passed in 1871. These tribal groups got officially "denotified" when the Act was repealed in 1952.[5] Even today people from these tribal groups are subjected to discrimination and humiliation in many ways. In Pindrukhi, the Pardhis are often seen as "trouble makers" for the neighbouring Tola residents. Men from the Pardhi Tola are frequently picked up by the local police for creating a "nuisance" in the village. Anand Pandian notes that the Criminal Tribes Act was the colonial state's way of managing a population of subjects assumed as criminal by nature and as organisms of instinct and impulse (2008). He also points out that the contemporary forms of such policing exist in the post-colonial state as well when the moral self-conduct of these communities are being governed. He equates it to Foucault's concept of "pastoral power": "the government of a population modelled on the relationship between a figurative shepherd and the individual members of a flock" (Pandian, 2008: 86).

The state's relationship with the Baiga Tola and the Pardhi Tola could be classified in two different ways. With the Baiga, the state takes the role of a benevolent protector by categorising them as the "protected" community. With the Pardhi, the state is the perpetrator by treating them as criminals. Both these relationships are the ways of the post orientalist orientation of its subjects where they are still considered to be part of the "civilising mission". In his novella *Heart of Darkness*, Joseph Conrad portrays how immense power and domination can be imposed on people in the name of civilising them. The novella centres around Marlow, a pensive sailor, and his journey up the Congo River to meet Kurtz, reputed to be an idealistic man of great abilities. Through Marlow, Conrad tries to show the greed and great thirst for power of the West while using the excuse of modernisation. Conrad in this novella looks into the dark sides of the "civilising mission" and its adverse effects on people who went through it. In the novella, Conrad uses two powerful symbols in his work which are the "sword" and the "torch" that refer to the ruthless force and the denial of the native culture by the pseudo light of civilisation (Conrad, 1899). The Baigas and the Pardhis, even today, in the post-colonial society, are reduced to such subjects who are yet to be "civilised". They are often defined in terms of what they "lack" and how they need to be "empowered" in the statist discourse.

Electricity and Infrastructural Power

To analyse the presence and the role of the state in this study, I draw on the concept of the "infrastructural state" from Michael Mann (2008) wherein he explains the duality in the power of the state. According to Mann, the state possesses two different kinds of power which are despotic power and infrastructural power. While Mann defines despotic power as a range of actions that the state elite is entitled to make without any consultation with civil society groups he describes infrastructural power as the capacity of the state to actually penetrate the civil society and implement its actions across its territories. He also notes that the state can be "strong" in two ways with the use of these two different kinds of power and modern democracies across the world tend to be despotically weak while they have more infrastructural power (Mann, 2008: 355). Mann describes four mechanisms which enable the expansion of the state's infrastructural power and those are: "increasing specialisation of activity; literacy, which facilitates constant communication of the state's message, including its legal order; measurement to facilitate exchange; and the expansion of technologies to facilitate the movement of people, goods and ideas" (as cited in Kale, 2014: 10).

As mentioned above, Kale (2014), in her book *Electrifying India: Regional Political Economies of Development* identifies electricity as both the object of and mechanism for the expansion of infrastructural power in modern states. Kale also states that electricity enables the state's message to fill the airwaves, aids in transportation and also has an indirect effect on the spread of education through improved schooling and studying (Ibid:10). She adds that the networked energy in particular allows the state to denote its spatial reach and marks its territories through electric poles and transmission lines. At the same time, she also points out that these energy grids could be the symbols that indicate the absence or bare existence of the state on the ground (Ibid: 11). This is where I find the first footing of my study and I attempt to explore a region—the Baiga Tola—where the state has not been keen to spread its infrastructural power. This study analyses the situation further and explores how the pre-existing social inequalities impact it and add to those inequalities.

Right to Infrastructure and the Politics of Claim Making

Interestingly, electricity, a tool which is generally used for the spread of the state's infrastructural power is absent in both these hamlets where the rest of the village was electrified a few years ago. My work explores this "darkness" and focuses on the question that the absence of the state here is an impact of the existing social inequalities faced by these tribal groups. The "action" part of my work explores the duality of the state's infrastructural power and facilitating a platform for claim making of its "subjects". In the sense that infrastructural power has the reciprocal characteristic that it also enables civil society parties and people to control the state through the claim making process (Mann, 2008). Through my action research, I have examined the delayed electrification and the process of claim making beyond the modernisation paradigm of the state as the benevolent provider of *sadak* 'road', *bijli* 'electricity', and *pani* 'water'.

The electrification of the Baiga Tola comes under the central government rural electrification scheme Deen Dayal Upadhyaya Gram Jyoti Yojana (DDUGJY) and as per this scheme the rural village households are entitled to free electrification. The scheme focuses on feeder separation (rural households and agricultural) and strengthening of sub-transmission and distribution infrastructure including metering at all levels in rural areas. This allows to provide round-the-clock power to rural households and adequate power to agricultural consumers. The earlier scheme for rural electrification, viz. Rajiv Gandhi Grameen Vidyutikaran Yojana (RGGVY) has been subsumed in the new scheme as its rural electrification component.[6]

Initially the Baiga Tola residents did not have any information regarding the electrification schemes they were entitled to.

Therefore, later along with them, I facilitated a collective platform that enabled discussions regarding the delay in the electrification process during the course of my action research. Weekly meetings were held to discuss the possibilities of a collaborative effort for the electrification in the hamlet. As a result of these discussions, we decided to use RTI (Right to Information) Act to demand information from the authorities regarding the electrification process and its delay in Baiga Tola. We prepared a RTI application and one of the Tola residents volunteered to file it in his name. Since the Dindori Electricity Board was 30 kilometres away from Pindrukhi, we decided to submit the RTI query to the Amarpur Block Office. As per the rules of the RTI Act, a person can submit his/her queries to the Panchayat or the Block Office and it is the duty of the office in charge to forward the queries to the corresponding department/section. But the authorities in the Amarpur Block Office were reluctant to accept the RTI query which we had furnished. They gave a number of irrelevant technical reasons to reject our query. Since we had a detailed discussions in our group meetings regarding the rules and provisions under the RTI Act, we resisted and demanded firmly that our application should be accepted. The office in charge was quite annoyed and offended since we dismissed the existence of the excuses he gave us not to accept our RTI query. After an hour long argument, the authorities finally accepted the application and gave us the receipt of its acceptance. Within three days of filing the RTI query, the Electricity Board officials reached Baiga Tola for the site visit and work estimation. After the site visit, I left Baiga Tola and from then onwards the Tola residents coordinated with the officials throughout the entire electrification process. My involvement with them after I left Pindrukhi was minimal. I used to make occasional phone calls and inquire about the progress of work. There were technical difficulties and delays in between as I was told, but the Tola residents made the necessary interactions and interventions with the officials and finally the 'light' arrived in their houses. Two months after the site visit, the electrification process of Baiga Tola was completed.

The RTI Act was used as the most significant tool for the access of the infrastructure (electricity) in Baiga Tola. The decision to file the RTI was made since there was no information available to the residents regarding the delay in the electrification process of the Tola. The RTI Act has been widely used for infrastructural access and justice across the country. Since its enactment in 2005, citizen groups of diverse socio-economic backgrounds have long since battled for the exercise of their rights in India. What makes this piece of legislation significant and unique is that the demand for it came through a grass root based struggle from rural India for a transparent system of governance (Mander and Joshi, 1999). The role of the RTI Act in demanding transparency and accountability in the infrastructural projects running across the country are huge currently.

There have been many instances where the RTI Act was used as a mechanism to attain knowledge about the delays and corruption involved in the service delivery system and in the infrastructural projects running in this country (Shreyaskar, 2014). It has been used to demand accountability from the public officials as well. The RTI Act was one of the best instruments for the Baiga Tola residents to make their claim for electricity in their households. Moving along with the RTI application has ensured strong participation from the Baiga Tola residents in this action research. The resistance from the officials while filing the RTI and the immediate impact it made in the electrification process have once again proved the power and efficiency of this legislation. However, the limitation of the RTI Act is also marked by this process as only the Baiga Tola residents were able to make the claim for electricity through it. As mentioned before, according to official documents, Baiga Tola was the only hamlet which did not have electricity access in Pindrukhi but was entitled to receive electrification. The administrative acknowledgement of the status of Baiga Tola's future of electrification opened up the way for claim making in Baiga Tola. The ambiguity in the administrative existence of the Pardhi Tola remained as a hindrance for the Pardhis to be a part of this claim making action for electrification.

In this backdrop, the study presents evidence that development is not merely artifactual but a transformative exercise of a process of 15 Baiga families coming together to discover a potentiality beyond the statist discourse of lack and empowerment. In the larger context, this study frames electricity within the notion of energy, and examines the politics behind the distribution of energy.

Why Electrification?

David S. Brown and Ahmed Mushfiq Mobarak (2009) in their article state that electricity is a publicly provided good which can positively affect the health, education, and economic growth simultaneously of a region. "Electricity affects a multitude of political, economic, and social outcomes. Access to cheap and reliable energy can directly affect economic growth by spurring industrial activity. Access to electricity can help education by lighting a school room or by allowing a child to read after dark and it can help health care provision by allowing the storage of perishable vaccines in health clinics" (Mobarak and Brown, 2009: 194). Kale, points out that electricity can drastically transform all kinds of productivity. She argues that the usage of electric power can make remarkable improvements in both the agricultural and industrial sector. She also notes that the access to electricity could also improve the quality of life. On a similar note, Akhil Gupta writes that electricity stands out from other infrastructural elements due to its role in lighting since it opened up the possibility of using the time after sunset for various purposes. He also points out that the presence of light, especially in rural India has made the streets safer and commutable at night. Yet, around 2 million people live in the dark in the developing countries (Gupta, 2015).

Can electrification of Baiga Tola act as the catalyst for a broader social change? The social character of each Indian state varies due to their socio-political histories and it accounts for the variation in their patterns of infrastructural development. The idea of rural electrification was emphasised when the rural constituencies became more politically influential in regional politics or when the farmers mobilised to demand a larger share of development resources (Kale, 2014: 1-23). Kale argues that although rural electrification profoundly impacted the agricultural productivity and improved the rural standards of living, it led to social inequalities, especially when the rural rich monopolised the use of electricity and the other communities could not access the benefits of it. Bikash Chandra Dash states that electric power is a vital commodity for the socio-economic development of the nation and therefore it should be made available and accessible to all irrespective of the poor and rich in the region. In fact he argues that equity in electric power distribution reflects as a good governance practice of a government (Dash 2006). He notes that a sizeable population in India are not being able to reap the benefits of electric power and the subsidies given for its usage. He also points out that the benefits of electricity ends with the lighting purposes in most of the electrified regions in rural India. The subsidies are provided for the good of the poor communities but often in rural India the poor do not even get connected to the grid and thereby nullifying its purpose (Ibid: 511-22).

The structure and the power distribution between the central and state governments of the Indian power sector also have resulted in the slow and inefficient electrification process across the country. Kale analyses the 2011 census and points out that even if we compute all the achievements made in Indian electrification since independence to the present, electricity still cannot be counted as a public good to all citizens. "Only 67.2 per cent of households can rely on electricity as a primary source of lighting; everyone else—close to 400 million Indians—rely on other sources of fuel like firewood and kerosene" (Kale, 2014: 160-79). She also mentions that other South Asian countries like China have fared better than India in providing this capital-intensive and technologically intricate commodity. The Chinese government estimates that only 1 per cent of households are without electricity access. She concludes her argument by stating that to finish the project "electrifying India" there has to be both "political mobilisation from below—by those who were left out of the first wave of infrastructure expansion in the countryside—and institutional restructuring from above" (Ibid: 179).

Thus, electrification of Baiga Tola not only eliminates the physical darkness but also urges us to look into the darkness created by the social inequalities around it. In Baiga Tola, the claim for electrification is a claim for well-being as well as a resistance against the injustice faced by the community. As mentioned above, electricity has the spillage effect on several other development concerns like health, education, etc. Therefore, working towards the achievement of electrification also gives the potential to open up the possibility of reclaiming their voice in their own living space.

The Conventional/Renewable Energy Dilemma

Deciding to take the conventional energy path for the electrification in Baiga Tola was a crucial and a complex task for me as an action researcher. I was asked by a few officials in the Dindori Electricity Board and the Block Office of Amarpur as to how the Baiga Tola residents would be able to afford to pay the electricity bills every month. There are subsidies and other benefits through the state and central government schemes but still they would have to pay the bill, even if it was minimal, on a monthly basis. Although this question was raised by those officials because of their caste-class prejudices and the stereotypical views on the Adivasis, it certainly remains valid and needs to be discussed.

According to Gupta, the relationship between electricity and the poor is quite troubled in the countries of the global south. He says that "the provision of free electric power in rural India is the product of electoral competition, populist politics and the organisational abilities of rich rural peasants and it increases inequality since the advantages of electricity other than lighting (such as motor pump irrigation, tube wells, etc.) are mostly affordable only for the rural rich" (Gupta, 2015: 561).

Thus he concludes his argument by stating that we need to re-imagine the future of electricity which does not simply add more and more people to the central grid. He urges the global south to experiment with different ways of using electricity. He states that "a combination of wind, solar, biomass, and electric power could meet all the community's energy needs and, whether we like it or not, that is the future of energy sustainability on the planet, since we cannot continue to burn the energy stored inside the earth" (Ibid: 565).

Looking through the above lens, one could argue that this action research should have been based on a sustainable and renewable method of electrification. However, this is not possible given the absence of electricity in Baiga Tola which did not just stand for the absence of a modern technology. The darkness in Baiga Tola was a symbol of inequality, discrimination and injustice. Baigas claiming for their existing right for electrification in their houses is their resistance against the society which dismisses even their mere existence and survival. Electricity in Baiga Tola therefore stands as the symbol of acceptance of their need for justice and well-being. As Gupta has pointed out that often in the rural areas, electricity leads to further inequality when the rural rich monopolise it for their benefits, these 15 Baiga families receiving electricity makes it less unequal. Gupta's urge for re-imagining the ways of producing and using electricity is certainly a way to think forward. But right now for the Baigas of Pindrukhi, the fight they put up for the electrification definitely added a milestone in the journey for the acceptance and recognition which they were denied for ages. There are successful renewable energy projects which have functioned among vulnerable communities. However, these are yet to reach many more people in the country so that the issue of energy poverty can be resolved to a greater extent. Therefore, taking the conventional energy path was right and necessary in this context.

Electrification, Energy and Development

India accounts for 2.4 per cent of world energy production and is at the eleventh position in the world in energy production. The country also accounts for 3.5 per cent of the total energy consumption and holds the 6th position in energy consumption (Osmani, 2014). There is a huge gap between energy production and energy consumption in the country. "India relies heavily on conventional energy sources, coal being at the forefront and the scenario seems to continue in the coming decades as well in order to feed one of the fastest growing economies, despite an ambitious push for renewable energy."[7]

Energy is humanity's fundamental source of power and the production and distribution of diverse forms of energy often creates levels of inequality across the globe. Timothy Mitchell (2011), in his work *Carbon Democracy*, talks about how the politics of energy often revolves around fiscal aspects rather than its process of production and distribution. Mitchell argues that it is not the fiscal part of energy production but the outcomes of particular ways of engineering political relations out of flows of energy that creates inequality in a democracy. He also points out that it is this inequality which limits the contemporary democracy from making energy as a decentralised commodity and we need to analyse it and overcome it for building solutions to the future energy needs (Mitchell, 2011).

Electricity is seen as a modern form of energy which has become an integral part in our day-to-day lives and yet millions of people still live in the dark. As an energy form, the production and distribution of electricity also needs to be analysed in the above manner as Mitchell has described. It is important to see how the existing social and economic biases affect its distribution and creates new biases from this unequal access. One of the lenses to understand this unequal access is the framework of 'energy poverty'. There are various reasons for energy poverty[8] such as in South Asia the major causes of energy poverty are: the difficulty and cost of providing conventional power infrastructure to reach the large numbers of people who live in rural areas; heavy dependence on traditional fuels for domestic use; and, at the national level, an undesirable dependence on (often imported) fossil fuels (Saracini, Krishnaswamy and Dubey, 2015). The current approaches of delivering energy, especially in the case of the production and distribution of electricity, have not addressed this energy poverty particularly in rural areas. Various policy interventions and subsidies which are aimed at reducing energy costs for the poor have not been successful in reducing the inequalities in energy access (Ibid: 16). The existing social and economic inequalities are further reinforced by these disparities in energy access.

The future energy policies should aim for a transition to low carbon energy production but this does not mean that the poor should be denied the energy access in the present. The report prepared by Greenpeace on climate justice reveals that "the considerably significant carbon footprint of a relatively small wealthy class (1 per cent of the population) in the country is unseen by the 823 million poor population of India, who keep the overall per capita emissions below 2 tonnes of carbon dioxide (CO_2) per year" (Ananthapadmanabhan, Srinivas and Gopal, 2007). The report says that the carbon footprint of the highest income classes earning more than Rs. 8,000 per month, representing a population of about 150 million people in the country, already exceeds sustainable levels of CO_2 emission. The study also argues that the rich consumer class of the country is hiding their CO_2 emissions behind the legions of the poor, most of who do not even have access to electricity (Ibid: 4). Therefore the report urges the Indian government to create differentiated responsibility for climate justice for various social and economic classes of society. The report also points out the fact that inefficiency and inaccessibility of clean and sustainable forms of energy put the poor in more danger of environmental changes and disasters. In short, the poor live with huge energy insufficiency and are also made to suffer from the hazardous effects of climate change caused by the over exhaustion of the conventional energy resources.

The access of electricity for the Baiga Tola residents becomes significant because of all the aspects discussed above. The delay in the electrification process at its first glance would seem like a bureaucratic inefficiency but when electricity is seen as the energy form which could make many positive impacts on a community, it requires a deeper analysis. The Baiga community in Pindrukhi village represents the poor and marginalised sections of people in the country and they are denied energy access due to their caste/class identities, geographical locations, economic incapability, etc. Although the "action" part of my research was confined as the Baiga Tola residents making a claim to be a part of the central grid and achieving the access of electricity, it was a relevant fight for the Pardhis in the village as well. It also indicates the bigger picture which obliges us to look at the energy poverty experienced by the poor in India and the inequalities which are impacted in its distribution. The Baiga Tola being attached to the central power grid is not going to resolve the issues in energy access to the poor and is also not a long term sustainable solution to their energy needs. For the future that creates wider access of clean and sustainable energy, it is important to go in the way of renewable sources for energy production but that does not resolve the issues which prevail on the distribution side.

Conclusion

The relationship between energy and humankind has always been a complex one. It has got furthermore complex and crucial due to the political relations which have emerged in the backdrop of energy distribution in the world. Currently we are in the phase of a crisis where the abundance of our traditional energy resources are deteriorating and resulting in an energy crisis and hazardous environmental alterations. The world is forced to make a move towards sustainable choices of energy production in order to save humankind from global warming and other environmental issues. It has been realised that the energy production has to take a turn towards renewable sources for a better and sustainable future. Scholars like Timothy Mitchell (2011) and Akhil Gupta (2015) hope that moving towards the renewable energy sources would also result in the decrease of inequalities that exist in the distribution of energy. The action research done in Pindrukhi raises a concern on that expectation and argues that changing the modes of energy production not necessarily eliminates the inequalities on the distribution end especially in the context of rural India. Therefore, there has to be a deeper understanding of the existing social inequalities and how the politics of energy reinforce these inequalities on the ground.

India is one of the countries that has high energy consumption levels and most of its primary energy needs are being met through imports and conventional energy sources. The country is keen on addressing the energy poverty in its rural areas and several policy measures have been taken to improve the situation. In the case of electricity access, the central and state governments have formulated and implemented various schemes and programmes to provide electricity for all. Although many of these schemes and programmes are targeting vulnerable sections in the society, often the success of it remains in theory, not in practice. There have been ample efforts from numerous non-governmental and private organisations in this field, especially in promoting renewable and sustainable energy consumption practices. Many NGOs and private organisations have come up with renewable energy programmes to provide clean and easy energy access for the vulnerable communities. Yet, there are millions of people who live in the dark in our country. This shows that the issue of energy poverty has not been addressed by looking at all its aspects and very often the people who suffer from energy poverty are the people who have been marginalised and discriminated based on their social and economic background. The energy sector in India is dominated by the state and increasingly non-governmental participation is being encouraged. A combined attempt from both the government and the non-governmental organisations are ideal and promising. However, the state policies need to be more focused and should be able to take the specificness and diverseness of each social context into consideration.

Another striking aspect that emerges from this research is the long-term affordability of a freely provided infrastructure by the state to the public. The residents of Baiga Tola have received their free and rightful electrification and they have started receiving the bills according to the meter readings. Now, the remaining question is the affordability of this infrastructural facility in the coming days. While Baiga Tola receiving electricity is certainly a milestone, the journey does not end there. The responsibility of the state seems to end once the free electrification and subsidies are in place. However the issue of energy poverty does not get addressed by that. Since economic poverty and energy poverty are linked with each other, the affordability of energy services stands as a hindrance for the rural poor. The Government of India has promised complete rural electrification by the year 2019 in its 2017-18 financial year budget[9] but the question of affordability does not go beyond the point of subsidies. This is not just the case with electricity. For example, on paper, Pradhan Mantri Ujjwala Yojana (PMUY) is a success and under this scheme, 50 million LPG connections were to be given to women belonging to families that fall below the poverty line[10]. The scheme has managed to cover around two crore households within 11 months from its launch in Uttar Pradesh. However, this has not made any increase in the overall LPG consumption since many families who received the gas connection under the scheme had not returned to refill their cylinders[11]. The reason for customers not returning for the refill after receiving the connection and cylinder free of cost is most probably attributed to the high cost of even a subsidised cylinder. The PMUY beneficiaries are also not required to pay the security deposit or any other overhead costs while taking LPG connections, and can also opt to pay in instalments for gas stoves and the first refill while getting a connection. However, these concessions do not apply for the second refill. The situation with free electrification is also very similar to the gas subsidies. Although each of the households in Baiga Tola are entitled to receive 25 units of electricity 110 free of cost every month, they have to pay a certain amount of money that is not less, to continue to avail of this facility. Therefore, economic security is a necessity for energy security as well. State-led initiatives to eliminate energy poverty among the rural poor do not really take this factor into consideration, so most of these schemes and policies fail to make any actual impact on the ground. These schemes in fact, further deepen the social and economic inequalities among the rural poor indirectly. Therefore, it is not merely a question of renewable or non-renewable energy but also a question of affordability that has to be analysed within the context of energy and economic poverty.

The participatory nature of action was instrumental in shaping the path of transformation—introduction of a tool of justice that can be used for other infrastructural claims. However, the larger question that remains to be explored is the increasing demands of energy, entry of non-state actors in renewable sectors of energy through civil society initiatives and the future of conventional energy in the context of climate change. Also, in the context of Baiga Tola it might be the access of an infrastructural facility that stands for justice but in many other parts of rural India, people are exploited in the name of infrastructural development. For example, the ongoing movement in Bhangar, West Bengal against the construction of a power grid substation in the village is the struggle by the villagers to save their land, livelihood, ecology and environment[12]. It is significant to note that on both these ends of infrastructural injustice, the poor and the marginalised sections are the ones who are at loss. On one end, their land is taken away with the false promises of infrastructural development and on the other end, they are denied basic infrastructural facilities and further marginalised. A deeper understanding of the role of the state in creating and reinforcing the social inequalities and its impact on infrastructural development is essential to change the axis of transformation in the area of energy and development.

NOTES

1. Here, a bus-stop implies where the buses come and halt. There is no physical marker which signifies the name of the hamlet.
2. Tripathi, Kartikeya. 'To Match a Thief' *The Times of India*. July 17, 2010, http://epaper.timesofindia.com/Default/Layout/Includes/CREST/ArtWin.asp?From=Archive&Source=Page&Skin=CREST&BaseHref=TCRM%2F2010%2F07%2F17&ViewMode=HTML&GZ=T&PageLabel=9&EntityId=Ar00900&AppName=1; Accessed on March 25, 2017.
3. Chakravartty, Anupam. 'Baiga Tribals Become India's First Community to Get Habitat Rights'. *Down to Earth*. January 14, 2016, http://www.downtoearth.org.in/news/baiga-tribals-become-india-s-first-community-to-get-habitat-rights-52452; Accessed on January 12, 2017.
4. http://www.dindori.nic.in/Profile.html. Accessed on October 5, 2016.
5. Rationalist, Debashish.'Criminal Tribes Pardhi'. Word Press, https://rationalistdebashis.wordpress.com/2011/07/25/criminal-tribes-pardhi/; Accessed on March 25, 2017.
6. http://powermin.nic.in/en/content/deendayal-upadhyaya-gram-jyoti-yojana-ddugjy. Accessed on January 14, 2017.
7. *Dembinski, Stanislas.* "Conventional Energy Sources Dominating the Power Mix." *Media India Group,* November 2015. http://mediaindia.eu/energy/conventional-energy-sources-dominating-the-power-mix/; Accessed on March 6, 2017.
8. Energy poverty is defined by the International Energy Agency as a lack of access to modern energy services in the form of access to electricity and to clean cooking facilities (fuels and stoves that do not cause air pollution in houses).
9. IANS, 'Complete Rural Electrification by 2019, Hike in MNREGA Fund: Arun Jaitley'. *The Times of India*. February 1, 2017, http://timesofindia.indiatimes.com/business/india-business/completerural-electrification-by-2019-hike-in-mnrega-fund-arun-jaitley/articleshow/56910067.cms; Accessed on March 16, 2017.
10. 'The Poor Got LPG Cylinders Under Modi's Scheme But They Can't Afford Gas Refills'. *The Wire*. June 28, 2017, https://thewire.in/152066/modi-lpg-scheme/; Accessed on June 29, 2017.

11. Jha K. Dhirendra.' Modi's Pet Ujjawala Scheme Wobbles as Many Beneficiaries Drop Out After Their First LPG Cylinder'. *Scroll. in*. June 11, 2017, https://scroll.in/article/839961/modis-pet-ujjawalascheme-wobbles-as-many-beneficiaries-drop-out-after-their-first-lpg-cylinder; Accessed on June 29, 2017.
12. Gangopadhyay, Bolan. 'State and Bhangar'. *The Indian Express.* February 7, 2017, http://indianexpress.com/article/opinion/columns/bhangar-kolkata-land-violence-pgcil-roadblockade-bengal-government-4511146/; Accessed on March 12, 2017.

REFERENCES

Ananthapadmanabhan, G., Srinivas, K. and Gopal, Vinuta. 2007. *Hiding Behind the Poor: A Report by Greenpeace on Climate Justice,* Bangalore: Greenpeace India Society.

Barnes, D.E. and Halpern, J. 2000. 'The Role of Energy Subsidies'. In *Energy Services for the World's Poor*, ed. World Bank 60-68. Washington, DC: World Bank.

Conrad, Joseph. 1899. *Heart of Darkness*, Reprint, New Delhi: Worldview Publications, 2015.

Dash, Bikash Chandra. 2006. 'Does Good Governance Matter for the Equitable Distribution of Electricity? An Analysis of the Indian Case', *The Indian Journal of Political Science*, 67 (3): 511-522.

Fisch, Michael. 2013. 'Tokyo's Commuter Train Suicides and the Society of Emergence', *Cultural Anthropology,* 28: 320-43.

Gupta, Akhil. 2015. 'An Anthropology of Electricity from the Global South', *Cultural Anthropology*, 30 (4): 555-568.

Kale, S. Sunila. 2014. *Electrifying India: Regional Political Economies of Development,* Stanford, California: Stanford University Press.

Larkin, Brian. 2013. 'The Politics and Poetics of Infrastructure', *The Annual Review of Anthropology*, 42: 327-43.

Mander, Harsh and Joshi, Abha. 1999. 'The Movement for Right to Information in India: People's Power for the Control of Corruption', *Commonwealth Human Rights Initiative.*

Mann, Michael. 1984. 'The Autonomous Power of the State: Its Origins, Mechanisms, and Results', *Archives of European Sociology*, 25: 185-213.

____ . 2008. 'Infrastructural Power Revisited', *Studies in Comparative International Development* (SCID), 43: 355-65.

Mitchell, Timothy. 2011. *Carbon Democracy*, London: Verso.

Mobarak, Ahmed Mushfiq and Brown, S. David. 2009. 'The Transforming Power of Democracy: Regime Type and the Distribution of Electricity', *The American Political Science Review*, 103 (2): 193-213.

Osmani, Ali Reja. 2014. 'Conventional Energy to Renewable Energy: Perspectives for India', *The NEHU Journal*, 2: 41-60.

Pandian, Anand. 2008. 'Pastoral Power in the Postcolony: On the Biopolitics of the Criminal Animal in South India', *Cultural Anthropology*, 23 (1): 85-117.

Saracini, Nadia, Krishnaswamy, Srinivas and Dubey, Sunita. 2015. *Energy for Development in South Asia: Addressing Energy Inequality Sustainably,* London: Christian Aid.

Shreyaskar, Pankaj K.P. 2014. 'Known Unknowns of RTI Legitimate Exemptions or Conscious Secrecy?', *Economic and Political Weekly*, XLIX (24): 32-38.

8

Sammamma's Seeds: The Price She Pays

Shalini Bhutani

Dedication

The name 'Sammamma' has been inspired by those in Andhra Pradesh and Telangana whose lives are impacted by the price of new proprietary seed technologies, such as transgenic Bt cottonseeds. When reference is generally made to farmers, all are lumped together in one category regardless of their scale, location, practices and gender. Female nomenclature is intentionally used here to symbolically represent the unsung and invisible women farmers in India's many rural landscapes who are struggling to keep their own seeds, biodiverse farms and (agri) cultures alive. Any resemblance to actual persons, real and living is therefore not merely coincidental.

Seed at the Centre

An important factor of production in village life is the seed; it plays a central role in the livelihoods of farming families and in the lives of those connected with them. This chapter takes a closer look at the problem of pricing of genetically modified (GM) seed from that viewpoint. It looks at the plethora of regulatory bodies dealing with the pricing of GM seeds.

The household—the smallest unit of micro level analysis, often gets lost sight of in the macro-level management of the big and complex seed systems and their many dimensions. More so, an important member of that household—the woman, is often rendered invisible. A large percentage of rural populations engaged in on-farm and in-house seed activities are women.[1] With industry-linked migration of the male population from villages, there has also been a feminisation of agriculture. Moreover, given the traditionally female roles vis-a-vis seeds, it is important that analysis of seed-related issues reflect the gynocentrism.

Women are not only at the centre of food in the home, but also at the centre of informal seed systems, though they may not be adequately recognised as such by the state. It is from the perspective of Sammamma—a small woman farmer in a rural household in the cotton belt of South India, that this chapter studies the dominant players in the seed industry that determine her seed choices and the price she pays for those seeds.

Price Regulation

The problem of seed pricing is in itself compelling. And that in part is the significance of this chapter. Price controls on seeds are justified by governmental agency, for the twin purposes of balancing the interests of seed producers and those of the end consumers—the farmers. In regulating seed prices, policy makers have to constantly contend with competing objectives. On the one hand decision-makers in government argue that lowering seed prices would disincentivise the big industry that markets new technologies, such as GM seeds. On the other hand, farmers groups ask governments to keep the input costs low to keep their farming economically viable. Yet not all public policy interventions with respect to price automatically lead to the betterment of the women farmers' situation.

There is a more fundamental concern for Sammamma. Within political circles and administrative offices of the agricultural departments the debates over seed have narrowed down to making 'good quality' seed available at reasonable prices to the farmer. Even in 2004 when the Central Government mooted the idea of a new seed legislation for the country, its stated objective was *to provide for regulating the quality of seeds for sale, import and export...*[2] This was again reflected in the National Policy for Farmers in 2007. That gives away the ideological bias of the government's seed policy. (It is another matter that the language of the proposed law is completely gender-blind.)

Though the sale of spurious seeds is a real and urgent problem for farmers, but quality control itself can put farmers' own seeds out of use and circulation. If seed quality is set as per industry standards, Sammamma gets converted from being amongst the original seed producers to being merely a seed consumer. This has happened before in the not so distant past, with the so-called 'Green Revolution'.[3] Local farmers' varieties were replaced by so-called high-yielding varieties (HYVs) released through the public sector. Apart from seed quality it was argued that the HYVs offer superior genetics. The National Seed Corporation was established in 1963 for the large-scale production of 'quality' seeds. The first seed law of the country—Seed Act, 1966, was passed in that era to regulate the quality of varieties notified by the government.

While there is no dispute about the role of the government in regulating the quality of seeds in the formal seed supply system, there is much debate in India about whether GM seed prices should be controlled by the government. It is in this background that the chapter examines orders on the pricing of GM Bt cottonseeds issued by governments, at the centre and state level. In analysing how the seed companies are responding to these regulations by the state, the motivations of the economic agents involved are unraveled.

The purpose is to continue to highlight the women farmer(s) as the key reference point. For apart from the economic system what is equally important is the political frame in which seed prices are determined. The international peasants movement—*La Via Campesina*, works for 'seed sovereignty' as part of their larger food sovereignty movement.[4] If the small seed keepers—many of whom are rural women are to be supported, mere price controls over products of seed corporations are inadequate to realise that. Sammamma's own seed 'science' and knowledge of plant breeding will need to be given as much law and policy support. There is a need to generate more gender-aware insights on seeds, apart from their mere price.

Seed prices have particular consequences on the small woman farmer and the sustainability of the agriculture she may choose to pursue. Law and policy interventions are used not simply for regulating prices of seed products of the large seed industry and the dominant player(s) in India, but for facilitating the dissemination of pre-selected technologies to the farmers. In the contemporary times seed policies, effected either through law or government programmes, are a powerful means of transforming the very seed systems in the village.

Technology Angle

Technology is central to seed production, and is a key determinant of the price at which seeds are sold. The choice of technology is a political one too. In making that policy choice, the decision maker also makes a choice of whose innovation to support and promote. Law and policy is then re-oriented to provide the institutional arrangements for the chosen technology.

In 2002 the Government of India allowed the commercialisation of modern biotechnology in the seed sector, by approving the use and sale of GM Bt cotton. The said seed technology is developed by the US multinational corporation (MNC) Monsanto Inc. Sammamma had no say in this decision.

In India in March 2003 Monsanto released three Bt cotton hybrids with its first-generation single-gene technology under the brand name Bollgard I (BG I). It did so in collaboration with the largest hybrid seed company in India—MHSCL (Maharashtra Hybrid Seeds Company Limited). The GM seeds were marketed through a joint venture between the two companies namely, Monsanto MAHYCO Biotech Limited (hereinafter referred to as MMBL).

After the failure of the 2003 harvest and the non-performance of its seeds, the company did not pay any compensation to the affected farmers. Neither did the government insist that this be done. But many farmers woke up to the reality of possible crop failures despite the highly-priced GM seeds. Meanwhile, the failure created grounds for the MNC to market another version of the technology. In 2007, MMBL released its second generation Bollgard II (BG II)—double-gene insect-protected cotton technology in India. It continued to license out the technology in a similar business model as it followed for BG I.

Seed technology has not always been available only through sale and licensing. Sammamma shares seeds. This is how it has been in her village and those around hers. The sharing allows for a steady flow of diverse context-specific planting material from the living environs of other farmers' fields. This is how farmers' seed know-how circulates amongst the informal sector. However, this is relegated by the state to being people's 'traditional' knowledge.

Sharing not only means giving a portion of something to others, but also using and enjoying something jointly with others. This is made possible only if one believes that the very thing to be shared—in this case the seed, cannot be private property. Farmers like Sammamma have either believed that seeds are the biological heritage of humankind or at least held them as common property resources.

In fact, the public sector has also benefited from this sharing; plant breeders in the national agricultural research system (NARS) have always had free access to farmers' seed innovations. These comprise the collections of germplasm now stored in national gene banks. International gene banks that collect and keep farmers' varieties in cold storage are also under obligation to maintain these seed collections as global public goods. The plant genetic material sourced from farmers is then passed on to either the public or private sector to develop new varieties to be further multiply the seeds for mass distribution. Now with the seed MNCs occupying a dominant position in R&D in seed technologies, they are reversing the trend. The MNCs in turn are the source of the seed technology, for which they charge. They do not share it for free.

For Sammamma sharing seeds is the norm. It can take place in many ways: gifting seeds, bartering seeds, exchanging seeds or even selling seeds. Both technology and ideology are now making this sharing impossible. At the physical level if the use of hybrid seeds is encouraged by government policy, then farmers get locked into buying them repeatedly every season (since hybrids lose their vigour in subsequent generations, saving them becomes pointless). Most GM varieties marketed in India are hybrids.

There is another assault on Sammamma's own seeds and the practice of sharing them; making the sharing illegal in certain situations.[5] This can happen through seed laws that outlaw saving of seeds and through intellectual property (IP) laws that make seeds the property of the 'inventor'/producer/technology provider. IP laws and policies originally meant to balance the interests of an inventor with larger public interest are now becoming a means to grant protection for proprietary technology. The very idea of sharing that is at the core of farmers' seed systems is undergoing change to make intellectual *property* the norm in this area.

Intellectual Property

Intellectual property is based on a belief system that the inventor is the sole owner of his/her invention, at least for the term permitted by law. The grant of IPR through a national or regional office, gives a set of economic rights to the developer/holder of the said technology. The extent of those rights is defined by law through intellectual property (IP) legislation. In the context of seed, patents and plant variety protection (PVP) are the two most commonly used IP concepts to control other's use of the planting material.

The idea of extending IP protection over seeds and planting material world over was planted by the multilateral system—World Trade Organisation (WTO). The WTO's Agreement on Trade-Related Aspects of Intellectual Property Rights (TRIPS) makes it mandatory for all WTO member countries to provide for IP in all fields of technology (including agriculture).[6] It incorporates the idea of having patents on seeds from USA, and also introduces the concept of plant breeder rights (PBRs) from a European Convention.[7] New IP standards extended to seed and planting material have been set by global trade rules; member countries like India are pushed into compliance.

For that reason there have both been changes in India's IP laws (such as amendments to the patent legislation) and new IP infrastructure specific to agriculture (such as the PBR law) that have been put into place. Though vide the amendment of the India's patent law in 2002, and insertion of Section 3(j) no patents on plants, including GM plants is allowed in India. Additionally, a new law—the Protection of Plant Varieties and Farmers' Rights (PPV&FR) Act, 2001, was legislated to provide intellectual property rights (IPR) to plant breeders. The irony is that this law also woos farmers into the IP system, by granting them similar breeder rights. This in effect gives farmers the legal right to exclude others, including farmers like Sammamma, from freely using and sharing the seed. Something that was held in common with other farmers—seed and planting material, is now being made the preserve of a single farmer or group of farmers, who first register the variety with the national level PPV&FR Authority.[8]

In India, while patents on seed *per se* are not legally allowed, they are allowed on particular GM constructs and microorganisms used by the plant biotech industry. This is how Monsanto exercises IPR over its GM products and processes in India. In fact, both MNCs like Monsanto and domestic seed companies apply and get PVP over crop varieties in India. Monsanto has IPR on the back of which it has been out-licensing its GM technology to Indian seed companies since 1997. The IP-protected technology becomes the seed major's rent-seeking property. MMBL has reportedly sub-licensed its proprietary Bt technology to about 50 seed companies in India for GM cottonseed production. The MNC's IP portfolio and the way it has and continues to use it, gives the MNC a near-monopoly position since its entry in the GM seed sector in India (Bhutani, 2016).

Price Setting

Technology fees have a direct impact on pricing. A business enterprise selling seeds will first as any other business want to recover its production costs. Pricing refers to all the methods that businesses use to set the price of their products. Another aspect of pricing is licensing. A technology-producer seed firm charges fees its downstream licensees. The licensees will predictably pass on that cost to their clients/customers, like Sammamma.

In India, the MNC has since 2004 been charging in the range of Rs. 1,100 to 1,200 for a seed packet of 570 grams (450 grams Bt cottonseed + 120 grams refugia) to be sown in an acre of land. By 2005 the company was charging Rs. 1,250 for the same packet. Cheaper illegal Bt cottonseeds were being sold in the market at prices between Rs. 800 to 1,200. The price of these GM seeds, whether legal or illegal, was higher than the conventional (non-GM) hybrid cottonseeds.

Theory also explains how the prices a firm can charge is related to elasticity of demand. This is best put by the economist Abba Lerner, who explains that the extent to which a firm can take advantage of its monopolistic condition will highly depend on the flexibility of its demand curve. If it is more rigid (steeper), it will only have to reduce its production in order to achieve a higher price. However the more flexible (flatter) the demand curve is, the less market power the firm has to increase prices.

The Monsanto group and its partners usually flex their muscle on that front near the planting season, when farmers are desperate to get seed in time for sowing. Although these firms have little maneuverability in pricing, each of them tries to fix a price for its seed products so as to compete with rival seed firms in the market and ensure large(r) sales. Yet they do not have room enough for strategic actions. As given the dominant position that Monsanto occupies in India, perfect competition does not exist.

In 2006 an official from the Union Ministry of Agriculture and Farmers Welfare (MoA&FW)'s Department of Agriculture and Cooperation (DAC) admitted that Monsanto in India was the sole provider of GM cottonseeds. Monsanto's own Annual Report of 2006 claimed that in India over 2 million smallholder farmers planted its Bollgard Bt cotton across 8 million hectares. In its own words, this was one of the largest year-on-year increases; this was because the total acres planted with this technology in India jumped 171 per cent from the prior year. By that time the company had begun charging much higher prices for its seeds.

From the point of regulation the power to set prices is shared between the centre and state governments. The centre and for that matter even the state officials can be quite out of reach for Sammamma. Yet they determine what her spending on seed will be. Cottonseed when included as an 'essential commodity' under the Essential Commodities Act (of 1955) empowers the Union Government to regulate production, quality, distribution, etc. of cotton seed and to curb the sale and spread of spurious seeds. The production, distribution, etc. aspects of cotton seed are also made subject to regulation under the *Seed Control Order, 1983* to regulate quality of seed irrespective of whether they are hybrids or GM or both.

It is under the Essential Commodities Act that the GoI through the MoA&FW issued the *Cotton Seed Price (Control) (CSPC) Order, 2015* on 7 December 2015. On 27 January 2016 a nine-member central price control committee was set up under the CSPC Order. On 8 March 2016 the said committee fixed a uniform price for Bt cottonseed for the financial year 2016-17 for the whole of India (see Table 1). There were different rates at which Bt cottonseed was being sold in the country. States such as Andhra, Maharashtra, Karnataka and later Telangana have state-specific laws to to fix the trait fees of GM seeds. But they had not imposed any cap on the sale price of a packet (450 grams) of these GM seeds.

Table 1: Prices Set by the Central Committee for 2016-17

Bt Cottonseed Price for	BGI	BGII
Seed Value	635	751
Trait Fees	0	49
Maximum Sale Price	635	800

Anti-Competitive Measures

There is a background to the current pricing problem of GM cottonseeds, which needs to be fully understood. The story commences in Hyderabad—city that is also termed as the country's seed industry capital. It is in the southern states of India that the GM technology was first introduced and it is also from that state that the 'price wars' began. In 2006, local farmers' groups complained to the state government about the rising price of Monsanto's GM seeds.

The Andhra Pradesh (AP) Government responded with raising the matter at the then Monopolies and Restrictive Trade Practices (MRTP) Commission. The Department of Agriculture in the AP Government initiated proceedings before the MRTP Commission, which was functioning under the Union Ministry of Corporate Affairs. [The MRTP law of 1969 and the Commission it set up, pre-dates the Competition Act, 2002 and the Competition Commission of India (CCI) and has since been repealed.]

This comprised a complaint against MMBL, Monsanto (USA), MAHYCO, Rasi Seeds, Proagro Seed Company Private Limited and Nuziveedu Seeds Limited (NSL). The state government, among other things:

- alleged that MAHYCO's price of Rs. 1,850 per packet was exorbitant and the component of Rs. 1,250 therein as 'trait value' was too large
- contended that the royalty fixed by MMBL was not proportionate to the actual cost incurred on the invention of the new technology
- accused Monsanto of imposing restrictive practices insofar as not allowing sub-licencees to transmit the technology to others.
- complained of "discrimination" in charging lesser trait value in the US (Rs. 108) and China (Rs. 34) for the same seed product.
- argued that there was no effective alternative to Bt cottonseed in the state, which forced farmers to cough up this high price.

On 11 May 2006, the Director General of Investigation and Registration (DGIR) of the MRTP Commission directed the company not to charge more than Rs. 900. The Commission also held that the MMBL was indulging in restrictive and monopolistic trade practices. This also as some sub-licensees like Nuziveedu Seeds Limited (NSL), were ready to sell the Bt cotton seeds at Rs. 800 but were forced by MMBL to instead sell them at Rs. 1,818. The Commission gave time until 10 June 2006 to MMBL to set a new technology user fee.

In the interim, the State Agriculture Minister in consultation with farmer leaders decided that the price for a 450 grams packet should not be more that Rs. 750 (inclusive of the technology fee). On 29 May 2006 the Agriculture Commissioner issued an order to that effect to MMBL's sub-licensees. In the same year MMBL filed a statutory civil appeal in the Supreme Court of India against the interim order of the MRTP Commission. The Supreme Court declined to stay the order of the AP Government, which had asked the company not to charge more than Rs. 750. (In 2009 the Supreme Court dismissed the company's appeal against the MRTP Commission order.)

In its home country USA too, the company has faced anti-trust proceedings. The Antitrust Division of the US Department of Justice (DoJ) in May 2007, required Monsanto and Delta & Pine Land Co. before proceeding with their proposed merger, to divest Monsanto's Stoneville Pedigreed Seed Co., multiple DPL cottonseed lines and other valuable assets, and to change certain cottonseed trait licensing practices.

The Competition Commission of India (CCI) functions as the anti-trust regulator post-MRTP Commission. It is meant to implement the Competition Act, 2002. This Act seeks to deal with issues such as price-fixing and limiting supply of goods, etc. regarded by this law as an 'abuse' of a dominant position. Acquiring a dominant position is not the issue, but abusing it is not permitted by law. Section 4 of the above-mentioned legislation clearly prohibits abuse of dominant position. In substance, 'dominant position' means the position of strength enjoyed by an enterprise (whether in the public or private sector) that allows it to act independently of competitive forces prevailing in the relevant market (Ramappa, 2006).

CCI itself is facing litigation from the seed industry. On 10 February 2016 the CCI held that there is *prima facie* case of contravention of Sections 3(4) and 4 of the Competition Act (abuse of dominant position) by the Monsanto group. Legal cases before the Delhi High Court, were filed by Monsanto against CCI's investigation orders. The MoA&FW had approached CCI in November 2015 to investigate the companies trade practices in India. Sammamma would have wanted to raise this matter herself, but she would also additionally expect governments to encourage farmers' own seeds, rather than leave them at the mercy of the market price. Farmers' seeds are competition for seed companies.

Legal Battles

A series of lawsuits on issues related to seed prices have also ensued at across different fora in India. Sammamma does not have the wherewithal to take the matter to court. Thus legal battles on seed-related matters either take the form of public interest litigation, or are undertaken by the seed companies who can afford it. In 2007 MAHYCO filed a writ petition before the High Court of AP due to the seizure by the seed inspectors of the hybrid cottonseeds being sold by MAHYCO without any authority.

The state government responded with passing the Andhra Pradesh Cotton Seeds (Regulation of Supply, Distribution, and Fixation of Price) Act, 2007 (hereinafter AP-CS Act). Other states like Maharashtra followed suit with similar state-level laws to deal with the issue of both price and assurance of quantity supplied. For example, in Maharashtra the affidavit to be submitted by a seed firm at the time of obtaining cotton seed sale licence requires it to fulfill the quantities of cotton seeds as mentioned in the District-wise marketing plan. This is to avoid any type of seed shortage situation in the market. Failure of compliance with this undertaking can lead to cancellation of license and legal action. The possibility of deliberate reduction in either production or supply to increase prices is also what needs regulatory oversight.

The seed industry also undertakes litigation to aggressively guard its IP, as its pricing tool. In 2008 MAHYCO filed a writ petition before the Delhi High Court, challenging the order passed by the Central Information Commission (CIC) directing the disclosure of information considered proprietary and confidential by MAHYCO. The High Court granted a stay against the order of the CIC.

In March 2013, the Agriculture Department of the Government of AP fixed the maximum sale price (MSP) of cottonseeds per packet of 450 grams as follows:

1. for GM Bt where non-Bt cotton seed is used as refuge seed
   @ Rs. 830 (with BG I Technology)
   @ Rs. 930 (with BG II Technology)
2. for GM Bt where red gram seed is used as refuge seed
   @ Rs. 762 (with BG I Technology)
   @ Rs. 862 (with BG II Technology)
3. for Conventional seeds @ Rs. 500

In April 2013, three domestic seed companies (sub-licensees of MMBL technology) along with the Seedsmen Association (representing about 400 seed producer companies and seed dealers in India) challenged the above MSP in a court of law. They filed a writ petition before the High Court of AP against the above-mentioned order. They were in particular aggrieved with the royalty (commonly known as 'trait fee'/'train value' in trade) fixed by the state government with respect of the two (BG) Bt cottonseed varieties. Though in principle they did not challenge the power of the government to fix the MSP, under the AP-CS Act, 2007. These sub-licensee companies were caught between what Monsanto charged them as royalty and what the state government ordered (see Table 2).

Table 2: Royalty Component of Sale Price Per Packet of 450 grams (2013-2014)

	For BG I Bt Cottonseeds	For BG II Bt Cottonseeds
As charged by Monsanto in India	Rs. 109.43	Rs. 163.28
As directed by High Court of AP	Rs. 50	Rs. 90

A decade after the legal battles on seed pricing continue. MMBL challenged the 8 March order of the MoA&FW, which capped the Bt cottonseed price. The MNC argued before the High Court of Delhi that the government had no role to play in setting the trait value. ABLE-AG also challenged the same price order in the Karnataka High Court.

The fiercest of legal battles are those being fought between the Monsanto group and the domestic seed companies that refused to pay any of outstanding high trait value fees to Monsanto. This led to an arbitration case filed by the MNC; it also brought IP infringement cases against its biggest sub-licensee Nuziveedu Seeds Limited (NSL). The Indian sub-licensee companies responded to this collectively by a case in the Mumbai High Court. These companies are members of the National Seed Association of India (NSAI). The NSAI members, with NSL at its helm approached the GoI to intervene. This led to the MoA&FW issuing the *Licensing and Formats for GM Licensing Agreement Guidelines, 2016.*

Through these guidelines, the central government sought to cap not only the upfront fee payable to the technology-licensing company, but also set the trait value that the licensor can charge to the licensees. The guidelines were withdrawn after the industry insisted that the trait value (license fee) is a matter of mutual agreement and must be based on the contract between the companies and not by government regulation. The biotech MNC threatens that unless "marketing freedom" is restored and "no official interference" is assured, it may have to pull out of India. But the question ought to be: how are Sammamma's interests to be protected?

Economic Agents

Even if seen from a purely economic point of view, at the receiving end of the pricing policies is the consumer-farmer; she is merely a price-taker. Sammamma has little or no influence in the politics of pricing. And she is perhaps the least powerful amongst those in the set of four economic agents particular to the problem at hand: herself the small woman farmer, the near-monopolistic foreign corporate who is the technology provider, the domestic seed producer companies and the governments (both at the centre and the state level) as the regulators.

Sammamma and other small farmers are targeted by industry as the consumer of the cottonseed. She is faced with two very different seed systems; the informal one in her village and the formal seed supply one. Both run on almost completely divergent principles. She and her kin may have spent many hours standing in endless queues to be able to even buy seed from the market. So she is also someone who is exploring a way out of market dependency on seeds. Till then her choices are limited to what the seed market offers—hybrids or GM seeds. What strategies and decisions the other agents adopt vis-a-vis pricing will directly affect her choices.

Secondly, there is the seed industry selling transgenic seeds within which the near-monopolistic corporate Monsanto has a dominant position. As a price-setting firm its payoffs are the profits it earns. Thirdly, there are relatively smaller firms in the seed industry that operate as seed producers in the market. The technology they choose and the scale of their operations tells on what and how much and what kind of seed they produce. In the present case these smaller firms get their technology from Monsanto. It is that market of GM seeds which is the subject matter of this chapter.

The fourth set of economic agents are the regulators, usually governmental agency that exercise oversight. The motivation of both the central and state governments is to ensure a steady supply of seeds to farmers, that too at reasonable prices.

Though in the problem at hand, it is both the executive and the judiciary that are seen regulating the price of seeds. So another set of actors who are having to take decisions on this subject matter are the judges before whom such cases are filed. The interplay between these economic agents determines the price at which seed technologies and seeds themselves are sold.

No Accidental Change

The understanding of near-monopolistic situations discussed herein, bolster the idea that there are no such things as natural monopolies (DiLorenzo, 1996). Just as he argues that the existence of economies of scale in water, gas, electricity or other 'public utilities' in no way necessitates either monopoly or monopoly pricing, likewise seed production too does not warrant near-monopolistic conditions. On the contrary it requires a non-centralised production system that is not concentrated in the hands of a few. Seeds need to be produced locally and consumed locally to be able to remain ecologically viable, culturally appropriate and politically relevant.

Moreover, monopolies can appear due to government intervention. It were the macroeconomic policies of the Government of India (GoI) that allowed MNCs like Monsanto's to get a foothold in the Indian market. In so much, the regulators should have anticipated the problems of price-fixing. The price wars that are recurrently fought are not between seed companies, but between the seed producers selling the GM seeds and the regulators at the state level. Yet as Murugkar, Ramaswami and Shelar (2007) show in their insightful survey of the Indian cottonseed market, the private sector has become an important supplier of varietal technology in agriculture. The power of proprietary hybrids is to charge a mark-up in price. So it is with GM seeds.

As far as the situation of small and marginal farmers in AP is studied, there is much to support the contention that apart from the issue of price, that of seed quality is critical. While farmers have the option to seek remedy under the Consumer Protection Act, 1986, but the seed industry lobbies the government to get its activities outside the purview of this legislation. In the vicinity of Sammamma's fields, some farming communities are experimenting with 'alternatives; through a participatory guarantee system (PGS), which seeks to give an assurance of organically grown organic seeds and grain for its network of domestic consumers.[9] This is in stark contrast to the information asymmetries that prevail for the consumers of the GM Bt seeds looked at in this chapter. This then goes to core of question—what remedies do farmers like Sammamma have if the seeds do not perform? Also, what if the GM seeds cause genetic contamination to neighbouring fields or her own non-GM crops? This makes the cultivation of GM crops even more risky.

It is low-risk low-investment farming that perhaps works best for small farmers like Sammamma. This also needs institutional arrangements that are low-cost (Patibandla and Sastry, 2004). To that it can be said that citizens of India now have a fundamental right to form co-operatives.[10] Given the high transaction and start-up costs involved with seed firms that merely offer 'techno-fixes' to small women farmers, another way of organising them is through locally organised co-operative seed collectives. Though in the interest of seed diversity a caveat is sounded against making these collectives simply one-variety producers/growers.

Women are generally not given an equal status as men in economic activities. One is in agreement with the line of thought that skill definitions are saturated with sexual bias and that 'economics' cannot be left unchallenged by the feminist critique (Phillips and Taylor, 1980). The value of women as seed keepers is constantly undermined. Seed legislation both in force and proposed are conceived of and implemented in a gender-neutral manner. This is despite the feminisation of agriculture (Vepa, 2005). Yet as Vepa conveys, one concurs with the viewpoint that there is fine balancing to be done between women their due recognition in the economy, while not overburdening them with seed work and conservation. The point being made is that they should have real choices.

But farmers' choices can actually be limited by grant of IP to seed companies. As planting material is made private property, restrictions can be imposed on farmers' access and use of seed and produce harvested from IP-protected seed. IP on seeds further the outgo of royalties for the breeder lines of the seed companies even though the basic raw material has been traditionally held by and therefore believed to belong to farmers. This is also where competition law and its enforcement also needs to come into play. There is little literature on the role regulatory bodies such as the CCI can play on this front. For previous analysis also shows that with stronger IPRs, the prices of GM seeds will rise (Basu and Qaim, 2007). High monopoly seed price can be a barrier for the small farmer. However, in one's view that could prove to be a blessing in disguise as it pushes farmers to seek alternatives and could take them towards the seed sovereignty they envision.

Much of the literature concerns itself with increasing access of small farmers to seed from 'outside'. However, this paper is to try and look at the possibilities within small farmer networks themselves. Farmers rely on multiple channels for their seed requirement. These include their own FSS, social networks, local haats, public sector and the seed companies. The latter cannot be allowed to become the sole suppliers. Meanwhile, as Basu and Qaim (2007) conclude, government has a role to play in order to ensure lower prices.

Choice in Name

Sammamma is the targeted consumer of cottonseeds. She has to buy the seeds from the formal market. Her budget constraints determine the quantity of seed she will buy. Theory tells us that as the price of seeds goes up, the money in hand also changes. This clearly has implications for her household budget. Having to allocate more of her limited income on seeds, implies that as seed prices and other related inputs go up, she has less and less in hand to satisfy other household needs.

The assumption here is that Sammamma is choosing to buy GM cotton seeds, though given the range of products available from different seed companies she has no preference for a particular companies' seeds. It is also assumed here that in the household the women are taking the decision, (for both literature and field exposure shows that oft men make seed choices and veer more towards cash crops).

The factual situation also indicates that there are not large differences between willingness to pay for new seeds amongst the women *sanghams*. Moreover a neighbouring farmer's choice can often influence one farmer's choice of seeds. If Sammamma buys a particular seed, by word-of-mouth, chances are her neighbours might buy the same one's too. This in economic theory is best explained by the Bandwagon effect.

Given the official neglect of local seed systems, which are interchangeably referred to as either farmer/informal/traditional seed systems; small farmers have to rely on the market for their seed needs. Else, the source of seeds is the barter or exchange amongst neighbours, relatives or small sales at the local grain markets/ village fairs. If local farmers start shifting to the formal seed supply system it disrupts the customary exchanges of seeds amongst the community. This is also because seed companies have the law on their side to prevent their IP-protected seeds from being sold or exchanged beyond a limit to maintain their market share.

When turning to the formal seed market Sammamma has to go by a value system dominated by economics. And it is not that she and the likes of her can negotiate a better price. In economics, a market is defined as collection of buyers and sellers that, through their actual or potential interactions, determine the price of a product. In this case, she has no say in determining the price of the seed products. She and the women sanghams may not always remain passive consumers, they may organise to approach the local administration and state government seeking intervention for affordable quality seeds. Apart from that they do not have an influence on the seed sellers. At most she and the *sangham* she is part of may collectively decide not to buy seeds from the market and try and grow, share and exchange their own seeds.

The public sector does not seem to be providing credible alternatives. Being one of the very few producers of the GM technology (the public sector bred GM cotton varieties have not done very well and are in no position to displace the space the MNC currently occupies) it has come to command a dominant position in the seed industry in the country. More importantly, there are no transition strategies to move to more agro-ecological farming systems, which also support Sammamma's choice of seeds.

Acceptance or Alternatives?

The GM seeds produced with the trait provided by MMBL is the one that has found wide acceptance in the market. That 'acceptance' too could have been engineered from its vantage point. For the business practices it engages in include:

- charging unreasonably excess prices.
- price discrimination across different locations (comparing USA, China and India).
- restricted selling/dealing of the product.
- product bundling, i.e. the companies seeds to be grown with a package of other agrichemicals also marketed by the same firm.
- seeking IPR and using them in a trade restrictive manner.

It could also be because of a lack of governmental and other support for the alternatives.

A monopoly is typically when there is one big seller who markets a unique product. It is also characterised by specialised information on the one hand and possible asymmetries in information on the other. Even though this is not a case of absolute monopoly, it points to information asymmetries at two levels. This itself is indicative of market failure. Sammamma does not have full information of the nature of the seeds. Due to this information asymmetry the small farmers cannot determine the quality of the seeds until they have bought and sown them.

The sellers of the product, in this case—transgenic cotton seeds, know their product much more than their buyers (whether the small farmers or the smaller seed companies). Thus, the consumers cannot make utility-maximising decisions when purchasing seeds/ accessing technology. And the law of the land does not offer them enough remedy in case of crop failure or failure of seeds. Even, the Right to Information (RTI) Act, 2005 gives cover to what business enterprises regard as 'confidential commercial information'.

Clearly with the information monopoly, at another level the

seller of the seed product knows more about its quality that the buyer does.

Over the years Monsanto has maintained its dominance in the GM crop market. Though it is not the size or market share of the entity that determines the dominance of its position. The law clearly lays down the factors to be considered by competition authorities when deciding this question of fact [Section 19(4) of the Competition Act, 2002]. The market shares of MMBL's competitors, the technological advantages it holds and the barriers to entry in the large seed market are some of the facts that need to be taken into consideration when not simply determining prices of seeds, but what seeds ought to be in circulation. But one legal provision that warrants specific mention is that of 'dependence of consumers on the enterprise' [Section 19(4)(f) of the Competition Act, 2002]. The consumers of MMBL and MAHYCO are not only the numerous Sammammas in Southern India but the many seed producing companies that use its Bt technology.

Yet the collusion in price fixing between Monsanto and the sub-licensee companies can also not be ruled out. It is interesting to read that the government pleader in the case before the AP High Court submitted that the petitioners are nothing but front people set up by the third respondent who had in fact filed a separate independent writ petition and having failed to get a favourable order therein, a fresh writ petition was engineered through the present petitioners under the guise of questioning the government orders of price fixation.

What is pertinent is that for their interests, the seed companies will come together. They co-operate, even though they may appear to compete in the market. Yet the industry would rather that the small farmers not come together in a co-operation. For that would give them more strength in lobbying the government for assured quality seeds and that too at reasonable price. Irrespective of the size and scale of the company, farm-saved seed (FSS) is the biggest competition to the big seed industry. Seeds are single-use goods. Sammamma needs them every season. If law and seed technologies do not encourage seed-saving, the farmer has to continually rely on external seed producers for her seed requirements.

Most economists believe that an optimum operation of the market leads to more welfare (Slot and Johnston, 2006). Agricultural policies in India liberalising the seed market, place much greater reliance on the market. Yet this is a case of market failure. Can Sammamma rely on the market to realise her 'seed sovereignty'? The seed market clearly shows that it cannot regulate itself—the market can not be left to decide Sammamma's fate. It is for such situations that regulation is required.

Situations for perfect competition also do not prevail in the seed market. The National Competition Policy (NCP) needs to address some these issues. The Draft NCP's Illustrative List of Parameters for Undertaking Competition Assessment includes checking if something 'creates and fails to address gender-based barriers'. Farmers' own seeds need to be encouraged. Another way to introduce more competition is for government policy to support farmer's own seed technologies to develop. Farmer-developed folk varieties are in fact used by (public and private) R&D as raw material from which to develop commercial products. This free-rider problem sans due compensation to the original seed producers needs to be reversed.

Moreover, issues around abuse of IP by powerful IP-holders need to be addressed. The PPV&FR law provides IP protection to the seed companies in question. The impact of this on competition in the seed market has to be assessed. The public sector has to step up with 'alternatives' to corporate seeds. This in turn requires agricultural R&D to be re-oriented to address the real needs of small farmers. Some of the women farmers like Sammamma are also involved in efforts to democratise agricultural research for development as it is defined locally.

Globally, new proprietary technologies in agricultural crops are fast changing the debate and the law is lagging behind. Given that an updated biosafety regime that also adequately factors in concerns of liability and redress is yet to be developed, the transgenic seed industry needs to be contained. The Biotechnology Regulatory Authority of India Bill, 2013 still under discussion seeks to provide for a regulatory framework for the use of GM seeds, but it does not deal with the issue of their price.

Agriculture policies stress too much on seed replacement ratio. This pushes farmers to use hybrid seeds (that come with a biological patent) that need to be bought every season thus guaranteeing profits for the companies while creating a recurrent expense for the small consumer-farmers, as Sammamma.

She and other women seed savers who are organising themselves need to be supported. This can facilitate the re-localisation of food and farm systems, with biodiverse multi-cropping which makes better sense for household nutritional needs in growing locally appropriate crops that are also more climate-adaptive. The need to encourage agro-biodiversity in seeds cannot be over-emphasised. Thus apart from attempting to insist on economic efficiency, the ecological rationality, social justice and political ideology too needs to considered. The country's new food security law also envisages a central role to women in household food security. It is important to realise the transformative power of gender-sensitive seed laws and policies and the implications of this for contemporary village India.

There is an express principle of policy that the Constitution of India directs the State to follow (Article 39):

The State shall, in particular, direct its policy towards securing

a. that the citizens, men and women equally, have the right to an adequate means of livelihood;
b. that the ownership and control of the material resources of the community are so distributed as best to subserve the common good;
c. that the operation of the economic system does not result in the concentration of wealth and means of production to the common detriment.

Thus the problem of seed pricing, and with it control over proprietary seed technology and the enterprises that market them, cannot be resolved simply by an economic perspective. 'Getting the prices right' is not enough. And while the rhetoric says that the market will take care of the farmers' seed requirements, it is shown here how in fact there are more than one condition present that point to market failure. This has a serious fall-out on the price that Sammamma pays for seeds. Forced to buy company seeds, she also pays the price of loss of her own seeds and with it her freedom.

NOTES

1. National Sample Survey Organisation data.
2. The Seeds Bill, 2004; full text available on the web site of the PRS Legislative Research: http://www.prsindia.org/uploads/media/1167468389/1167468389_The_Seeds_Bill_2004.pdf
3. William S. Gaud, the Administrator of the United States Agency for International Development (USAID) used the term 'Green Revolution' for the first time in the 1960s.
4. La Via Campesina Notebook No. 6 Our Seeds, Our Future May 2013 https://viacampesina.org/downloads/pdf/en/EN-notebook6.pdf
5. In PVP laws there are restrictions on the sale of seeds by farmers if the crop varieties are IP-registered.
6. Article 27(1) of TRIPS.
7. UPOV Convention, 1961.
8. The official data for the number of applications received from farmers and the number of plant variety certificates granted to registered farmers' varieties is available with the PPV&FR Authority in New Delhi and on its web site here: www.plantauthority.gov.in
9. http://ddsindia.com/pdf/PGS_certification_logo.pdf
10. The Constitutional (97th Amendment) Act, 2011 makes forming a *cooperative* society a *fundamental right* under Article 19(1)(i) of the Constitution of India.

REFERENCES

Basu, Arnab and Qaim, Matin. 2007. 'On the Adoption of Genetically Modified Seeds in Developing Countries and the Optimal Types of Government Intervention', *American Journal of Agricultural Economics*, Vol. 89, No. 3 (Aug., 2007), pp. 784-804, Oxford University Press on behalf of the Agricultural and Applied Economics Association.

Centre for Sustainable Agriculture. 2005. *Seed Sector in Andhra Pradesh*, International Institute for Environment and Development.

DiLorenzo, Thomas J. 1996. 'The Myth of Natural Monopoly', *Review of Austrian Economics*, 9(2), pp. 43-58.

Karl-Gustaf Löfgren, Torsten Persson and Jörgen W. Weibull. 2002. 'Markets with Asymmetric Information: The Contributions of George Akerlof, Michael Spence and Joseph Stiglitz', *The Scandinavian Journal of Economics*, Vol. 104, No. 2, pp. 195-211.

Mehta, Pradeep S. (ed.) 2007. *Competition and Regulation in India*, 2007, Jaipur: CUTS CIRC, XIX, 219.

Murugkar, Milind, Ramaswami, Bharat and Shelar, Mahesh. 2007. 'Competition and Monopoly in Indian Cotton Seed Market', *Economic and Political Weekly*, Vol. 42, No. 37 (September 15-21), pp. 3781-3789.

Patibandla, M. and Sastry, T. 2004. 'Capitalism and Cooperation: Cooperative Institutions in a Developing Economy', *Economic and Political Weekly*, Vol. 39, No. 27 (July 3-9), pp. 2997-3004.

Phillips, Anne and Taylor, Barbara. 1980. 'Sex and Skill: Notes Towards A Feminist Economics', *Feminist Review*, pp. 79-88.

Pindyck, Robert S., Rubinfield, Daniel L. and Mehta, Prem L. 2006. *Microeconomics 7th Edition*, Pearsons.

Pionetti, Carine. 2005. *Sowing Autonomy: Gender and Seed Politics in Semi-arid India.* International Institute for Environment and Development.

Pray, Carl E., Nagarajan, Latha, Huang, Jikun, Hu, Ruifa and Ramaswami, Bharat. 2011. 'Impact of Bt Cotton, the Potential Future Benefits from Biotechnology in China and India', *Genetically Modified Food and Global Welfare.*

Ramappa, T. 2006. *Competition Law in India: Policy, Issues and Developments,* Oxford.

Slot, P.J. and Johnston, A.C. 2006. *An Introduction to Competition Law*, Hart Publishing.

Swarna S. Vepa. 2005. 'Feminisation of Agriculture and Marginalisation of Their Economic Stake', *Economic and Political Weekly*, Vol. 40, No. 25 (June 18-24), pp. 2563-2568.

9

From Polyvalent Knowledge to Monovalent Knowledge: A Social Constructivist Account of Agricultural Knowledge Transition in a Village in Telangana

Chandri Raghava Reddy and Prasanth Kumar Munnangi

For centuries cultivation has been a way of life shaping the social, cultural, political and economic spheres of human organisation. Till the advent of crop sciences farming progressed by imitation. Improvements in the practices of crop cultivation were isolated random accidental improvisations which spread through the word of mouth and got established as practices over a period. The occurrence of these accidental inventions and innovations were sporadic and spatial, and communities worked hard on their adaptation and adoption. The improvisations added to the cumulative knowledge of cultivation and the accumulated knowledge was transmitted or passed on to the next generation. However, the most significant shift in the knowledge of cultivation occurred due to the emergence of crop sciences which provided a scientific understanding of crop physiology, soil, pest and diseases, weather, and nature's role in cultivation. Crop science, through its principles evolved certain standard practices which have proved to be advantageous over the practices hitherto used by farmers. Thus, over a period, the scientific knowledge on crop production marginalised community knowledge in all aspects of cultivation.

The epitome of scientific knowledge in agriculture is the Green Revolution. Byres (1981) observes that before the Green Revolution agriculture was based on indigenous knowledge where farmers used to grow crops with the cumulative traditional knowledge. But the Green Revolution turned agriculture into 'knowledge-based farming', as the new technology demands appropriate knowledge levels to achieve the desired productivity and efficiency. In the post-liberalised era, owing to multiple factors, agriculture in India is undergoing radical changes. With the opening up of the agriculture sector for private players cultivation became knowledge-intensive, commercialised, competitive and globalised.

India's agriculture is predominantly practised by small and marginal farmers operating small holdings for livelihood and survival. With the growing capitalisation of agriculture, Vasavi (2012) maintains that, these farmers are caught by the 'web of risks' such as low risk taking ability, lack of required technical knowledge, lack of access to working capital and marketing networks, low investment, low productivity and weak market orientation. The most significant feature of today's marginal and small farmers is that they entered into agriculture in their lifetime. They are new to the practice of agriculture, although their forefathers were involved in the cultivation of crops for others. Agriculture as an enterprise is new to these farmers. They entered into cultivation when agriculture was on the threshold of the second Green Revolution. Lured by the prospects of higher economic returns through self-cultivation by adopting commercial agriculture these sections of farmers have entered into cultivation. However, what is important to be noted is that their disposition towards knowledge of cultivation and the elements of cultivation like soil, water, seeds, etc. are different from that of those farmers who have already been into cultivation since a long time. It may be said that the young farmers who have entered into cultivation in the last two decades have a different worldview as regards cultivation from that of the farmers who have been there since three to four decades.

Besides, it is also important to note that the agricultural practices promoted by market forces and multinational corporations are leading to 'taylorisation of agriculture'. Farmers' aspiration for upward mobility through higher yields results in the adoption of the so-called modern scientific practices without a wholistic understanding of cultivation. It may be observed that farmers have shifted to crops that fetch them quick returns as has been witnessed in the sharp rise in the area under cotton and other commercial crops across the country. As a result, the traditional knowledge that was inclusive of all the elements of cultivation, i.e. soil, environment, biological organisms, cattle and farmers in a holistic manner is increasingly being replaced by knowledge that aims at yield and productivity only.

The marginal and small farmers who have newly entered the agricultural sector lack knowledge about new agricultural practices and are unaware of making 'choices' (Vasavi, 2012). Farmers' aspiration for upward mobility and the need to raise their income levels may be considered as another factor pushing farmers to adopt new agricultural technologies, new crops without adequate knowledge. As a result, the intensity of risk is increasing. The risk is inversely placed with the extent of landholding. In traditional agriculture, collective decision-making at the community level insulated risks to a greater extent (Omvedt, 1991).

In the context of increasing commercialization of agriculture, the intensity of competition among agribusiness players and the growing distance of the state from extension services has meant that agricultural practices are increasingly dictated by market-led ideology of higher yields. The result is the new norm of 'more yield per acre', forcing farmers to apply an undue amount of fertilisers in order to achieve higher yields. Such absorption and adaptation of fads, while displacing their own local knowledge systems, has also led to increasing 'agricultural deskilling' (Stone, 2007), which is the inability to use appropriate and relevant knowledge and practices.

Knowledge in Transition

Historically, the local agricultural practices, which were drawn from a shared repository of knowledge, were transferred within the region and were replicated and advanced. The knowledge system that evolved in tune with nature—soil, living organisms, crops, water usage, etc., over centuries has been rendered irrelevant as external input-intensive agriculture has crept into the technological frame of farmers. Crop rotation, intercropping, trap crops, use of cattle for agricultural and related operations, have become obsolete as they do not seem to augment yield directly. As scientific knowledge in agriculture, evolved in the research stations being privileged and transferred in the form of best management practices, the regional and local specificities of crop production have been given a go by leading to the maladies in agriculture.

Traditionally, agricultural knowledge and practices in India are shared among the community of farmers and passed down to the next generations through social and cultural practices. Such knowledge was local-specific, communitarian, open and embedded in the culture specific to the region. Knowledge was local-specific in the sense that cumulative knowledge was developed based on trial and errors of farmers in that region. It addressed the concerns of farmers with respect to suitable seeds, methods of cultivation, pests and diseases, etc. It was communitarian because it evolved through the collective enterprise of farmers. Such knowledge was available to all the farmers of the region either directly or indirectly. The local knowledge was also embedded in culture as many practices of cultivation were closely intertwined with religious, cultural, ethical dispositions of the farming community of the region. Although quipped for the stagnation of agriculture for a long period, the local knowledge must also be credited for the sync it achieved with the environment of the region.

Prajapati and others (2014) suggest that agriculture is moving to a knowledge-intensive mode of cultivation. They suggest that the transition in agriculture occurred in three stages. The traditional agriculture characterized by subsistence farming, transcended to preliminary modern agriculture. The preliminary modern agriculture was basically a market-oriented agriculture. This led to an advanced modern agriculture, which is said to be knowledge-oriented agriculture.

State and agri-business directed agendas that support market based inputs in agriculture and which seek to alter the very ecological bases of agriculture have promoted the erosion of local practices and knowledge. Local agricultural patterns and practices typically drew from a shared repository of knowledge, much of which were transmitted and reproduced through the social and cultural structures of agricultural regimes, having given way to use of external inputs. Vasavi (2012) contends that this has induced increasing dissonance between knowledge and know-how among farmers.

Polyvalent knowledge, according to Etzkowitz and Riccardo Viale (2010), refers to the emerging nature of knowledge that results from the interplay of theoretical, practical and interdisciplinary implications forming a common centre of gravity. The paper adopts the term polyvalent knowledge referring to the knowledge that considered different elements of cultivation, namely, farmers, soil, climate, biological organisms, cattle, etc in a holistic manner. It is argued that traditional knowledge was polyvalent as it placed all the elements of cultivation in an equilibrium and in sync with the local specificities of cultivation. The opposite of the term used is monovalent knowledge that emphasizes only one element of cultivation, i.e. yield. It is argued that the emerging nature of knowledge in agriculture, emanating from the institutions of sciences, emphasizes yield ignoring all other elements of cultivation. This knowledge is privileged over the traditional knowledge in the name of efficiency. Such knowledge is being made available to farmers by formal means of agricultural extension, i.e. state department of agriculture, and the agricultural scientific community, and informal sources of agricultural communication, i.e. input dealers, progressive farmers, etc. As a result of the privileged position of monovalent knowledge, polyvalent knowledge is obscured and is on the verge of extinction. The technological frame (Bijker, 1995) in the agriculture research, extension and market is oriented towards yield alone.

Bijker (1995) suggests that the technological frame is better understood as a 'frame with respect to technology'. The technological frame is the shared cognitive frame that defines members' common interpretation of an artifact. A technological frame can include goals, key problems, current theories, rules of thumb, testing procedures, and exemplary artifacts that, tacitly or explicitly, structure group members' thinking, problem solving, strategy formation, and design activities (Bijker 1995, 125). A technological frame may promote certain actions and discourage others. The present paper uses the technological frame referring to the knowledge on cultivation emerging from the agricultural scientists and corporate forces as the one that guides actions, and thinking of farmers vis-a-vis cultivation. The technological frame on cultivation aiming at yield alone provides the rationality for actions, and goals and structures farmers' thinking on cultivation. Using the social constructivist (MacKenzie and Wajcman, 1999) approach it attempts to understand the technological frame that guides the cultivation practices in the study village. Constructivist account helps us to understand the values and standards which evolve into the technological frame and have a bearing on farmers within the village context.

Profile of the Study Village

The study was conducted in Nainala village in Warangal district of Telangana which falls under the semi-arid tropical climate zone. The village has a long history of agriculture as its major occupation. It is located about five kilometres from the revenue headquarters indicating the greater amount of exchange of communication with the outside world. For decades, farmers in the village have cultivated multiple crops in irrigated and dry land. Major crops grown in the village are paddy, maize, cotton and turmeric. Crops are cultivated in both seasons, namely Kharif and Rabi.

Landholding Pattern

Landholding pattern in the village reflects the traditional socio-economic and political hierarchy. Based on the land ownership the households in the village may be divided into landholding and landless. The official records of the village of 2012 show the total geographical area as 1,554 acres, out of which the cultivable land is 1,143 acres (80 per cent). The cultivable land comprises 725 acres of dry land (cultivated under rainfed conditions) and 418 acres of irrigated land, and the remaining 411 acres (20 per cent) of land comprises houses, pond and barren land. Village pond (spread over 50 acres) and tube wells (numbering about 350) are the major sources of irrigation.

Data suggest that 437 (80 per cent) households own land and 109 are landless. Most of the land is in the possession of Yadava, Gowda, Madiga, Munnuru Kapu and Reddy castes. The numerically dominant caste (Yadava caste with 127 households) holds 389 acres of land constituting about 34 per cent of the total land in the village. The Gowda caste has 82 households who own 135 acres of land (12 per cent of the total land). Madiga and mala are the Scheduled Castes who hold 269 acres of land out of 1,143 acres of total land (constituting to about 24 per cent). The Reddy caste households are 16 who hold 92 acres of land with a share of 8 per cent of the total cultivable land. The Vaddera caste holds 25 acres of cultivable land. The Dudekula caste holds 39 acres (about 3 per cent) of land in the village. Vadrangi, Kamsali and Yanadhi castes hold less than one percentage of the total land holdings of the village.

Table 1: Caste-Wise Distribution of Irrigated and Rain-Fed Land (in Acres)

Sl. No.	Caste	Land in Acres			No. of Households
		Irrigated	Rain-Fed	Total	
1	Yadava	114	275	389	89
2	Reddy	78	14	92	16
3	Gowda	55	80	135	72
4	Madiga	40	170	210	71
5	Munnru Kapu	40	15	55	22
6	Chakali	30	53	83	31
7	Mala	22	37	59	9
8	Mudhiraj	16	18	34	52
9	Vaddera	14	11	25	53
10	Dudekula	6	33	39	13
11	Mangali	2	8	10	6
12	Kamsali	1	9	10	1
13	Vadrangi	-	1	1	1
14	Yanadhi	-	1	1	1
	Total	418	725	1143	437

Source: Village Panchayat Records, 2012

Data on landholding also reveal that about 63 per cent of the land is under rain-fed cultivation. The irrigated land constitutes to about 37 per cent which is largely owned by the dominant castes like Reddy and other OBC castes like Gowda, Mala, Chakali and Yadava, Mudhiraj and Munnuru Kapu. Yadava caste households own 114 acres of irrigated land, whereas 170 acres of land are possessed by Madiga caste households. Classification of farmers based on the extent of land cultivated suggest that nearly fifty per cent of the holdings are less than two and a half acres. About thirty-one per cent hold less than five acres while about twenty-one per cent hold more than five acres.

Table 2: Distribution of Land

Category of Farmers	Percentage of Farmers	Percentage of Land
Marginal Farmers (less than 2.5 acres)	48	24
Small Farmers (2.5 to 5 acres)	31	31
Semi-Medium Farmers (5 to 10 acres)	17	30
Medium Farmers (10 to 25 acres)	4	15
Total	100	100

Cropping Pattern

The major crops cultivated are paddy (*Oryza sativa*), cotton (*Gossypium Sp*), turmeric (*Curcuma Longa*), mirchi (*Capsicum Anmum*), groundnut (*Arachis Hypogoca*), and maize (*Zea Mays*).

Cotton, which can be grown under rain-fed as well as irrigated conditions (semi-dry), has emerged as the important non-food commercial crop in Telangana. In the study village cotton is cultivated in 380 acres (33 per cent of the total area under cultivation). The average cotton acreage is 2.71. Besides paddy and cotton, the most important crop in the economy of farmers of Nainala village is turmeric (*Curcuma longa*). It is cultivated in 190 acres by 189 farmers (17 per cent of the total area under cultivation). The average area under turmeric is 1.05 acres. The other important crops of the village are mirchi cultivated by 80 farmers in 140 acres, with an average of 1.75 acres and maize (35 farmers in 70 acres). Other crops like groundnut and pulses (green gram, red gram) are cultivated by 50 farmers in 63 (5.51) acres of land.

Table 3: Major Crops Cultivated

Crop	Area Under Cultivation in Acres (Percentage of Area to the Total Area Cultivated)	No. of farmers*
Paddy	300 (26)	220**
Cotton	380 (33)	140
Turmeric	190 (17)	189
Mirchi	140 (12)	80
Maize	70 (6)	35
Other Crops#	63 (6)	50
Total Area	1143	

* Each farmer may grow more than one crop in a particular season. This data is for the Kharif season 2012.

** Actual number of farmers.

\# include crops like groundnut and pulses like green gram, red gram, and beans.

The cropping pattern indicates the prevalence of commercial cultivation. Cotton is grown under rain-fed conditions by farmers belonging to all castes. Paddy as a food crop occupies the next position in terms of acreage, while turmeric emerges as the third most preferred crop. Cotton, turmeric and mirchi are the commercial crops cultivated by farmers for monetary returns. Paddy is cultivated in two seasons. Over the years because of the undue emphasis on paddy in the successive state policies, and by the Green Revolution paradigm paddy emerged as the most reliable crop.

Rise of Commercial Agriculture

Akin to the changes widespread across the country the study village presents the rise of commercial agriculture. Farmers in the village took to commercial cultivation in the late 1990s. Warangal district is one of the districts in Telangana where cotton and mirchi cultivation began on a commercial scale in a big way. Black soils are most suitable for cotton and mirchi cultivation as they have more water retention capacity. Even under rain-fed conditions these crops fare well in black soils. The commercial cultivation of these two crops started in the districts like Guntur, Prakasam and other districts of the erstwhile Andhra Pradesh along with paddy cultivation during the Green Revolution period. However, in Telangana, commercial cultivation of cotton and mirchi was not found till the 1980s. Cultivation of these crops began with the entry of entrepreneurial farmers from coastal Andhra into cultivation in Warangal district by taking lands on lease from local farmers. As the commercial cultivation of cotton yielded favourable results for these migrant farmers, local farmers began emulating them. The success stories of the migrant farmers reaping lucrative profits spread across the district attracting the attention of large and medium farmers. Initially, commercial cultivation of cotton began with the large and medium farmers and later on spread to the small and marginal farmers as well. More importantly small and marginal farmers began cultivating in the red soils as well under rain-fed conditions inviting troubles.

The commercial cultivation of cotton underwent severe stress in the post-liberalized period, which coincided with successive droughts (from 1993 to 2003). Unable to withstand crop losses on which farmers have invested heavily, many small and marginal farmers committed suicides. The entry of Bt cotton may be considered as another watershed in the commercialisation of agriculture in the district. What began with a small step Bt cotton cultivation spread like wild fire and today the situation is that about 95 per cent of cotton cultivating farmers use Bt varieties only.

Bt cotton cultivation in the village led to drastic changes in the cropping pattern. Farmers find it profitable to cultivate cotton and other cash crops than food crops since the returns from these crops is high. Farmers had to learn the new ways of cultivating these cash crops on commercial lines. With the entry of commercial cultivation farmers' orientation to cultivation changed to profits and yields. Cereals, pulses and other crops which were grown earlier gave way to cotton and mirchi.

Landholding and Education

A sample of a hundred farmers was selected out of 278 farmers (as per the official records, households owning land are 437, however, only 278 farmers are the actual cultivators while the rest have given their land on lease). The sample was used to observe linkages between landholding, education and years of experience in cultivation. Data on education reveal that out of 100 respondents 32 have no formal education. Out of these 32 respondents 31 belong to the marginal and small farmers' category. Out of 20 respondents who have studied up to primary level, twelve belong to the marginal farmers' category, five belong to small and three belong to the semi-medium farmers' category. In all, 52 respondents have less than primary education and out of these, 48 are marginal and small farmer categories. Out of 78 respondents from marginal and small farmers' categories 31 respondents (about 40 per cent) have no formal education.

Table 4: Landholding and Education Among Sample Respondents

Landholding	No Formal Education	Primary	Secondary	Intermediate	Graduation	Above graduation	Total
Marginal	20	12	11	3	2	-	48
Small	11	5	10	3	1	-	30
Semi-Medium	1	3	7	3	1	-	15
Medium	-	-	1	1	4	1	7
Total	32	20	29	10	8	1	100

Years of Experience in Cultivation

Apart from categorising farmers on the basis of landholding, the study also considered years of experience in cultivation as an important parameter to understand the shifting nature and pattern of cultivation. Experience in cultivation indicates the depth of knowledge farmers have on inputs and practices involved in farming. The study assumes that experience in cultivation has a direct bearing on the farmers' disposition towards cultivation. The technological frame which guides the actions, thinking and the outlook of farmers is dependent on their experience in cultivation. Disposition towards use of inputs and resources in crop production is influenced by farmers' experience in cultivation. It may be said that farmers who have been cultivating for the past three to four decades must have witnessed changes in cultivation after the introduction of the Green Revolution closely. They are also witnessing the changes taking place now. Thus, these farmers' understanding of cultivation practices and the rationale they offer would be different from the younger ones. Accordingly, based on the years of experience farmers are categorised into young, middle-aged and senior categories. Those who have less than ten years of experience in cultivation are categorised as young farmers, those with eleven to thirty years as middle-level farmers and those with more than thirty years of experience as senior farmers. A representative sample of hundred farmers from among the four categories of farmers namely, marginal, small, semi-medium and medium was selected.

Table 5: Years of Experience in Cultivation

Category of Farmers (years of experience in cultivation)	Percentage of farmers	Percentage of land
Young farmers (less than 10 years)	20	16
Middle Level Farmers (11 to 30 years)	50	54
Senior Farmers (more than 31 years)	30	30
Total	100	100

Landholding and Experience in Cultivation

Data suggest that there are 50 middle-level farmers and 30 senior farmers. Middle-level farmers are those who have cultivation experience in the range of eleven to thirty years. Out of these 50 middle-level farmers 38 belong to marginal and small farmers' categories. Out of 30 respondents who are categorised as senior farmers (who have more than 30 years of cultivation experience), 24 belong to marginal and small farmers' categories. There are only 20 young farmers among 100 respondents and 16 of them belong to marginal and small farmers' categories. It may be pointed out that the young generation across all categories of farmers is disinclined to be engaged in cultivation.

Table 6: Landholding and Experience in Cultivation

Landholding	Young	Middle level	Senior	Total
Marginal	7	24	17	48
Small	9	14	7	30
Semi-Medium	4	8	3	15
Medium		4	3	7
Total	20	50	30	100

Agricultural Knowledge and Information Sharing

To understand the prevalence of knowledge of cultivation in the community cognitive domain, data on the patterns of sharing agricultural information and knowledge were collected from the respondents. Generally, the successful practices get into the public domain within the village as farmers in the village forums share their experiences in the casual conversations and discussions. These open discussions often help disseminating the knowledge to reach farmers in the village. However, the extent to which knowledge is shared between farmers across caste and class categories is socially conditioned. In order to understand the issue of sharing agricultural knowledge, respondent farmers were asked whether agricultural knowledge is shared.

It may be ascertained from data that out of a hundred respondents sixty-seven reported that they do not share the information or knowledge with other farmers in the village. Out of these sixty-seven farmers who do not share, a large majority (36) are marginal farmers and 24 are small farmers. It is important to note that 75 per cent of marginal farmers (36 out of 48), and 80 per cent of small farmers (24 out of 30) do not share information with fellow farmers. On the other hand, a large majority of the medium and semi-medium farmers share information with other farmers in the village. Further probing on the patterns of sharing agricultural information and knowledge revealed that medium and semi-medium farmers belonging to castes like Yadava, Reddy, etc. share with other farmers in the village. Another important observation of the study is that most of the young farmers are open to sharing information and knowledge with other farmers when compared to senior farmers.

Table 7: Sharing of Agriculture Information

Category of Farmers	Sharing Agriculture Information with Fellow Farmer		Total
	Yes	No	
Marginal	12	36	48
Small	6	24	30
Semi-Medium	8	7	15
Medium	7	0	7
Total	33	67	100

In the evolving agrarian relations, the role of the community is declining as individuation in increasing at a fast pace. Farmers in today's context rely on information and knowledge sources which lie outside the village rather than on the sources within the village. As the community knowledge is claimed to be becoming irrelevant farmers appear to be disinclined to share knowledge with fellow farmers. Increasing importance to non-food crops, commercial cultivation, and market-linked production strategies have overtaken the practices which evolved within the community over a period in the village. But what is important to note here is the absence of information and knowledge sharing among farmers, particularly those belonging to small and marginal categories. It was observed by the researcher that anxieties of farming, for example, getting higher yields than other farmers, risks associated with advice or suggestions, incomprehensible practices (in the case of Bt cotton, farmers do not understand the scientific basis of insecticidal properties of the Bt cotton seed) contribute to the poor levels of knowledge and information sharing between farmers. It is also pertinent to mention the declining public, open spaces in the villages for the farmers to assemble.

Pest Management

Knowledge disposition towards pest management has witnessed a significant change over the years in the study village. Farmers were observed to be aware of the pesticides to control insect pests and fungicides for diseases on crops like paddy, groundnut, chilli, cotton, etc. Among the crops for which pesticides are used cotton stands at the top followed by chilli. Paddy and groundnut are also cultivated using pesticides, but to a lesser extent. Among the respondents, young farmers were observed to be using more pesticides than senior farmers. The reasons for more usage were time, efficiency, and availability of material. Young farmers reported that chemical pesticides are available in the market and are easily procured. Application of pesticides involves spraying of the chemical pesticide in the recommended dosage. However, farmers seldom follow the recommended dosage. Most of the young farmers were observed to be using more than required. What is important from the point of view of the present work is that despite the lacunae or gaps in the knowledge available with farmers regarding the usage of pesticides, all of them view it as an easy method to control pests. Knowledge about the alternative methods of pest control like trap crops, lighting fires at night, and crop rotation has declined. Some senior farmer respondents mentioned the usage of trap crops like marigold, castor, etc. in different crops, particularly in cotton. However, with the advent of pesticides farmers never bother about such knowledge as they feel that pesticide usage produces a more superior effect than other methods. Although the externally sourced pesticides cost more, farmers prefer them as there is an instant result. In their anxiety to get more yield farmers tend to favour practices which give immediate results. The traditional knowledge available with senior farmers has become irrelevant in the present context, not because the methods are ineffective, but the absence of instantaneous results, and lack of ready availability of material when compared to pesticides.

Declining Interest in Animal Husbandry

Animal husbandry has been an integral part of Indian agriculture. For centuries, Indian agriculture witnessed close linkages between crop production and livestock. Cattle not only serve the needs of farmers in cultivation but are also a symbol of status. Farmers who owned more cattle derived higher social status when compared to those who do not. Similarly, sheep rearing has been a common interest among farmers. Till the introduction of machinery in agriculture, cattle were attached to farmers' social status. A number of religious or seasonal rituals and ceremonies accord a prominent place for cattle. However, over a period there has been a significant change in the attitude of farmers towards cattle rearing. With the introduction of tractors and tractor-drawn tools farmers have lost interest in cattle rearing. The other important contribution of cattle and sheep was manure, which is called farm yard manure. It was an essential part of cultivation as every farmer collected and applied farm yard manure in the field.

Table 8: Caste-Wise Distribution of Livestock

Sl. No.	Caste	No. of Cattle	No. of Sheep	No. of Goats
1	Yadava	70	500	200
2	Madiga	42	40	25
3	Gowda	38	20	9
4	Reddy	27	-	-
5	Chakali	22	-	-
6	Munnuru Kapu	22	-	-
7	Mala	16	20	15
8	Dudekula	10	15	6
9	Mudhiraj	9	-	-
10	Mangali	4	-	-
Total		260	595	255

It may be observed that the Yadava caste respondents own more livestock than other caste farmers. Similarly, the Madiga caste respondents also own livestock but to a much lesser degree than the Yadava caste respondents. It was reported by farmers that at least till two decades back there used to be the system of community grazer, who would take care of the grazing of cattle in the common grazing lands of the village. The person was hired by all the farmers by giving foodgrains at the time of harvest. Such a system collapsed with the emergence of cash economy, Green Revolution and the decline of grazing lands in the village. The decline in grazing lands is due to the increase in cultivable area under borewell irrigation which entered the village in the late 1980's. As a result, every farmer who owned cattle had to hire an extra hand to rear cattle or spare extra time of his own.

With the onset of nuclear families, cattle rearing has become burdensome. Sparing time and labour on rearing cattle is viewed as a burden by the farmers and their family members. It was observed in the study that women in these families do not show much interest in rearing cattle. As women, who play a critical role in maintaining milch cattle, do not show interest, men in the family are disinclined to rear cattle. While senior farmers and their family members appreciate rearing cattle for milk and manure, the younger generation appears to be showing disinterest. Perrumalla Narasaiah, aged 60 years, a marginal farmer, belonging to the Gowda caste observes that,

> In the past ten to fifteen years the number of livestock in the village has decreased. Farmers, particularly the younger ones, are not willing to spend time and energy on cattle rearing. They prefer hiring a tractor for ploughing and chemical fertilisers than rearing cattle. It is also a fact that the small and marginal farmers do not have space near their houses to rear cattle. Moreover, the common grazing land has shrunk over the years. What once used to be fallow land, is now converted into cultivable land.

It was reported by farmers in the village that they are aware of the benefits of organic manure like farm yard manure. In fact, there is a heavy demand for it in the village. But lack of its availability forces them to opt for chemical fertilisers. Small and marginal farmers can neither afford to maintain cattle, nor can they buy farm yard manure. A young farmer respondent observed that

> organic manure packets should be made available in the shops where we buy chemical fertilizers. If the government gives financial support to rear cattle for producing manure, farmers would be encouraged. Instead of giving a subsidy on chemical fertilizer the equivalent amount can be shared with farmers which will encourage them to rear cattle and sheep which will make the organic manure available in the village itself. This will definitely help to improve soil fertility significantly.

What is interesting to note here is that farmers are also aware that continuous usage of chemical fertilisers depletes soil quality over a period. They have reported their observation on soil losing its fertility levels in the last two to three decades. In spite of this, farmers were observed to be using chemical fertilisers in order to increase yield. It was also observed that farmers are aware of the beneficial impact of the organic fertilisers like farm yard manure, green leaf manure, etc. All the respondent farmers suggested that organic manure enriches soil fertility. However, the results, in terms of high yield, are witnessed after the continuous usage of organic manure for a long time. Senior farmers are well aware of the potential of organic manure as they use it regularly in the field. The young farmers are more interested in instant results and tend to use chemical fertilisers.

Young farmers find it convenient to apply chemical fertilisers rather than organic manure for the reason that the preparation of organic manure, transferring it to the field and its application is time and labour-intensive. Therefore, they favour using chemical fertiliser rather than organic manure. As organic manure preparation, for example, farm yard manure, demands prior planning for preparation and is linked to own cattle, and also that organic manure does not show immediate results young farmers prefer chemical fertilisers which can be sourced instantly from the market and give instant results (in terms of high yield). Young farmers were reported to be unaware of the long-term benefits of organic manure. Disinterest among farmers in general towards organic manure is also due to its non-availability in the village as the cattle population is fast declining. Joint families allowed cattle rearing as the old people, women and often children of the family used to take care of the cattle. With the disintegration of joint families, a farmer living with his wife and children feels burdensome to rear cattle. Villages are now witnessing a shift towards decoupling of cattle rearing from farming as well as social status. Tractors replaced cattle as the status symbol in the agrarian social structure. In fact, farmers who rear cattle are seen as traditional. Every farmer, irrespective of the extent of landholding, prefers to use tractors for all the farm operations. The use of cattle for ploughing was stopped long ago in the village. As the time taken for ploughing using a tractor is less when compared to a cattle-drawn plough, farmers prefer the former. It may be mentioned that farmers prefer spending less time in farm operations.

Changing Nature of Work

Farming is the primary activity for rural people in the country. Agriculture employs more than 50 per cent of the total workforce in India (*Economic Survey, 2017-18*). Nevertheless, within the rural economy, the percentage of income from non-farm activities has also increased. In other words, engagement of rural population in non-farm occupations has increased. It is important to note that although the area under cultivation has increased the amount of time people spend in non-farm occupations are increasing. This was witnessed in Nainala village.

It was reported by farmers that earlier they used to spend more time in the field. They used to start the day at six in the morning attending cattle and irrigating the crop. They used to come for lunch around eleven and rush back to the field where they spent time till six in the evening. But now, respondents report that, farmers, including the small and marginal would not like to spend more time in the farm. Although they cultivate on their own using family labour, they neither prefer to spend the whole day in the farm nor for a long time during the crop season. It should be mentioned that farmers, including the small and marginal, have turned to commercial cultivation which require more investment than food crops. Despite this, farmers prefer to spend less time in the field. The reasons were ascertained from the respondent farmers. It was mentioned that a majority of the farmers—small, marginal, and even semi-medium—would like to undertake other income-generating activities, either in agriculture or in non-agriculture, to earn extra money to support their families.

After the launching of the Mahatma Gandhi National Rural Employment Guarantee Programme (MNREGP) farmers find it convenient to take up such employment in the pre-lunch time and perform agricultural activities in their fields in the latter part of the day. In fact, farmers suggest that entry of MNREGP changed the whole notion of work and employment in the village and even in the region. The other important reason for spending less time in the field is reported to be mechanisation. As machines for different activities have entered the village all categories of farmers prefer hiring machines to complete the task early and take up income-generating activities which will support the family till the crop is harvested. Offering their labour for daily wages is also linked to the changing economic and agricultural situation in the village. As discussed, farmers have undertaken commercial agriculture in a big way necessitating huge investment by their economic standards. To meet the investment needs, farmers offer their labour to earn cash. The other reason is that farmers are well aware of the risks associated with commercial agriculture. As any crop loss would incur debts, farmers prefer to save some money earned through wage labour. It was also observed that because of the increased transportation facility between their village and the nearest town farmers prefer to opt for wage labour work in the town. Most of them were reported to be engaged in house construction work.

Owing to increased opportunities for wage labour, the marginal and small farmers take up such work instead of spending time in their farm. To compensate for their absence, they encourage their family members, particularly wife, to take care of the farm. It was found more prominently among the small and marginal farmers, especially from the Dalit and other backward castes in the village. It is important to note that such a trend is largely confined to young men from these castes. At the time of important operations in cultivation, men visit the fields. Farmers from other castes having more than five acres of land are found to be spending more time in their farm and visit the farm regularly, at least once a day when compared to small and marginal farmers. It was also found that senior farmers have a great reverence for and attachment to their farms and thus visit them regularly when compared to young farmers.

It was observed in the study village that the availability of agricultural labour has been shrinking progressively every year. Many senior farmers have complained about the present situation of agricultural labour while young farmers are coming to terms with it through mechanization. Senior farmers from the medium and semi-medium category observe that the present generation of agricultural labour is not skilled in agricultural operations. *Chatla Sathaiah*, one of the senior farmers, complains that the 'present youth have no stamina that we used to have at that age. A young agricultural labourer cannot handle laborious works for a long time during the day. That is why they prefer mechanization. I think that they have no stamina because what they eat today is chemical-based food. We used to consume all types of cereals produced without using chemicals. Hence, we had greater endurance and resistance.'

On the other hand, young men and women, whose parents were agricultural wage labourers, feel that it is not worth spending the whole day out in the field bearing the hot sun (or rain or cold) doing agricultural operations. Given a chance they prefer taking up non-farm-based works. It was observed that many landless labourers and even some of the small and marginal farmers go to work outside the village, in the nearby towns, by autorickshaw for daily wages. The wages are more when compared to agricultural works. And also, the payments are immediate when compared to farm labour. Increasing opportunities for work outside the village is one of the reasons for the shift from agricultural work. Also, the increased transportation facilities enabled greater mobility from the village.

Conclusion

The agricultural knowledge before being scientized was local-specific, communitarian, open and embedded in the culture. Knowledge was local-specific in the sense that cumulative knowledge was developed based on trial and error of farmers in that region. It addressed the concerns of farmers with relation to suitable seeds, methods of cultivation, pests and diseases, etc. It was communitarian because it evolved through collective enterprise of farmers. Such knowledge was available to all the farmers of the region either directly or indirectly. The local knowledge was also embedded in culture as many practices of cultivation are closely intertwined with religious, cultural, and ethical dispositions of the farming community of the region. With the adoption of the Green Revolution, such knowledge became irrelevant to a great extent.

Changes in the content of inputs altered the contours of knowledge of cultivation radically. Inputs such as improved seeds, fertilisers, insecticides, herbicides, and use of mechanical power have become important factors of cultivation in the Green Revolution paradigm. And knowledge about these new inputs became obligatory. They have substituted organic manure, animal power and farm-retained seeds (Kumar, 2016). The knowledge system that evolved in sync with nature—soil, living organisms, water, etc., over centuries has been rendered irrelevant as external input intensive agriculture made into the technological frame of farmers. Indigenous knowledge in agriculture is a cumulative body of practices evolved over centuries based on observation and experimentation. Indigenous knowledge reflects the technological frame of the given culture or society. It is passed down or transmitted from generation to generation through social and cultural structures and practices. With the introduction of the Green Revolution paradigm and the commercialization of agriculture, the shift from indigenous practices to the scientific knowledge-based practices has taken place.

It was observed that farmers' practices or knowledge of such practices is not directly received from the extension personnel or agricultural scientists. Rather, it came through several sources like progressive farmers, input dealers, extension personnel, fellow farmers, etc. Knowledge thus received has undergone several modifications and farmers adopted the practices based on social, economic and cultural factors. For instance, a small farmer adopts cultivation of cotton (using Bt cotton seed) in dry land (which is rain-fed). Cotton cultivation in dry land using high-cost Bt cotton seeds is a risky practice because any delay or unseasonable rain would affect the crop growth and yield drastically. Moreover, the usage of chemical fertilisers for cotton crop, in the absence of assured irrigation is nothing but inviting trouble. However, small and marginal farmers were observed to be adopting such practices in the study village.

The reason for the evolution of such knowledge is located in the technological frame within which farmers as a community carry out cultivation in the village. First of all, in the commercialisation of agriculture crop is seen as a means to earn more money by selling the produce in the market. In other words, cultivation of crops is associated with the economic aspirations of farmers and their families. Related to this is the understanding of farmers on productivity and yield. It was observed that in the interactions between farmers, the discussion always centred on yield. In fact, yield was observed to be a key discussion point which is used as a parameter to assess a farmer's social and economic standing. The farmer who gets more yield is privileged over others. As yield is directly linked with the income the farmer is going to make, those farmers who reap more yield stand tall among fellow farmers in the village. Those who cannot make such yield attempts to emulate the successful one without bothering to look at his/her economic and farm conditions.

The technological frame that evolved over a period, after the introduction of commercial agriculture was observed to have influenced other practices of cultivation. The technological frame within which farmers operate now has replaced the earlier notions of cultivation rooted in tradition. It was observed that all the farmers, irrespective of caste, size of landholding and educational background have used chemical fertilisers to augment yield. Farmers use chemical fertilisers to increase productivity per acre and yield per acre. All farmers in the study village use chemical fertilisers, although they are aware of the increased cost of production. It may be mentioned that farmers associate chemical fertilisers with greater yield.

It may be said that there is a perceptible change in the understanding of farmers towards crops and their cultivation practices. The change is prominent in the usage of seeds, chemical fertilisers, pesticides, and in the cropping pattern. Mechanisation or use of tractors in cultivation has been on the rise. Notions on cattle, use of organic manure, non-pesticidal control of pests, etc. have been witnessed to be declining in the study village. These changes are the resultants of evolving knowledge forms among farmers. The reason for the evolution of such knowledge is located in the technological frame within which farmers operate. The knowledge which privileges time, efficiency and productivity has replaced the knowledge which was sustainable and in tune with nature. It may also be said that the technological frame, which guides the thinking and actions of farmers, has evolved as a result of changes in the wider social and economic context. In other words, increasing nuclear families in the village caused the decline of cattle population and the increased usage of chemical fertilisers. Similarly, commercial cultivation emphasizes yield rather than the long-term impact of inputs on soil fertility.

It was observed that there is a significant change in the disposition of farmers, particularly young farmers, towards cultivation. First, they see cultivation as an entrepreneurial activity with the sole aim of making more money by increasing yield. Second, soil is viewed as a mere medium for cultivation without bothering about the fact that it is a host to many beneficial biological organisms. Third, decoupling of cultivation from cattle rearing. Cattle rearing is seen as a time-consuming burdensome activity with limited returns. The beneficial effects of cattle are ignored. Fourth, time spent on cultivation practices. Farmers, particularly the young farmers, are disinclined to spend more time in the farm or on cultivation-related activities, and hence the increased usage of tractors, chemical fertilisers and pesticides.

The paper finds that there is a shift in the knowledge base of the farmers from the one that considered all aspects of cultivation, namely, soil, crops, other biological organisms, the environment to the one that considers yield alone. If the traditional knowledge focused on the optimum usage of all the inputs of cultivation the scientific knowledge focused on maximum usage of input for maximum yields. The knowledge that evolved over centuries recognises the limitations set by nature on cultivation. However, modern scientific knowledge in agriculture views cultivation in terms of factory production. The scientific knowledge stresses higher yields ignoring the cost of cultivation or suitability of certain practices. Thus, it may be said that the emerging knowledge form is monovalent in the sense that it focuses only on yield while the traditional knowledge was polyvalent as it emphasized the holistic approach to cultivation. The nexus between nature and its flora and fauna, climate (rainfall) of the region, cattle and associated animals, and farmers has been broken. The 'taylorisaiton of agriculture' that has crept into the villages emphasizes yield, and time spent on cultivation operations.

The paper also finds that although modern scientific knowledge is privileged, traditional knowledge has not been replaced completely. The displacement of traditional knowledge was appeared to be varied across the spectrum. Senior farmers who have seen cultivation before the entry of the Green Revolution are more inclined to preserve traditional knowledge. It was witnessed that this section of farmers still follows certain practices which are labelled as traditional. However, young farmers, who entered cultivation after the beginning of the Green Revolution, are disinclined to adopt the traditional practices not just because of the fact that they have not witnessed the beneficial results of traditional knowledge but also because of their anxiety for getting more yields. They tend to associate traditional knowledge with low yields.

In the process of prioritisation of productivity and yield, which got into the technological frame of farmers, indigenous knowledge appears to have become irrelevant or inadequate. The empiricist positivist Green Revolution paradigm substituted the knowledge that is non-positivist, holistic and polyvalent. The erosion of the traditional knowledge base in cultivation is gradual and significant. In crops like paddy, wheat, maize, cotton the use of traditional knowledge is marginalised to a great extent. Adopting the constructivist method, the paper attempts to understand the social and cultural factors influencing the transition in the knowledge on cultivation of crops. The paper finds that the evolving nature of knowledge is monovalent in the sense that it focuses only on yield replacing the polyvalent knowledge that was holistic.

REFERENCES

Bijker, W.E. 1995. *Of Bicycles, Bakelites, and Bulbs: Towards a Theory of Sociotechnical Change*, Cambridge, MA: MIT Press.

Byres, T. 1981. 'The New Technology, Class Formation and Class Action in the Indian Countryside', *The Journal of Peasant Studies*, 8(4): 405-454.

Economic Survey 2017-18, Government of India.

Etzkowitz, Henry and Viale, Riccardo. 2010. 'Polyvalent Knowledge and the Entrepreneurial University: A Third Academic Revolution?', *Critical Sociology*, 36(4), pp. 1-15.

Kumar, Vijaya S. 2016. 'Institutional Failure and Farmers' Suicides in Andhra Pradesh', *Social Change*, Vol. 36, Issue 4, pp. 1-18.

MacKenzie, Donald and Wajcman, Judy. (eds.) 1999. *The Social Shaping of Technology*, Buckingham: Open University Press, pp. 28-40.

Omvedt, Gail. 1991. 'Towards Greening the Revolution', *Economic and Political Weekly*, November 16, 2613-2614

Prajapati, M.M., Patel, R.N., Dhandhukia, R.D. and Solnaki, K.D. 2014. 'Impact of Agricultural Modernization on Sustainable Livelihood Among the Tribal and Non-Tribal Farmers', *Journal of Agricultural Extension and Rural Development*, 6(4), 138-142.

Stone, Glenn D. 2007. 'Agricultural Deskilling and the Spread of Genetically Modified Cotton in Warangal', *Current Anthropology*, Vol. 48, No. 1, pp. 67-103.

Vasavi, A.R. 2012. *Shadow Space: Suicides and the Predicament of Rural India*, Gurgaon: Three Essays.

10

From Grain to Gain: Mapping the Socio-Cultural Dynamics of Agribusiness in a Village of Uttarakhand

Santosh K. Singh

Introduction

'Agriculture', wrote David Ludden (1999: 19) very perceptively, 'is humanity sculpting the earth, designing habitats, making a landscape as a kind of architecture, and producing symbolic domains that form the spatial attributes of civilisation.' The traditional agricultural environment and its universe were woven into religion, caste, deities, symbols and values. Lands, seeds and humans were as much units of production as elements of larger religio-cultural universe. The culture of agriculture displayed sharp dichotomised spaces of the sacred and the profane. Use of agricultural produce for gain and trading was considered sinful, ploughing by women was considered profane and while some grains could be indispensable part of religious rituals, others were strictly prohibited.

What is interesting, however, is that traditional societies in the past everywhere have shown similar inclinations. The idea of business and profit making or gain clearly had an aura of illegitimacy associated around it in most of the traditional societies. Catholic churches' annoyance with the business activities has been legendary. The Roman Church had always regarded the merchants and their activities with a dubious eye. Heilbroner (1967: 13) wrote: "The idea of gain, the idea that one should ceaselessly strive to better his material condition is an idea which was quite alien to the great lower and middle strata of Egyptian, Greek, Roman and medieval culture, only scattered through Renaissance and Reformation times and largely absent in the majority of Eastern civilisation. In the Middle Ages, for example, the church taught that 'no Christian ought to be a merchant and behind that dictum lay the thought the merchants were disturbing yeast in the heaven of society.' Not only is the idea of gain by no means as universal and ancient as we sometimes suppose, but the social sanction to the notion of profit and gain is even more modern and a recent development. Even to our pilgrim forefathers, the idea that gain might be a tolerable-even a useful-goal in life would have appeared as nothing short of doctrine of the devil." The central argument here is that the idea of profit was not as much a pursuit diffused throughout the society earlier as much as it developed in modern times.

The Indian context too is no different. This is most visible in the domain of agriculture. For instance, the universe of agriculture has traditionally been more of a part of the religious domain with every process and even equipment carrying sacred connotations. References in the ancient texts about land, seeds and human labour have been deeply enmeshed in a religio-sacred environment. Agrarian relations and the factors such as land, seed and human labour have been found to be intimately linked and embedded into the larger religio-cultural contexts and rituals and thus are a very defining part of the normative structure of society. It perhaps explains why grains or crops are treated with so much reverence. The seeds, therefore, as a product of the agricultural realm are as much a social product.

There is a plethora of studies available noting the normative inter linkages of the domain of agriculture and the elements such as eating and cooking to the larger societal culture (Douglas, 1966; Khare, 1976; Vatuk, 1978). These studies essentially underline that food is not a neutral object within Indian culture. Food, for instance, is perceived to have more than nutritive qualities as it lays the foundation of both the physical and moral fibre of an individual (Belliappa and Kaushik 1978). Similarly there are references about *satvik* and *tamsik* food mainly highlighting the causation between the kind of food one eats and its resultant qualitative impact on the personality of an individual (Vasavi, 1994, 1999; Daniel, 1984). In a similar vein, land has been likened to 'mother nature', as a woman and notions and cycles of reproductive behaviour patterns in human beings mark the nomenclature of agrarian discourse and its harvesting patterns. Radhika Chopra provides a glimpse of this interlocking between culture and agriculture from her work in rural Punjab:

> Upturning of the first furrow was undertaken by married men; the Punjabi term for cultivator is *khasam*, which is also the term for husband, and it would perhaps be more accurate to translate the term *khasam*, when used in the context of agriculture, as husbandsman. It is the husbandsman who parted the earth (*cheer*: furrow; as well as the verb for making furrows or partings), with the ploughshare (*phala)*, paying particular attention to the first field, the *lari*, also a term for a bride. *Phalayee* was the term for the copulation of cows and buffaloes and it is related to the word phalanx, the organs of generation which propagate *phal* or fruit (Chopra, 1994: 85).

The role of agriculture as a connecting link between man and nature is clearly manifested through these analogies to reproduction. Chopra further writes:

> Just as the bullock plough or tractor was driven by the husbandsman, the seed was also sown by men. The term for seed, *bi* was also the word for spermatozoa and it was clearly the task of the husbandsman. The ploughing of at least the first field, the *lari,* and the sowing of the *bi* by the husbands man acquired their meaning when juxtaposed with the prohibitions upon those prevented from performing these tasks-women and bachelors (Ibid., 85).

The primacy given to the staple diet and cereals for internal household consumption, in contrast with the crops meant to be marketed and money oriented is another representation of how the idea of profit and gain are construed as violative of the religio-sacred arrangement between nature and man. Instances of certain crops considered impure and inauspicious by virtue of the fact that they were grown primarily for the market further corroborate the thesis that agriculture in its pure sense remained largely averse to the instinct of profit making. The simultaneity of the rhythm of the agricultural cycle to the pattern of the socio-cultural and religious calendar has been well documented (Srinivas, 1976; Chopra, 1994; Vasavi, 1999) and it is another significant occasion where the organic and symbiotic relationship between agronomic domains with the larger socio-cultural universe is on display.

The grain was understood not merely in terms of its physical qualities, weight, form or colour, but also in terms of the quality of the future and the potential of prosperity inherent in it. Pierre Bourdieu also observes a similar trend in his study of an Algerian peasant community where he finds a link between the significance of staple grains and the quality of future prosperity they evoke (Bourdieu, 1963; Chopra, 1994). The manner in which, for instance, potato which is a cash crop in Punjab is treated in a non-sacred manner; in sharp contrast to the food crop like wheat which is surrounded with many rituals from field to home only establishes that the market is clearly considered the domain of profane. Reactions towards hybrid seeds, for example, articulate similar sentiments of aversion towards technology, market and profit-orientation in a traditional agricultural universe. Vasavi's ethnographic work from Bijapur in Karnataka highlights this orientation:

> Just as associations were made between strength and dry or organic grains, and between weakness and wet grains, the evaluation of hybrid seeds is extended to both the physical and moral effects of consuming them. Noting that hybrid seeds are delicate, susceptible to disease, and need expensive chemical and technical inputs, village residents, especially those of the older generation, refer, to the current period as 'hybrid period' (*hybred kala*) and to themselves as 'hybrid people' (*hybred mandi*). Unlike the sturdy organic (*Javari*) seeds, they are like the hybrid seeds that they now sow-'delicate (*sukshme)*, diseased *(rogi*) and needing constant attention' as one woman put it' (Vasavi, 1999: 121).

It is therefore amply demonstrated that the traditional agricultural universe has a strong notion of sacrality associated with its elements and processes. The idea of purity and sacredness is eminently pronounced. Any surplus or amassing of food was considered sinful and inappropriate and it was advised to be given to the needy.

The above discussion clearly shows the overwhelming and intimate proximity between the universe of agriculture and the culture of a society. Most prominently it shows a largely unambiguous social proscription for the idea of gain and profit making. Agriculture was considered more of a cultural and social activity rather than a purely economic enterprise. Representations of its activities, tools and nomenclature about land, labour, seeds and crops sufficiently display its organic interconnections with the community life and its cultural context. Land, for instance, has always been seen as a status symbol; something representing family's honour. Hence, buying and selling of land in traditional agronomic discourse was always an occasion with intense emotional quotient symbolising the vicissitudes of fortunes in cultural and social terms more than its implications in terms of pure economic transaction and exchange. Land was living, organic and a social capital (Bolle, 1969; Srinivas, 1976; Bhattacharya, 1976; Vasavi, 1999). Similarly attitude and response towards seeds, especially hybrid ones, has been skeptical. The farmers carry forward these understandings from one generation to another. There is a distinct bias and inclination for 'natural', 'old' and 'consumption-orientation' as they are perceived to be morally rich and correct as per societal norms.

Purba Village: Story of an Agribusiness Farm

The intimacy that the universe of agriculture shares with the traditional and the normative framework of a society, it is understandable that the departure towards agribusiness with a contrasting weltanschauung would exhibit signs of ruptures and a complex web of adjustments, accommodation and alterations. More importantly, the pull of tradition, history of conventions and folk-wisdom's reluctance to the idea of business out of something that had been quintessentially enveloped within the ethos of sacrality would naturally therefore be full of dramatic consequences and impacts. The story of Purba captures those moments of inertia, change and challenges as a part of the village makes transition from Grain to Gain.

This chapter, an ethnographic study of a family-based agribusiness farm in a foothill village in the Terai region of Uttarakhand, examines the socio-cultural dynamics involved in the way agribusiness farm negotiates, both normatively as well as in terms of physical and social landscape, the pressure of being different or non-traditional. The chapter attempts to capture the nuances of multiple ruralities that come to define the intra-village social geography. It also highlights the contrasting ways in which, not just the two generations within a family understand or make sense of the universe of agriculture, but also how starkly the family who does agribusiness differs from others who are still part of the old arrangement. The presence of two communities with differing ethnic roots in the village add to the complexities involved as it interrogates some of the prototype essentialisms about a village such as its communitarian homogeneity and unity.

The study essentially originates from my long association with a village, first as part of my doctoral field work in the early years, beginning the year 2000, which included intermittent but intensive study of families engaged in agribusiness activities in selected villages of the Terai region of Uttarakhand. However I continued to be in touch with this particular village and the families, to get an extended longitudinal view of the processes that were simply difficult to map in the duration of a few years. By 2017, the Purba Village and the Batra farm demonstrated remarkable consistency, in terms of the larger status quoism that defined the former in general and the sheer expansion and growth of the latter. Following standard ethnographic protocol, pseudonyms for the village and its respondents have been used here.

Purba located at Haldwani-Ramnagar road in the district of Nainital is a well-known village on the map of Terai region of Uttarakhand. The village happens to be the seat of the most successful and advanced commercialized farming in the form of Batra farm. In fact, like elsewhere in the Terai region, this family farm has become the paramount identity of this village. Predominantly a Pahari (meaning related to hills) village, with more than 90 per cent inhabitants from the hills, in terms of demographic composition,

Batra farm represents the 'zone of prosperity' or 'mini pocket of the Green Revolution' on the village topography. The high visibility of the farm owes largely to the round-the-year intense agribusiness activities that take place on Batra farm.

It is interesting to note how with the growth and phenomenal expansion, Batra's residential landscape has been clearly bifurcated into two blocks: One, his personal space where his family stays including the kitchen area and second, from where the Batras operate their agribusiness activities which include papaya cultivation, vegetables and floriculture . Adjacent to their personal residential block a much corporatised office establishment has come up which is fully equipped with computer, tele-fax and internet facility through which the Batras interact with their domestic and global partners especially in the Netherlands. As one stands outside Batra's corporate space of the residential area, the sight of bullock cart driven ploughing in the neighbouring field, barely at a distance of not even half a kilometer, instantly reminds one of the phrase 'bullock cart-capitalism' used by a social anthropologist in a different context.

My first visit to the Batras was in the month of December. The Batras, as it appeared, were the most famous family of the area and hence locating them was not a problem. In fact the bus conductor who ferried people between Ramnagar and Haldwani knew the Batras very well especially their identity as 'phool bale' or 'flower-farmers'.

This was certainly a compliment to a family who had moved into this area as refugees just a few decades ago. On my first visit, I met Shri B.K. Batra, 70, the Senior Batra, as the locals would call him, who had first come to this land in the 1950s, after partition, from Rawalpindi, Pakistan. Pt. Govind Ballabh Pant, the first chief minister of Uttar Pradesh, when offered this area to these migrants from across the border, Batra family grabbed this opportunity. Senior Batra recounted: "The prosperity and good time were preceded by harrowing tales of fights with the deadly pythons and a man eater tiger, as this area was initially a dense forest infested with malarial parasites. Sheer hard work smeared literally with sweat and blood went in to the making of this journey from rags to riches."

Batra's only son, Pranjal Batra, was away to attend some agribusiness fair in Delhi during my visit. As I waited for Sr. Batra, I was informed by his attendant that he was having bath in his pool. This surprised me as I never ever expected a swimming pool in a village. Senior Batra attributed his success to *Punjab di matti*, the soil of Punjab, his ancestral land.

As I was about to leave in the late afternoon, I wanted a few sticks of gladiolus or gladiola, as locally known, and other flowers from Sr. Batra. Sr. Batra obliged me with a bunch of fresh flowers and as I was about to thank him for his gesture he very politely quoted me a price. A paltry sum of about Rs. 20 only, but I must confess it caught me unaware. I certainly had expected a generous parting gesture. In any case as I paid him the money, Batra's face remained firm and emotionless.

The family seemed to have inherited the art of delinking personal from pure commerce without much ambiguity from the very beginning. The Batras understand the value of money and believe in 'boond boond se ghat bhare' (economic reasoning which believes in accumulation drop by drop, where each unit counts). Senior Batra, therefore, embodies his struggle, his ordeal by fire post partition and hence there is this constant and insatiable urge for 'security' and more security leading to the perpetual quest for better avenues and new experiments. It appears that the scar of being uprooted once and having faced the adversity thereof has been instrumental in their entrepreneurial proclivity including agribusiness activity like floriculture etc. Says Batra: "Yes it is right we have seen the worst in our early days and so we understand the value of money. Sometimes local Paharis here try to denigrate us by calling us refugees but the fact is we are what we are today also has to do with our experience of uprootedness as a refugee. The experience made us brave and of strong resolve. This also enabled us not to fear taking risks."

This is a significant comment as it tries to establish a link between the culture of the refugees and the experience of up rootedness to the agripreneurship. It also provides some sociocultural reasoning as to why most of the successful agriculturist families and innovators in the area are all post partition settlers from the Punjab region.

It is however interesting to note how the new generation, that is Pranjal, son of Senior Batra, approaches his life and its economic conditions. It would be important here to mention that the villagers in Purba rates Pranjal Batra as more social and more instrumental in bringing the Batra farm to this level. Senior Batra comes across as a staunch minimalist who would not like to part with even a single grain to someone where he sees no possibility of any return.

Pranjal Batra in contrast can be called a modern farmer who instead believes in broad basing his profit generating avenues, through collaboration, experimentation and networking. In other words, his idea of successful business lies in opening more and more resource generating opportunities rather than emphasizing on under consumption and small savings, symptomatic of subsistence agriculture. Pranjal, a graduate from a local college underlines the importance of the 'right kind of education' and the role of technology like computer, fax machines, internet etc. in modern agribusiness. He explains: "Whatever my father earned, earned through sheer hard work, he grew conventional crops like wheat, sugarcane and rice as per his best marketing acumen but things have changed, times have changed, sweating in the field alone does not guarantee anything now."

Understandably real change in fortune came with Pranjal joining his father's profession. Pranjal's profile speaks volumes about his sharp agriprenurial mindset and his understanding of agriculture as a profession. He not only made it a point initially to attend all the state and national level agricultural fairs and workshops but also attended an advanced floriculture training course in the Netherlands in the year 1991 which was sponsored by the government. Pranjal elaborates: "I learnt a lot by attending these fairs and seminars on agri-business where I met people from different states with different experiences. Also I learnt about variety of new seeds and crops and about techniques. Most importantly by attending these seminars and meeting these successful people I realized it was possible to be successful." He further adds: "Through these meetings I got to know the rules of the game and the market networking techniques. Apart from floriculture what actually was like hitting the goldmine for us was papaya cultivation, especially papaya seed cultivation. The business of our papaya seed brand turned out to be very successful and it can now be found with all the major seed distributors of the country. About papaya also I learned in one of the agribusiness fairs which later turned out to be a source of our initial capital strength".

Pranjal executes the marketing of his seeds through coloured brochures and pamphlets highlighting the special qualities of the seeds. After a successful stint in papaya seed cultivation, Pranjal is now planning to enter in the litchi export business which he says his wife, Neetu Batra, will look after. Apart from his village based farm activities, the Batras have floriculture farms in Padampuri (where lilium is grown to be exported to the Gulf and European countries) and Bhavali near Nainital.

As the idea of these ventures seems to be trying too many things Pranjal clarifies: "Now that the children are grown up and they go to schools, my wife will have enough time to supervise the venture and help us." This is approved by Neetu Batra herself as she confides that she always wanted to share his burden (referring to Pranjal), and now comes the opportunity to use her education and show Pranjal that she can also prove her worth in his domain. And before you think that Pranjal is too calculative, he corrects you immediately, as he puts it: "This is not being calculative, this is human resource management at home; best utilisation of one's team whether they are your family members or outsiders."

Clearly Pranjal Batra applies his knowledge of the latest management techniques in his own home first. In response to a question as to why she did not marry a doctor or an engineer despite coming from a rich background with boarding school education, Neetu Batra shared: "This never ever occurred to me; in any case agriculture has always been the mainstay of our family and a proud profession. So getting married to an agriculturist was in no way considered inferior to a doctor or an engineer. In fact I am proud of Pranjal and his farms, especially when the news about his crops or flowers appears in the newspapers I feel very honoured."

Neighborhood and the Seeds of Mistrust

The most critical part of Purba, however, happens to be Batra's relationship with his neighbors, mostly Paharis. This is reflected amply in the way Batra's immediate neighbors and general villagers react to the question: 'why don't you people also grow papaya which will fetch you good returns even in the domestic market?'

A typical answer would be this: 'Batras, who sell seeds to *videshis*, meaning outsiders, give us fake seeds and not the original ones so that we remain in poverty'. The negativity against Batra is very strong in Purba. Moreover these comments, more often than not, are pointed towards Sr. Batra and not as much to Pranjal Batra. Not that Pranjal is completely absolved but he is still acknowledged by the villagers as mixing and helping. The latent meaning behind this negativity is very typical of an Indian village which is that prosperity anywhere in the village is considered a joint venture. People tend to expect and be acknowledged for being merely a unit of the village. Hence the common villager in Purba wants to be acknowledged for Batra's farm fortunes. It seems Sr. Batra's fixation with his 'Punjab di matti' identity and local Paharis' refusal to treat them as one of their own ran like two parallel lines all these years. Sr.Batra's frugality and indifference to local village issues also seems to have made the boundaries of Batra farm rather rigid. As a result and quite expectedly, Sr. Batra explains local Paharis' disinterest to agribusiness activities thus: "These people do not want to work and slog. Yet they would feel envious of others' success and would want some share in it."

The Paharis consider themselves the real owners of this area and they still refer to the Batras as "refugees". The Uttarakhand movement which led to the formation of a new state of Uttarakhand seems to have further sharpened the inter-ethnic divide. Majority of the Pahari youths and families seem to be more interested in petty government jobs even if that means selling a few acres of land in the bargain. In fact Batra's immediate Pahari neighbor has given their land to Batras on a subcontracting arrangement for a fixed sum of money annually. While taking land on subcontracting is a pure economic decision for the Batras, the Pahari owner of the land looks at it differently. They take pride in the fact that the Batra's family 'work on their land'. Here 'work on their land' has a connotation that flows from the traditional attitude where the tiller used to be considered inferior to the land owner. Thus even though the Batras live in opulence in local social context they do not enjoy high status.

As one young Pahari man casually remarked: "Kya faida aise paise ka, agar bahu-betiyon sahit chaubees ghante kam pe lage raho" (There is no point in having that kind of money which engages your entire family, even your women, on work round the clock).

That also shows how traditional agronomic discourse has that inbuilt notion of 'enough' and any proclivity shown for excess was considered a sign of greed and avarice. This is perhaps why the term 'baniyoti' or baniya -like was frequently applied for the Batras, meaning behaviour akin to Banias who have been traditionally stereotyped to be highly appropriative in their business-behaviour. Also it suggests that social honor in village is not necessarily coterminous with one's class position. The reason why the Batras do not occupy high status in the village hierarchy is because the social esteem is contextual. This is further explained by the way the local patriarchal culture and tradition understood and related to the 'mobility of women' outside the personalised, familial and household domain as sign of lower level peasantry. Those with 'enough' and 'more than enough' would consciously choose to restrict their women's movement as a sign of their upward mobility. Interestingly, the culture of agribusiness as represented by the Batras cannot afford such pretensions.

It is not that Pranjal Batra is not aware of the hostility and discontent of his village men around his farm. In fact during one of my visits I found the Batra family in the eye of storm for reasons which were thrust on them. The whole controversy had started after one of the migrant laborers from western Uttar Pradesh who was working on Batra farm for some time, eloped with a woman of the village. Expectedly the overall mood in the village was against the Batras. Villagers in general stoked the fire by saying that when it comes to choose between 'gaon ki izzat' (honor of the village) and his migrant labourers, the Batras still back their workers. Another malafide campaign, it seems, to score over the Batras was on.

As it appeared, the villagers anyway did not quite appreciate and encourage the outsiders and especially migrant workers who were seen as intruders to village social and cultural life. Since the Batra's agribusiness took off, they depended heavily on these workers for their loyalty. According to the Batras, the local labour force was susceptible to the vilification campaign triggered by the village politics every now and then. In contrast the settled presence of these migrant laborers from distant underdeveloped places suited the Batra, for they could be trusted and relied upon. Also more distant a place the labour belongs to and comes from; less prone they are to absenteeism which is rampant among the locals. On one pretext or the other the local laborer would abscond for days without any information and appear one day with lame excuses expecting favours citing familiarity and local relationships. And if not accommodated they join the Batras' opponents. Another reason why the Batras prefer migrants is that since they invest and work hard on their training, it really hurts when they (locals) do not value these inputs.

It is not that migrant laborers are a new phenomenon to this area. Even earlier when agriculture was the ' rice-wheat-sugarcane' type migrant labourers used to come for work for a certain period, earn their wages and return to their home states(mostly from Bihar and UP). But now with round the year engagement required by floriculture and other market-oriented cash crops, they are almost settled here with family members taking it in turn to visit their home towns. This trend has not been quite liked by the majority in the village (mostly traditionalist farmer). They considered them (labourers) a nuisance for the village. No wonder these migrant labourers are soft targets for the disgruntled elements that are always on the lookout for some issue to embarrass the Batras and settle the score with them. Batras are naturally very patronizing towards their workers when it comes to taking sides which is again considered and projected by their adversaries as a sign of disloyalty to the village.

Pranjal Batra regrets this aspect of his farm life but cannot help it either. To prove a point, Pranjal introduces his accountant; an educated and computer literate Pahari boy who Pranjal argues is there with him not because of his ethnic identity but because of his qualification and ability. Agribusiness requires skilled manpower which is difficult to get from the traditional quarters of the village. Recently he had to advertise for the post of lab-assistant in a local newspaper with the essential qualification of post-graduation in organic chemistry for his tissue culture lab. For this, he has shortlisted a candidate from Kanpur. 'This is inevitable, argues

Pranjal, 'as modern agribusiness cannot sustain itself in a traditional 'familistic-reciprocal' environment.' The ethos of agribusiness thrives on universalistic principles, to employ Sociologist Talcott Parsons' phraseology, which has no place for elements like obliging someone to cater to particularistic expectations of village life. Unlike his father, who considers Paharis 'aalsi' or lazy, Pranjal feels that Paharis are certainly less enterprising when it comes to agriculture which he reasons may be because of the minimalist-subsistence kind of low scale agriculture that they have been used to in the hills for ages.

Pranjal's understanding echoes in what a septuagenarian old Pahari woman had to say about agriculture in the hills: 'Waha kya kheti hogi. Din bhar khet me kam karo, aur sam me peechhay dekho to wahi ke wahi'.

(What is there in the hills to think of in terms of agriculture? You work there the whole day on your land and in the evening when you look back you realize you have hardly moved).

It would not be wrong to argue that the ages of small-scale cultivation for mere subsistence have affected and shaped the hill people's understanding about agriculture in a particular way which is minimalist, limited in scope and non-entrepreneurial. Even the thought of any business out of agriculture is considered weird and creation of a feeble mind in the villages in the interior of the hills.

Pranjal Batra, however, on his part tries hard to dispel some of these misgivings. Though not so successful, he explains his endeavours: "As I get very busy and occupied with my various farm activities in the village and elsewhere and whatever little time that I am left with after attending workshops and agro-seminars, I want to devote at least some time to my family and especially children. Now I agree this has certainly affected my interaction level and frequency with my village folks but I feel sad when this is perceived and constructed as snobbery."

Interactions with the Batras' neighbouring Pahari families indicated a pre-dominant preference for army jobs followed by petty government jobs in banks and other state government establishments. The most cherished dream job of any Pahari youth is joining Indian military. That almost all the Pahari families in Purba have at least one man in the Indian army; reflects their fascination for army jobs. Both the Kumauni and Garhwali folk songs are full of melancholic references to a mother's urge to meet her son who was serving on the border. In other words, agriculture has never been accorded any significant place in hill society traditionally. Pranjal Batra, apart from the element of non-entrepreneurial culture of the Paharis, attributes the following factors for lack of agribusiness initiative in the village: 1-Local hostile environment 2-Local politics, especially the panchayat election which seems to have further divided the village on caste and community lines. 3-Sharpened Pahari-non Pahari identity articulations accentuated by local politicians who have been rendered issueless after the formation of the new state of Uttarakhand.

That Batra farm's success story could not travel beyond its boundary suggests that there has been an almost negligible centrifugal tendency in the agribusiness currents in Purba. The Batra farm can be visualised as an island of prosperity amidst vast ocean of subsistence agriculture marked by apathy, gross indifference, hostility and almost fatalistic attitude of 'kaun jhamela leta hai' (why take this headache). Traditional farmers mostly verbalized their complacency by saying 'theke par jamin de do aur mast raho' (give the land on subcontracting and relax). That is, land never appears to them as an asset. In fact there is an increasing tendency among the Pahari families to sell their lands in Purba and buy cheap land near the emerging towns as after the formation of Uttarakhand these Terai-based small local towns have become hot property and land prices have shot up and it is being seen as lucrative investment for the future.

Apart from the Batras' own initiative and acumen for agribusiness what seems to have helped their ventures immensely is the way they have used various support schemes like easy bank loans provided by the government. They also seem to have used their image of progressive farmers of the area to elicit encouragement and positive favour from the politicians, bureaucrats and banking sector high ups to create the required infrastructure on their farms. This was amply evident from Pranjal's proud possession of photographs with the politicians and bureaucrats at various occasions, some of which donned the walls of his house in prominent positions. In fact he admitted that the government was encouraging people to start such projects but very few showed an interest. He has keenly followed the developments and seeking governmental support by personally meeting the officials and others who are promoting new commercial projects in agriculture in Uttarakhand. Again this is seen by the common villagers as misappropriation of govt. funds meant for the development of the entire village. This of course again is a misplaced perception as to average villagers government projects mean freebies and hence the view.

Over the years, Purba became witness to significant change and transitions. This was not merely in terms of mere expansion of the Batra's floriculture-based business beyond Purba in the distant hill areas of Nainital but also the phenomenon of extreme corporatization that his office near his residence in Purba had undergone. While Pranjal Batra was chatting with his clients and business partners on the internet, the newly appointed lab technician Mr. Ram Moorthy, a young south Indian who had graduated from the Pant Nagar Agricultural University seemed busy in a highly sophisticated lab. What has made all this technical paraphernalia look extraordinary is its coexistence with a rather contrasting setting marked by traditional technical knowledge form and way of life in Purba.

There were, however, visible signs of discontentment amongst Batras vis-à-vis his Purba co-villagers as evident in the gradual strategic shifting of farm base from Purba to nearby areas. As Pranjal Batra explained: "We do not want to add new enterprises in this village. Other than the limited level of papaya seed cultivation and our residential and office establishment we are shifting our base to nearby areas in the hills. The kind of flowers that we want to grow, these areas near hill side provide better weather conditions and congenial social and political environment. It is easy to work there as a neutral unacquainted person."

He made further interesting contrasts between his Terai Purba base and other new bases nearer to the hills around Nainital: "People at my new bases in the hills unlike Purba feel obliged and favored as the farms have provided them with regular job opportunities. And secondly there is absolutely no local politics and leg-pulling there. Being 'neutral people' there makes life much easier. We carry our work there without bothering about who will feel what and whether we are meeting their expectations or not. There is less social strain in conducting your activities in such areas." Pranjal explained it further which also captures the sentiments of growing inter-ethnic divide in the area: "People of the hills are generally simple and helpful but those who have settled in the plain Terai region have become politicised and think on ethnic lines."

Not quite surprising therefore that when it comes to using 'land' or agriculture in general towards profit maximization the mood is clearly discouraging among the Pahari population. The traditional thinking treats modern agribusiness like floriculture as a pursuit of the 'profane' world. This negativity surrounding agribusiness among the Paharis especially, may not be the only important factor but it certainly has considerable influence on the people who have been too cushioned by the status-quoism and comforts of subsistence agriculture.

No wonder the Batra farm in Purba appears like an island insulated from all sides. It has over the years created its own culture of agriculture which is modern, dynamic, entrepreneurial and profit-driven. Now the third generation of the Batra family, Shamant Batra, son of Pranjal, who is barely 19 years old but shares his father's dream of becoming the country's top name in floriculture business. Pranjal is grooming him into this by associating him in the activities of his new Padampuri (near Nainital) orchids farm. He smilingly says: "I will help him and provide him free consultancy for the initial two years. After all he is my son. But after that I will charge him with my consultancy fee." But before you try and take it in a lighter vein, Pranjal surprises you by this: "I am very serious. Please do not mistake me as I firmly believe that anything which comes free of cost is not taken seriously and less valued. So I will help him initially to stand on his feet in this sector and then leave him to take his own decisions, make mistakes and learn from them."

Neetu Batra, his wife, nods in agreement as Pranjal elaborates it further: "My father did not get anything on platter. He worked hard but I worked doubly hard on whatever he passed on to me. Now it is the turn of the new generation to carry it forward and actually better it given the fact that they have had substantial background."

This actually goes to show to the extent the Batras have mastered the art of disassociating their 'emotional world' from their 'professional' agriprenurial domain which is characterized by pure reasoning and instrumental rationality. Most importantly, there is absolutely no dilemma in all this. This family is working on their future with a vision. It would not be a big deal for them to send their children to any high profile business schools or in any engineering colleges imitating the dominant trend among most of the affluent around who would take pride in the fact that their children were studying medicine or engineering, even if in some substandard institutions. Reasons Pranjal: "After all children will ultimately join my business which I have created with such an effort. What is the point in specializing in engineering as it will be of no use? There are more opportunities in agriculture. So we are preparing them for the future with practical exposure."

Pranjal Batra's story is the story of a man who chased his dream of becoming a successful agriculturist by dint of sheer diligence and with a rare skill of negotiating and networking with both the man and nature made odds. His shifting the farm base from Purba to other places shows his adaptability and flexibility in the approach to his work. These new places provide him with congenial neutral settings away from the hostility of Purba. Unfazed by the local challenges, he is busy pursuing his business, visiting places like Belgium, Taiwan and the Netherlands to explore new opportunities and trends in the global flower market.

While the Batras are busy chasing newer dreams, the rest of Purba enjoys afternoon nap cushioned by safe, secure and simple life of conventional agriculture and its uninterrupted, non-risky world. Purba and its village dynamics around Batra farm reveals some of the socio-cultural conditions which make it difficult for conducting or taking up agribusiness model of doing agriculture.

Purba Today: Some Concluding Remarks

Today (2017) Purba farm has expanded its base to multiple sites on the higher planes of the hills towards Bhimtaal. These sites are being managed by the two young sons of Pranjal Batra. They now grow and export exotic variety of flowers from a factory like establishment that they have built in these new locations.

Fully-equipped with all the modern-corporate paraphernalia like seminar rooms, Wi-Fi linked workshop spaces, hostels and high-end infrastructural networks to scale up the business opportunities and expansion plans, these plants are signposts of success brought by decades of sheer hard work and perseverance against all odds. Back in Purba, the village has hardly changed, except the Batra farm, which has experienced a phenomenal growth over the years. Senior Batra, now in his 90s, continues to remain active. He remains rooted in his philosophy of hard work and higher aspirations within a traditional framework, while the younger generation follows the modern work ethic inspired by Pranjal. Tradition and modernity seem to effortlessly coalesce in this case to consolidate the agribusiness route to prosperity. The dynamics of two almost contrasting landscapes of Purba village underlines the critical role played by the local socio-cultural context and how different communities respond to the idea of gain differently. In other words, Purba reminds us that it is not always through the lens of logic, rationality and economic reasoning that people makes choices; often it is the history, local ethno-cultural context and other cultural indices that determine the trajectory of journeys. Purba is a cautionary note that while espousing any idea of transforming the villages of India one must not follow any standardised template or model of development; rather it must, at all times, be attentive to the diversity and the nuances of the local-regional cultural context. For a vast majority of villages of India, especially its marginal farmers, the idea of Gain is obviously imperative but its routes through agribusiness have to be properly assessed, planned and culturally mapped out with sensitivity to community's history and locations, both geographical and social.

REFERENCES

Appadurai, A. 1989. 'Transformation in the Culture of Agriculture'. In *Contemporary Indian Traditions: Voices on Culture, Nature, and the Challenge of Change* (ed.) by C. Borden, Washington: Smithsonian Institution Press.

Baudrillard, J. 1975. *The Mirror of Production*, St. Louis: Teleco Press.

Beals, A., 1974, *Village Life in South India: Cultural Design and Environmental Variation*, Chicago: Aldine.

Belliappa, J. and Kaushik, M. 1978. 'The Food of Well-being'. SSRC/ICSSR Conference on Welfare and Well-being in South Asia, Delhi. (mimeo).

Bhattacharya, S. 1976. *Farmers' Rituals and Modernizations*, Burdhwan: N.C. Roy Publications.

Bolle, Kees. 1969. Speaking of a Place. In *Myths and Symbols: Studies in Honour of Mircea Eliade* (ed.) J.M. Kitagawa and Charles H. Long, Chicago: University of Chicago Press.

Bourdieu, P. 1963. 'The attitude of the Algerian Peasant toward time'. In J. Pitts-Rivers (ed.), *Mediterranean Countrymen*, London: Mouton.

Chopra, Radhika. 1994. 'Voices from Earth: Work and Food Reproduction in a Punjab Village', *Sociological Bulletin*, 43(I), March.

Clifford, J. 1988. *The Predicament of Culture: Twentieth Century Ethnography, Literature and Art*, Cambridge MA: Harvard University Press.

Daniel, V. 1984. *Fluid Signs; Being a Person the Tamil Way*, Berkeley: University of California Press.

Douglas, M. 1966. *Purity and Danger: An Analysis of Concepts of Pollution and Taboo*, London: Routledge and Kegan Paul (RKP).

Entrepreneurship. 2008. A Study by the National Knowledge Commission, Government of India Document, Delhi.

Gupta, Akhil. 1998. *Post Colonial Development: Agriculture in the Making of Modern India*, Delhi: Oxford University Press.

Gupta, Dipankar. 2005. Whither the Indian Village?: Culture and Agriculture in 'Rural' India, *Economic and Political Weekly*, February 9.

Gurumurty, K. 1986. 'A Cultural Ecology: Study of Selected Villages in North Karnataka Region', Department of Environment, Government of India.

Halliburton, Murphy. 1998. 'Suicide: A Paradox of Development in Kerala, *Economic and Political Weekly*, September 5-12.

Heilbroner, Robert L. 1967. *The Worldly Philosophers*, New York: Washington Square Press.

Hobsbawm, E.J. et al. (eds.) 1980. *Peasants in History: Essays in Honour of Daniel Thorner*, Delhi: Oxford University Press.

Khare, R.S. 1976. *Culture and Reality: Essays on the Hindu System of Managing Food*, Simla: Indian Institute of Advanced Study.

Khare, R.S. and Rao, M.S.A. (eds.) 1986. *Food, Society and Culture: Aspects of South Asian Food Systems*, Durham, NC: University of North Carolina Press.

Ludden, David. 1999. *The New Cambridge History of India*, IV. 4. *An Agrarian History of South Asia*, New Delhi: Cambridge University Press.

Madan, Vandana. (ed.) 2002. *The Villages in India*, Delhi: Oxford University Press.

Marglin, F.A. and Marglin, Stephen A. (ed.) 1990. *Dominating Knowledge: Development, Culture, and Resistance*, Oxford: Clarendon Press.

Marriott, M. 1976. 'Hindu Transactions: Diversity Without Dualism'. In *Transaction and Meaning: Directions in the Anthropology of Exchange and Symbolic Behavior* (ed.) B. Kepferer, Philadephia: Institute for the Study of Human Issues.

____. 1989. Constructing an Indian Ethnosociology, *Contribution to Indian Sociology*, 23, 1-39.

Mies, Maria 1987. *Indian Women in Subsistence and Agricultural Labour*, New Delhi, Vistaar Publications.

Mohanty, B.B., 2005. We are Like the Living Dead: Farmer Suicides in Maharashtra, Western India, *The Journal of Peasant Studies*, Vol. 32, No. 2, April.

Moore, Jr. Barrington, 1966. *Social Origins of Dictatorship and Democracy: Land and Peasant in the Making of the Modern India.* Penguin Books.

Murton, B. 1981. *Traditional Systems of Agricultural Knowledge and Contemporary Agriculture Development in India in the Perspectives in Agricultural Geography*, Vol. 5 (ed.) N. Mohammed, New Delhi: Concept Publishing Company.

Ohnuki-Tierney, E. 1990. *Culture Through Time: Anthropological Approaches*, California: Stanford University Press.

Panini, M.N. 1999, Trends in Cultural Globalization: From Agriculture to Agribusiness in Karnataka, *Economic and Political Weekly*, Vol. XXXIV, No. 31, July 31.

____. 1995, The Social Logic of Liberalization, *Sociological Bulletin*, 44(i), March.

Pathak, Shekhar, 1993, *Kumaon Himalaya—Temptations*, Nainital: Gyanodaya Prakashan.

Ramanujan, A.K., 1989, Is There an Indian Way of Thinking? An Informal Essay, *Contributions to Indian Sociology*, 23, 41-58.

Ray, Shovan. (ed.) 2007. *Oxford Handbook of Agriculture*, Delhi: Oxford University Press.

Rogers, E.M. et al. 1998. *Social Change in Rural Societies: An Introduction to Rural Sociology*, Third Edition, New Jersey: Prentice Hall, Inc.

Scott, James C. 1987. *Weapons of the Weak: Everyday Forms of Peasant Resistance*, New Haven and London: Yale University Press.

Sen, Sucharita and Raju, Saraswati. 2006. Globalization and Expanding Markets for Cut-Flowers: Who Benefits? *Economic and Political Weekly*, June 30.

Shiva, Vandana. 1999. *The Violence of the Green Revolution: Third World Agriculture, Ecology, and Politics*, London: Zed Books.

Singh, Sukhpal. 2004. Crisis and Diversification in Punjab Agriculture: Role of State and Agribusiness, *Economic and Political Weekly*, December 25.

____ . 2005. Contract Farming System is Thailand, *Economic and Political Weekly*, December 31.

Srinivas, M.N. 1976. *The Remembered Village*, Delhi: Oxford University Press.

Vasavi, A.R. 1994. Hybrid Times, Hybrid People: Culture and Agriculture in South India, *MAN*, *Journal of the Royal Anthropological Institute*, Vol. 29, No. 2, June.

____ . 1999. *Harbingers of Rain: Land and Life in South India*, New Delhi: Oxford University Press.

Vatuk, S. 1978. 'The Food of Well-being'. SSRC/ ICSSR Conference on Welfare and Well-being in South Asia, Delhi. (mimeo).

11

Infrastructural Development in Rural Punjab: Understanding Social Impacts of Planned Interventions on the Stakeholders

Sukhwant Sidhu

Since independence Punjab has performed remarkably well in remodelling its rural social structure. Its rural economy has grown from strength to strength under planned government interventions. But the overutilisation of natural resources, lack of crop diversification, problems of agricultural labour coupled with erratic climate and weather extremes has led to the disenchantment of youth from agriculture. The process of land acquisition disfavoured earlier is now being looked as a panacea by the farmers. This chapter attempts to assess the social impacts of land acquisition on the stakeholders in rural Punjab. An attempt is being made to restructure, transform and modernise rural India into smart villages. The social impacts experienced by the stakeholders that are involved in land acquisitions are diverse and long lasting. There is need for understanding the social consequences of projects, programmes and policies. Social Impact Assessment (SIA) as a technique and methodology is being practised throughout the developed nations for minimising the negative impacts and maximising the positive impacts of development. The Government of India enacted the Right to Fair Compensation and Transparency in the Land Acquisition Rehabilitation and Resettlement Act (RFCTLARR), 2013. This act makes it mandatory to conduct Social Impact

Assessment of any development project in India. Although, the act is still being debated and has become a contentious issue. The involvement of the Project Affected Population in the decision-making process is crucial to avoid any unintended consequences on the stakeholders. The government should be able to identify all the stakeholders involved in any land acquisition and should ensure distributive and compensatory justice to all.

This chapter highlights the social impacts of the land acquisition on the stakeholders. The land has been acquired from a village located at the periphery of the 'City Beautiful'—Chandigarh. The ramifications of this acquisition of land is not only limited to the land owners but is extended to all those who are directly or indirectly associated with it.

The governments around the world strives effectively and efficiently to implement the programmes and policies for the welfare of its citizens. Development of rural areas has been one of the prime concerns of the government of independent India. Punjab has enthusiastically adopted and implemented the planned interventions introduced by the Government of India. The hardworking, resilient and entrepreneurial Punjabi people were the forerunners to adopt new techniques of agriculture. It led to the overutilisation of the natural resources diminishing the positive impacts of the Green Revolution. Agriculture is no longer seen as a profitable calling by the farmers leading to massive urbanisation. The urban centres on the other hand are expanding and entering the rural landscape. The land around the periphery of the cities is being acquired by government and private agencies for infrastructural development. The farmers are more than willing to part with their land and migrate to cities with the compensatory money they get from the government or project developers. It is assumed that all interventions intend to improve or uphold the social functioning of the populations. (Dolgoff and Stolnik, 1997).

The social impacts of infrastructural development are complex and multidimensional. These include all types of "social and cultural consequences to human populations of any public or private actions that alter the ways in which people live, work, play, relate to one another, organise to meet their needs, and generally cope as members of society. Cultural impacts involve changes to the norms, values, and beliefs of individuals that guide and rationalise their cognition of themselves and their society. (ICPGSIA, 1994)".

The process of acquisition of private land for public purposes is present around the globe and India is no exception. Land acquisition can be defined as an act of the government whereby it acquires land from its owners in order to pursue certain public purposes or for any private enterprise. The compensation is paid to the owners or persons associated with land. This can be distinguished from simple purchase of land from the market, either by the government or private players. "Land acquisitions by the government agencies are generally compulsory in nature, not paying heed to the owner's unwillingness to part with the land. (George, 2009)".

The genealogy of land acquisition by government agencies in India goes back to the early nineteenth century when the British enacted various acts in the then presidency towns and later expanding across the country to facilitate the land acquisition process for the construction of roads, canals and other 'public purposes' with compensation to be determined by specifically appointed arbitrators. (Law Commission of India, 1958).

The British used land as a tool to capture India's economic independence and to destabilise the social institutions. The traditional land ownership patterns were modified and legislated by the British government in order to facilitate acquisition of land by English businessman. Private ownership of land was encourage as opposed to joint (community) ownership. The British favoured the Zamindari system over Jajmani system and introduced the Permanent Settlement Act 1793, through which land was subjected to tax. The result of this system was that the land was concentrated in the hands of a few landlords. The landlords, in turn, acted as intermediaries between the British and the poor Indian citizens and followed the appeasement policy that suited the British. The British introduced the Land Acquisition Act, 1894 that was supposed to bring some sort of uniformity in the acquisition process. It meant to amend the law for acquisition of private land for public purposes and private enterprises. (Ray and Ray, 2011).

Independent India adopted the Land Acquisition Act of 1894 by the "Indian Independence (Adaptation of Central Acts and

Ordinances) Order" in 1948. A number of laws and amendments after independence such as abolition of the Zamindari system, town planning, land reforms, slum clearance, resettlement of refugees, etc., have been enacted. (Wahi, 2013). New cities of Jamshedpur, Chandigarh, etc., were constructed and acquisition of land took place under Nehru's modernisation model.

It was repeatedly felt by the government that the Right to Property was a roadblock in land acquisition as it was a fundamental right. In 1978 the government through the 44th amendment to the constitution abolished the right to property as a fundamental right but it declared that it would remain a legal right. This act was amended by Act 68 of 1984, which came into force with effect from September 24, 1984. The effect of this amendment is that in case of breach of this Right, an aggrieved person may approach the High Court (under Article 226) and not the Supreme Court (under Article 32), an option that was available earlier that ensured speedy remedy (Singhal, 1995).

There has been an increase in the public outrage regarding the land acquisitions especially for the reward of fair compensation, valuation of land, definition of 'public purpose' and other issues since independence. There has been massive displacement of traditional communities, tribal people and environmental damage that has resulted in many conflicts throughout India. This lopsided development has created an India in which islands of prosperity are glimpsed through a sea of poverty. (Gadgil and Guha, 1995). The Land Acquisition Act, 1894 in spite of amendments has been draconian because the government does not account for the emotions or sentiments of the displaced. (George, 2009).

The government has amended The Land Acquisition Act, in 1984 and after two decades notified the National Rehabilitation and Resettlement Policy, 2007 (in October 2007), and followed that up with the Rehabilitation and Resettlement Bill 2007 and the Land Acquisition (Amendment) Bill 2007. It was amended and represented in the union cabinet which cleared in December 2012, (Iyer, 2009). The bill after being discussed in both the houses got the assent of the President and the Right to Fair Compensation in Land Acquisition, Rehabilitation and Resettlement Act came into force on January 1, 2014.

Social Impact Assessment

The Government of India acceding to the pressure and outrage of the citizens and complying with the guidelines of the international funding agencies made it mandatory to carry out Social Impact Assessment (SIA) of every developmental project involving land acquisition.

Social Impact Assessment originated in USA as a part of the 1969 National Environment Policy Act (NEPA). The Environmental Impact Assessment (EIA) became an imperative component of environmental planning and decision-making and has enjoyed a remarkable rise to prominence in academic and applied social science literature. SIA has been evolving from its modest beginnings in the early 1970s when a few guidelines were available, and a Social Impact Assessment was generally carried out as an afterthought to Environmental Impact Assessment. (Barrow, 2001).

The planners, decision-makers and the government across the globe have recognised a need for better understanding of the social consequences of projects, programmes and policies. In response to this need a group of social scientists formed the Inter-organisational Committee on Guidelines and Principles for Social Impact Assessment (ICGPSIA), with the purpose of outlining a set of guidelines and principles that will assist state agencies, private parties and the stakeholders in fulfilling their obligations under NEPA. The term 'Social Impact Assessment' was first used when the Department of the Interior, of United States was preparing the report on Environmental Impact Assessment for the Trans-Alaska pipeline in the early 1970s. (ICGPSIA, 2003).

The, International Association for Impact Assessment, (IAIA) defines Social Impact Assessment as: "A process of analysing, monitoring and managing the intended and unintended social consequences, both positive and negative, of planned interventions (Projects, Policies, Programmes or Plans) and any social change processes invoked by those interventions. Its primary purpose is to bring about a more sustainable and equitable biophysical and human environment". (ICGPSIA, 2003)

This definition of IAIA not only incorporates the concept of a priori assessment of social impacts, but also includes post facto components. The terms monitoring and managing are crucial in dealing with the social effects of development. There is a lot of difference between preparing a technical report regarding the future social impacts on one side and initiating a process to manage and minimise the social impacts of a developmental project.

SIA is best understood as an umbrella or overarching framework that embodies the evaluation of all impacts on humans and on all the ways in which people and communities interact with their socio-cultural, economic and biophysical surroundings. The social impacts of the developmental projects should be the most important consideration of any government. Adverse social impacts can decrease the intended benefits of a proposal, and can even threaten its viability. In such cases, a social impact assessment is carried out along with Environmental Impact Assessment (EIA). This approach is used to analyse the impacts of a proposal on individuals and communities, and to minimise the adverse effects and enhance the positive effects. It also provides a framework to manage social change.

Social impacts are the consequences faced by people of any proposed action that changes the way they live, work, relate to one another, organise themselves and function as individuals and members of society. It includes social-psychological changes, for example to people's values, attitudes and perceptions of themselves and their community and environment. Indeed, some SIA practitioners consider social impacts to be only 'as experienced' (e.g. stress, disruption, hunger) and differentiate these from the causal processes (e.g. over-crowding, infrastructure pressure, poverty) (ICGPSIA, 2003).

F. Vanclay (2002) stresses that social impacts include all human impacts including—"aesthetic, archaeological and heritage, community, cultural, demographic, development, economic and fiscal, gender, health, indigenous rights, infrastructure, institutional, political (human rights, governance, democratisation, etc.), poverty-related, psychological, resource issues (access and ownership of resources), the impacts of tourism and other impacts on societies", (Vanclay, 2002: 190-91). The social impacts may be positive or negative or both. These bring about changes in income, standard of living, employment patterns, sources of livelihood, place of residence, environment, political systems, health and well-being, perception, attitude and aspirations. With the increase in the number of developmental projects in the developing countries more and more people are being displaced affecting their social milieu in more than one ways.

Types of Social Impacts

Social impacts are impacts of developmental interventions on human settlements. Such impacts not only needed to be identified and measured but also need to be managed in such a way that the positive effects are magnified and negative ones minimised.

1. Time-Based Impacts: These impacts are related with the life cycle of the project. An infrastructural development project generally passes through four major stages according to ICGPSIA. Each and every phase has its own relevance and requires different types of consideration for the impact assessment. These are—Pre-Construction Phase, Construction Phase, Post-Construction Phase and De-Commissioning Phase.

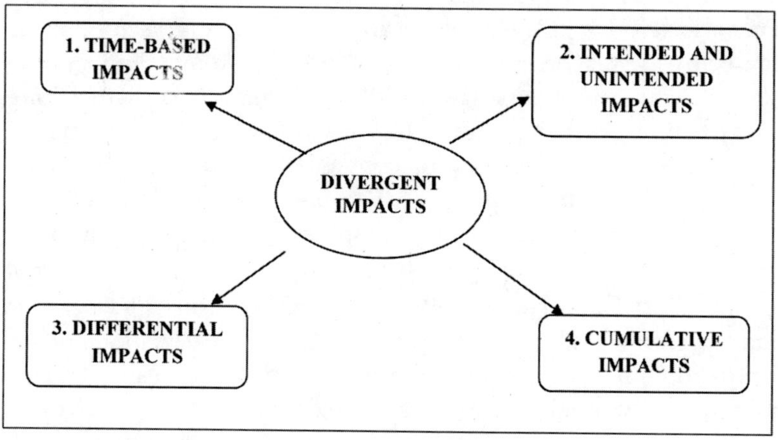

Source: ICGPSIA, 1994

(a) Pre-Construction or Planning Phase: This is the initial phase and commences with the proposal to pursue a particular project. Once the proposal is made public all sorts of speculations are spread by the media and local leaders. The social, economic, political, cultural systems are affected immediately after the announcement of a project (Walker et al., 2000).

The initial impacts are psychological in nature and are generally related with the perception. The local people are eager to gather information about the nature and magnitude of the project. The speculations run very high and people try to gain financially by spreading rumours related to the location of the project. The local leaders become active and try to lobby with the developers to meet their political ends. (Burdge and Johnson, 1994). These are future oriented impacts generally related with the perception, displacement, compensation, rehabilitation in the anticipation of development and change (Walker et al., 2000).

(b) Construction Phase: In this phase the actual work of acquisition of land takes place. There may be unwilling residents who would not like to part with their land. The land is finally cleared and the construction work is initiated. There is a large influx of vehicles and migrant construction workforce at the site. There may be health concerns for the people living in proximity to the construction site (Burdge and Johnson, 1994). The commuters may also face the problem of traffic jams. There may be pollution caused by the machines or the mixers used for mixing sand, gravel, cement. The contractors have to deal with onlookers that curious to gather information about the development. The impacts of this stage may have far-reaching consequences from displacement, change in occupation, loss of traditional source of livelihood, change of neighbourhood and geographically severing of old social ties.

(c) Post-Construction Phase or Operation Phase: The construction phase is followed by the Phase of development or Operation phase during which the positives are realized. The community stabilizes, there are benefits of new infrastructure, wealth generation, employment opportunities and new patterns of social organization emerge (ICGPSIA, 2003).

(d) De-Commissioning Phase: The de-commissioning takes place once the project becomes operational. These impacts can be felt depending on the region or the situation of the community. There may be loss of employment for local labourers, environmental degradation, community composition may change, and local industry and business may need to adapt to the new socio-economic set-up.

2. Intended and Unintended Impacts: Intended impacts are those impacts that are obvious and intentional that may be experienced by stakeholders. The intended impacts may be displacement and rehabilitation of population, health and environmental issues on one side and positive impacts such as employment generation, stimulation in economic activities of the area, fostering transportation, energy and improvement in social services (construction of new schools or hospitals).

Unintended impacts may include those impacts that may be not visualized at the initial stages of the project. These are generally experienced by those individuals who are not directly affected by the acquisition of land or dislocation. These may be marginal landless labourers who may not be the owners of the land but depend on that land for their livelihood. The population of nearby areas may be affected by construction of roads, transmission lines, and increased vehicular traffic and by other associated works. There may be an impact on the business of the local community because of the project. People might face stress or tensions and other socio-psychological problems due to the project.

3. Differential Impacts: These are the impacts on the most vulnerable groups of society like women, elderly, differently able and ailing residents. The psychological impacts (stress, perception, attitudinal changes) on these sections of society may have far-reaching consequences on their personality. These impacts may be identified through Gender Impact Assessment, Vulnerability and Resilience Mapping.

4. Cumulative Impacts: The planned interventions do not take place in isolation from the surrounding region and communities. There may be a number of different Projects, Plans and Programmes (PPP) being undertaken in that region and the impact of these disparate actions will interact with each other in unexpected ways (Barrow, 1997).

The intensity of impacts may increase as the life of the project is extended, as the time passes more external factors such as new Projects, Plans and Policies could be undertaken and these would interact with the existing ones in an unprecedented ways (Geisler, 1993).

Cumulative effects may last for a long time, affecting the social milieu directly and increasing the exposure to foreign culture. It may further lead to the erosion of traditional beliefs and values.

The Assessment of the Cumulative Impacts is very difficult and a complex process. The Cumulative Effects Assessment Working Group (CEAWG) observes that the Cumulative Effects Assessment (CEA) involves the identification and active involvement of all the stakeholders that are the valued components of the project. The valued components are based on societal beliefs and local knowledge of the life world.

There is no single factor responsible for cumulative impacts so these are complicating in nature. These impacts may not only be felt on the local population but may spread to the entire region. In order to deal with these impacts the cooperation of all proponents, regulators and government is required.

Development Projects and SIA

The notion of inclusive growth along with involvement of stakeholders in any development project has become a sine qua non of policy makers in developed and developing countries (Ramos and Ranieri, 2013). More and more emphasis is being given to facilitate dialogue between the policy makers and other stakeholders involved in the Projects. According to Giddens (1984) the stakeholders are active social actors with three features: firstly, practical consciousness derived from life experience, secondly, their own theories about social relations and power and finally, systems of reflective monitoring on working of things in day-to-day life.

The identification of all the stakeholders involved in any planned intervention is an essential aspect of assessment of impacts on PAPs. The success or failure of Impact Assessment depends on a judicious identification of all stakeholders. IAIA has prepared a set of guidelines that assist in the identification of stakeholders, these include:

- The people who have to be rehabilitated because of the project and whose land will be acquired.

- The people who are directly or indirectly dependent on the land that has been acquired.
- The vulnerable groups that belong to the socio-economic weaker sections, women, aged, differently abled and ailing people
- The inhabitants of the locality where the displaced people shall be relocated.
- People from nearby communities, villages whose livelihood may be threatened as a result of the project.
- The residents who ought to suffer due to increase in vehicular traffic, transmission lines and any other associated work.
- The labourers working at the site and their families.
- The residents where the construction workers will be located.
- The natives who may have religious attachment to land or building near the construction site.
- The environmentalists who may be concerned with the ecological conditions that may be threatened by the project.

All these stakeholders may face negative consequences of development and may be directly or indirectly affected by the project. On the other side the beneficiaries of the project that may be the developer, associate contractors, local or state governments also form a part of stakeholders and they should also be involved in the process of impact assessment (Vanclay, 1999).

Social Impacts on the Inhabitants of Village Jheur Heri in SAS Nagar, Punjab

The village Jheur Heri is situated at the periphery of the City Beautiful, Chandigarh, capital of Punjab and Haryana in district Sahibzada Ajit Singh (SAS) Nagar. The land from this village and the adjoining villages was earlier acquired in 1950s for the construction of an Air Force station. The domestic flights operated from a part of this Air Force Station. In 2008 the Government of India acquired 308 acres of land adjoining the domestic airport that belonged to this village. It was acquired to upgrade the existing domestic airport into an international airport. The land was acquired by the Punjab government and the compensation amounting to Rs. 1.5 crore per acre was given to the land owners. The acquired land is adjoining the residential place of the villagers. There were wide ranging social impacts on the Project Affected Population that are as follows:

Impact on Demographic Structure

The demographic structure has undergone profound changes after the acquisition of land. The data from Census 2001 and 2011 is compared because the land acquisition took place in 2008, hence the social impacts post acquisition can be observed in Census 2011. A comparative analysis of the demography of the village is depicted in Table 1. It indicates that that there has been an increase in 10.58 per cent population of the village indicative of the fact that not many people have left the village post land acquisition. There is negative growth of 1.87 per cent in total population below six years and a much higher negative growth in 12.2 per cent in the population of girls below six years. This decrease in the female population can be attributed to the fact that the villagers after getting compensation were in a position to opt for Pre-Natal determination tests and must have gone for female foeticide.

Table 1: Comparative Demographic Profile of Jheur Heri (Census 2001 and 2011)

	Census 2001	Census 2011	Transition (+/-)
Number of Households	145	185	+ 40
Population (Total)	894	991	+ 97
Male %	52.8	53.48	+ 0.68
Female %	47.20	46.52	+ 0.68
Below 6 years % (Total)	13.98	12.11	– 1.87
Below 6 years % (Male)	52.8	65.0	+12.2
Below 6 years % (Female)	47.2	35	- 12.2
SC % (Total)	33.0	36.8	+ 3.8

Source: Census 2001 and 2011

The villagers deny carrying out any unethical practices and they believe that the increase in the ratio of male children is due to the fact that they have become more health conscious and the tension or burden of work on both males and females has decreased considerably since the acquisition of land.

Impact on Relations with Neighbouring Villages

There is a feeling of relative deprivation among the residents of adjoining villages as they are amazed by the hefty compensation paid by the government to people of village Jheur Heri. The people of this village were small farmers and were known for selling milk to make their ends meet. The villagers from surrounding areas were reluctant to interact with the people of Jheur Heri village because most of them were debt-ridden and they considered them misers.

Post acquisition of land the people in this village became arrogant, and now look down on the people of neighbouring villages. They now drive recklessly, their newly purchased SUVs in the narrow lanes endangering the lives and property of other residents.

Impact on Literacy Rate

There has been an overall increase in literate population from 79.45 per cent in Census 2001 to 83.35 per cent in Census 2011. There has been a negative growth of 1.74 per cent in the male literacy rate of the village and a positive growth of 1.75 per cent in the female literacy rate of the village. This is due to the fact that after being financially strong the parents of the land owning community were now willing to send their daughters to schools and colleges. The comparison of literate population is highlighted in Table 2.

Table 2: Comparison of Literate Population

	Census 2001	Census 2011	Transition (+/-)
Literate Population % (Total)	79.45	83.35	+ 3.90
Literate % (Male)	57.12	55.37	- 1.74
Literate % (Female)	42.88	44.63	+ 1.75

Source: Census 2001 and 2011

The villagers now act as absentee landlords and have bought properties in nearby towns. The boys, especially those belonging to the land owning community have stopped studying either after clearing their matriculation exams or some have left the schools midway and are engaged in business. They are of the view that being a matriculate or a graduate would not guarantee them any job, especially in the government sector.

Impact on Occupational Structure

Most of the villagers who earlier sold milk in the nearby towns/ cities, have now stopped selling milk. The number of the milching animals (cows and buffaloes) has also gone down. The women belonging to the families whose land has been acquired are now free, earlier they used to assist their husbands in milching animals. Many families have bought agricultural lands in other villages. They now act as absentee landlords and rent out their lands to the other cultivators..

The landless labourers now go to other villages, town and cities in search of work. Some of them unload the material from trucks that bring raw material (cement, bricks, sand, gravel, etc) to the construction site.

The women of these labourers work as domestic help in the houses of the land owning community. They are distressed as their husbands after unloading material from the truck get drunk or take drugs. The social milieu of the village has been disturbed and the village is divided into factions. The plight of the landless community of the village is deplorable. The women of the community have no option left but to work as domestic help in the houses of the land owning community.

Impact on Socio-Political Relations

The socio-political relations amongst the villagers were adversely affected. There was around 54 acres of common land (*Shamlat*) of the village that belonged to the Panchayat. The amount of compensation for this land that turns out to be more than Rs. 80 crore is lying in the treasury. This common land known as *Shamlat* is used for common purposes. The land owning community generally contributes a small portion of their land for the *Shamlat*.

The division or sale of this land is prohibited. The Panchayat controls the land and the income generated from this land is used to carry out development works in the village. There was the dispute regarding the distribution of the compensatory money of the *Shamlat*. The cheques were to be issued in the name of the land owners who contributed the land to the *Shamlat*. The landless community of the village wanted the share in the compensatory money as the land now belonged to the Panchayat and hence was common land of all the villagers. The matter is now sub-judicious and the money is lying in the treasury. The relations amongst the villagers have soured and socio-political tension prevails in the village.

Conclusion

The acquisition of land results in changes at the structural and institutional level of the Project Affected Population (PAP). The Land Acquisition Acts concentrated on 'Public Purpose' and 'Public Consent' without involving all the stakeholders involved in the project. The Right to Fair Compensation in Land Acquisition, Rehabilitation and Resettlement Act, 2013 (RFCTLAR&R Act, 2013) is an initiative taken by the government to ensure inclusive development. The inclusion of a woman member in the SIA team is a welcome step towards ensuring the participation of women in the developmental process.

It is evident that the PAPs of the Jheur Heri village have witnessed many changes at the structural and institutional level. Some of the villagers have come to terms with these changes but others, especially the elderly and women face several problems. Major gainers from the land acquisitions are the people, who already have control over the resources, i.e. those who owned the land. The landless agricultural workers have been reduced to the level of daily wage earners. Their women have no options but to work as domestic help in the houses of the landed gentry. Some of their wards have to give up their studies in between for the dearth of money and to contribute economically in the family.

The process of development is essentially centralising. It increases the marginalisation of the already marginal sections. It is highlighted in the study that people belonging to marginal sections are by and large at the receiving end and victims of disruptions caused by the financial windfalls of land acquisitions. It is regretful that the development carried out for the public purpose is of no use for the local public, especially the weaker sections but are only for the elites.

The governments and the policy makers should try to comprehend the rural complexities and should work in curtailing the loss to traditional knowledge, disorder in social relations, minimising the negative impacts on the marginal sections and at the same time ensuring transparency, inclusiveness and distributive justice in land acquisitions. The government should try to win the hearts of all the Project Affected Population (PAP) through participative techniques such as Social Impact Assessment (SIA).

REFERENCES

Barrow, C.J. 1997. *Environmental and Social Impact Assessment*, London: Arnold.

____ . 2000. *Social Impact Assessment: An Introduction*, London: Arnold.

Burdge, R.J. and Johnson, S. 1994. 'Socio-Cultural Aspects of the Effects of Resource Development', in *A Conceptual Approach to Social Impact Assessment,* ed. Rabel J. Burdge, 25-40. Middleton, WI: Social Ecology Press.

Dolgoff, R., Feldstein, D. and Skolnik, L. 1997. *Understanding Social Welfare,* 4th ed., p. 5, New York: Longman, http://web.hku.hk/~hrnwlck/introsocwelfare/welfareconcepts.htm> (May 12, 2016).

Geisler, C.C. 1993. Rethinking SIA: Why Ex Ante Research Isn't Enough? *Society and Natural Resources*, 6 (4): 327-338.

George, Robin. 2009. Constitutional Validity and Land Acquisition Act, 1984. < http://www.legalserviceindia.com /article/ 1295-Land-Acquisition-Act.html> (May 4, 2016).

Giddens, Anthony. 1984. *The Constitution of Society*, Berkeley and Los Angeles: University of California Press.

ICGPSIA. 1994. Guidelines and Principles for Social Impact Assessment. US. Dep. Commer., NOAA Tech. Memo. NMFS-F/SPO-16. <httpwww.iaia.org/publicdocuments/.../IAIA-SIA-International-Principles.pdf> (Mar 5, 2015).

____. 2003. Principles and Guidelines for Social Impact Assessment in USA, Prepared by ICGPSIA, Impact Assessment and Project Appraisal. 21(3):231-250 <http://www.nmfs.noaa.gov/sfa/ reg_svcs/ social%20guid&pri.pdf> (Mar 5, 2015).

Iyer, Ramaswamy R. 2009. 'Land Acquisition (Amendment) Bill: A Slow But Sure Step Forward', *The Hindu.*

Law Commission of India. 1958. Tenth Report. Law of Acquisition and Requisitioning of Land. Government of India, Ministry of Law, 1-6. <http://lawcommissionofindia.nic.in/1-50/Report10.pdf> (March 3, 2016).

Ray, Ishita Aditya and Ray, Sarbapriya. 2011. 'B.R. Ambedkar and His Philosophy of Land Reform: An Evaluation', *Afro Asian Journal of Social Sciences*. 2(2.1): 1-16.

Singhal, M.L. 1995. 'Right to Property and Compensation Under the Indian Constitution', *J.T.R.I. (Judicial Training and Research Institute) Journal*, I(2) http://ijtr.nic.in/articles/art41.pdf> (March 5, 2016).

Vanclay, F. 1999. 'Social Impact Assessment', *International Handbook of Environmental Impact Assessment*, 1: 301-326.

____. 2002. 'Conceptualising Social Impacts', *Environmental Impact Assessment Review*, 22: 183-211.

Wahi, Namita. 2013. Land Acquisition, Development and the Constitution, <http://india-seminar.com.../namita_wahi.html> (March 7, 2015).

Walker, J.L., Mitchell, B. and Wismer, S. 2000. 'Impacts During Project Anticipation in Molas, Indonesia, Implications for Social Impact Assessment', *Environmental Impact Assessment Review*, 20: 513-535.

Contributors

Anjana John is a PhD research scholar at the Department of Sociology and Social Anthropology in Central European University, Vienna, Austria. Her PhD research focuses on understanding the network of state-led electricity distribution in India through the lens of its indigenous communities to examine the power-Relationships between them and the state.

Anup Dhar is Professor of Philosophy, School of Liberal Studies and Director, Centre for Development Practice, Ambedkar University Delhi. His co-authored books include *Dislocation and Resettlement in Development: From Third World to World of the Third* (Routledge, 2009), *The Indian Economy in Transition: Globalization, Capitalism and Development* (Cambridge University Press, 2015) and *World of the Third and Global Capitalism: Between Marx and Freud* (Palgrave Macmillan, forthcoming). His co-edited books include *Breaking the Silo: Integrated Science Education in India* (Orient Blackswan, 2017), *Psychoanalysis in Indian Terroir: Emerging Themes in Culture, Family, and Childhood* (Lexington Books, 2018), *Marx, Marxism and the Spiritual* (Routledge, 2020) and *Clinic, Critique, Culture: Philosophy and Praxis of Psychoanalysis in India* (forthcoming: Orient Blackswan, 2021).

Bhavya Chitranshi is currently a PhD fellow at the Institute for Culture and Society at the Western Sydney University. She is the co-founder of an adivasi (indigenous) single women's collective, Eka Nari Sanghathan, in Odisha, India.

Bidhan Chandra Dash is an Assistant Professor at the School of Liberal Studies, Ambedkar University Delhi. He completed his PhD from the Department of Humanities and Social Sciences, Indian Institute of Technology Bombay on Dalit Movement and Globalization, focusing on the role of media and information flows across organizations and networks. Dr. Dash's research interest includes subaltern religious traditions, Dalit political mobilisation in the era of globalisation and science and technology studies.

Chandri Raghava Reddy is a Professor in the Department of Sociology at the University of Hyderabad. His areas of research interests include science, technology and society studies (STS) and sociology of disability.

Dev Nath Pathak teaches Sociology at South Asian University, New Delhi (India). He has contributed articles to the various journals, chapters in edited books, and he is co-editor of the journal *Society and Culture in South Asia* and the editorial board of *Journal of Human Values*. A couple of his very recent publications include: *In Defence of the Ordinary: Everyday Awakenings* (Bloomsbury, 2021); *Living and Dying: Meanings in Maithili Folklore* (Primus, 2018), *Another South Asia* (Primus, 2017), in addition to the coedited books such as *Neighbourhoods in Urban India* (Bloomsbury, 2020), *Culture and Politics in South Asia: Performative Communication* (2017); *Intersections of Art, Anthropology and Art History: A Conversation with Parul Dave-Mukherji* (2016) and *Narrating Nations, Performing Politics: A Conversation with Vasudha Dalmia* (2017), *Decoding Visual World: Intersections of Art, Anthropology and Art History in South Asia* (2019).

Ishita Dey teaches at the Department of Sociology, Faculty of Social Sciences, South Asian University, New Delhi. Her research interests are food, labour, senses, migration and technology. She has been working on the life of sweets and sweetness in South Asia. She has co-anchored an art research project on smells of the city with a focus on Delhi supported by Kiran Nadar Museum of Art, Delhi. She is an editorial board member of the journal *Society* *and Culture in South Asia* (Sage), and has published her work on food in edited volumes, *Oxford Compendium to Sugar and Sweets* and *Gastronomica*. She has coedited a book *Sustainability of Rights after Globalisation* (Sage, 2011) and co-authored a book *Beyond Kolkata: The Dystopia of Urban Imagination* (Routledge, 2013).

Ishita Mehrotra holds a PhD in Development Studies from School of Oriental and African Studies, University of London. She completed her MA and M.Phil in Political Science from Jawaharlal Nehru University. Winner of the Sanjay Thakur Young Labour Economist Award (2013), Dr. Mehrotra has taught at graduate and postgraduate levels. Presently, she is Assistant Professor at the School of Undergraduate Studies at Ambedkar University Delhi, India. Her research and teaching interests include the political economy of agrarian relations, caste and gender, rural labour relations, labour movements and development theory.

Prasanth Kumar Munnangi is a UGC Post-Doctoral fellow in the Department of Sociology, University of Hyderabad. His research interests include science, technology and society studies, sociology of scientific knowledge and rural society and agrarian change.

Priyasha Kaul is an Assistant Professor of Sociology at Ambedkar University Delhi. Her research interests include media, gender, migration and religion. She has a doctorate in sociology from Bristol University, UK, Masters Degrees in sociology and management from Delhi School of Economics (DU) and Bristol University, respectively. She has previously taught undergraduate and postgraduate courses at Miranda House, Hindu College (DU), Bristol University, FLAME University, and IGNOU.

Santosh K. Singh holds MA, MPhil and PhD degrees in Sociology from JNU, Delhi. Formerly with Dr. B.R. Ambedkar University Delhi (AUD) where he joined as one of the founding faculty members of the Sociology and Global studies programme and served for almost a decade in various capacities, including as the Dean, Student services of the university, Dr. Singh is currently a faculty with the Post Graduate Department of Sociology at Government College for Girls, Sector 11, Chandigarh. He has published his decade-long research work among the Ravidassia and the Dera phenomenon in Punjab in various national and international journals and book chapters. He is currently working on a monograph based on his research in Punjab. He regularly contributes lead articles in the prominent English dailies and opinion web-portals on themes of topical sociological relevance.

Shalini Bhutani is a legal researcher and policy analyst based in Delhi, while her work pans across the Asia region. Her areas of interest range from global trade rules and their impact on peoples, to how science and technology policies deal with grassroots innovation. She publishes on a wide range of issues including free trade, intellectual property, seed laws and agricultural biodiversity. She is member and legal counsellor for the *Apna Beej* network and supports the Indian Alliance for Seed Sovereignty. She also gives guest lectures on legal and regulatory affairs at various universities.

Sukhwant Sidhu is an Assistant Professor with the Post Graduate Department of Sociology at Post Graduate Government College for Girls, Sector-11, Chandigarh. He has been awarded PhD from Punjabi University, Patiala for his work in the field of Social Impact Assessment of a village in Punjab. His areas of specialisation include sociology of development, gender and social theories.